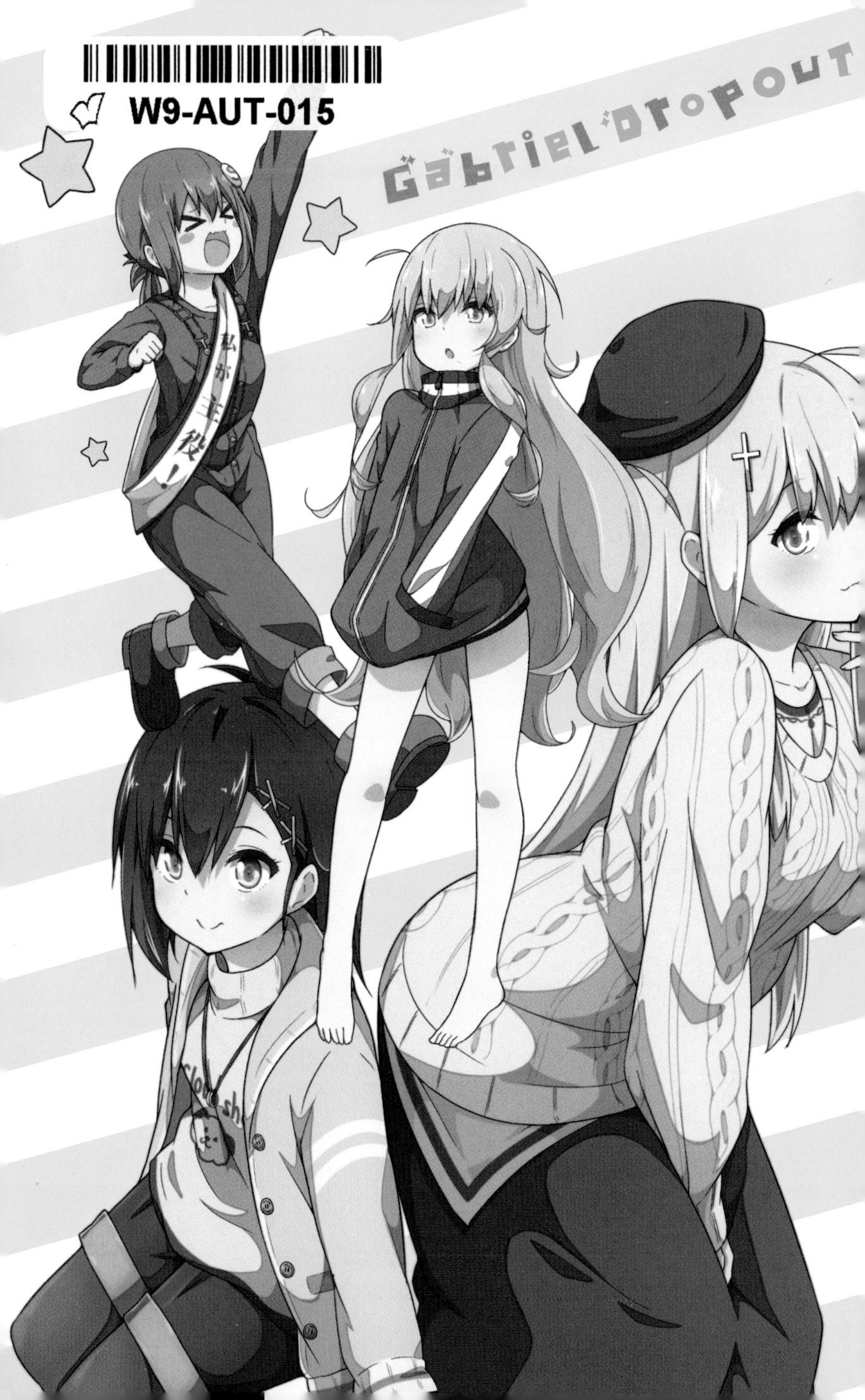
Gabriel DropOut
私が主役！

Contents

Gabriel Dropout

5

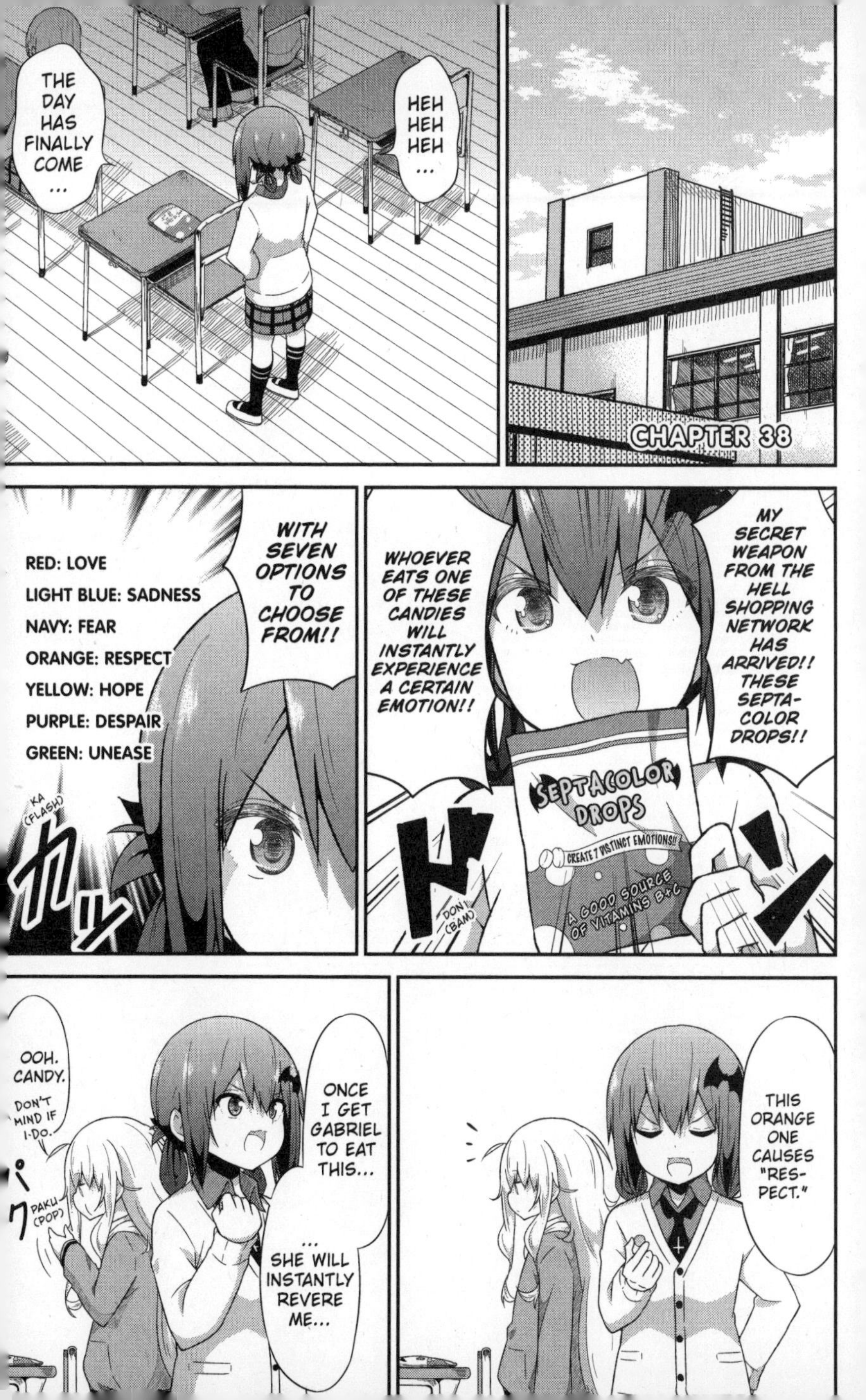
CHAPTER 38
HEH HEH HEH ...
THE DAY HAS FINALLY COME ...
MY SECRET WEAPON FROM THE HELL SHOPPING NETWORK HAS ARRIVED!! THESE SEPTA-COLOR DROPS!!
WHOEVER EATS ONE OF THESE CANDIES WILL INSTANTLY EXPERIENCE A CERTAIN EMOTION!!
SEPTACOLOR DROPS
CREATE 7 DISTINCT EMOTIONS!!
A GOOD SOURCE OF VITAMINS B+C
DON (BAM)
WITH SEVEN OPTIONS TO CHOOSE FROM!!
RED: LOVE
LIGHT BLUE: SADNESS
NAVY: FEAR
ORANGE: RESPECT
YELLOW: HOPE
PURPLE: DESPAIR
GREEN: UNEASE
KA (FLASH)
THIS ORANGE ONE CAUSES "RES-PECT."
ONCE I GET GABRIEL TO EAT THIS...
... SHE WILL INSTANTLY REVERE ME...
OOH. CANDY.
DON'T MIND IF I-DO.
PAKU (POP)

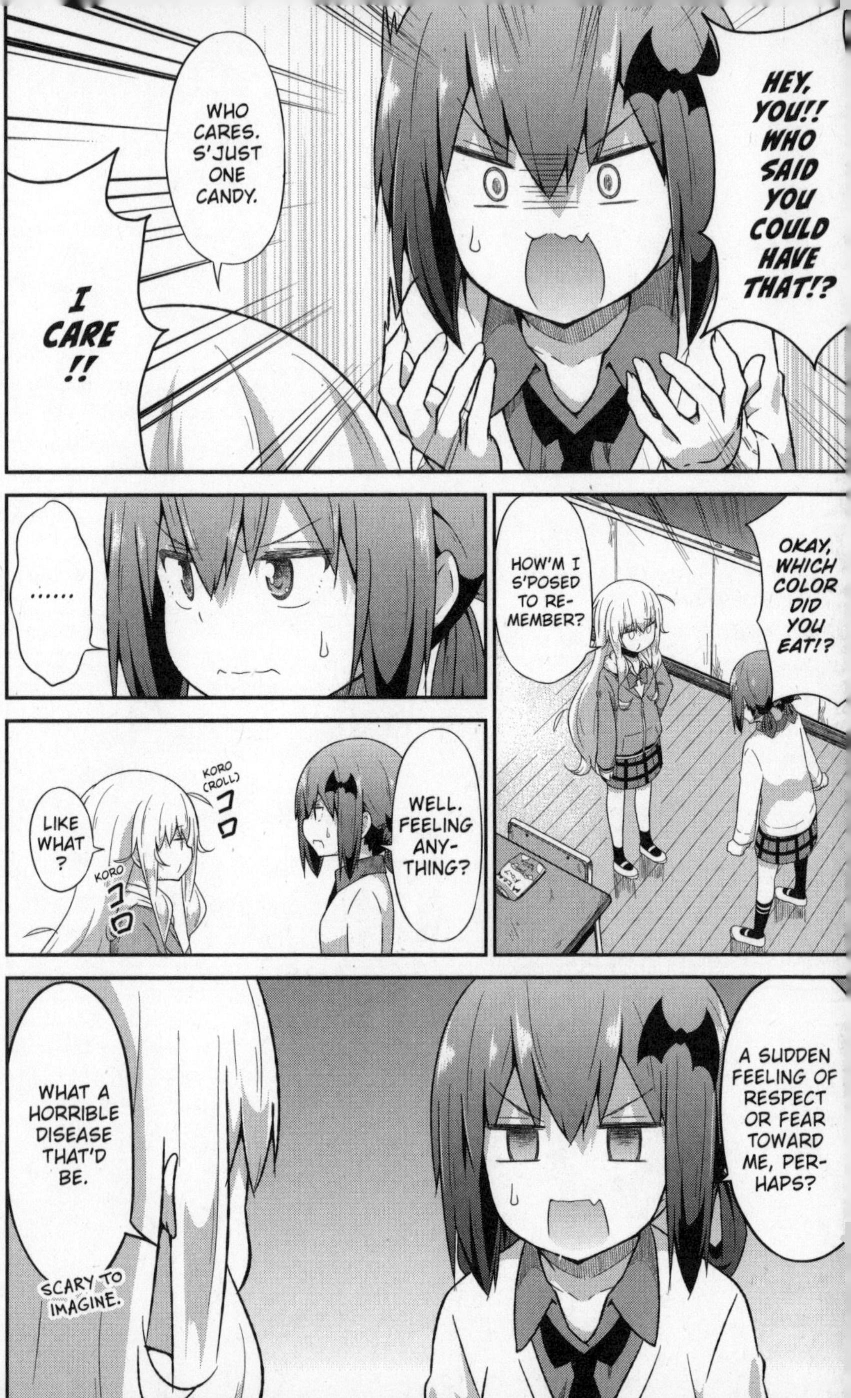
HEY, YOU!! WHO SAID YOU COULD HAVE THAT!?
WHO CARES. S'JUST ONE CANDY.
I CARE!!
OKAY, WHICH COLOR DID YOU EAT!?
HOW'M I S'POSED TO RE-MEMBER?
......
WELL. FEELING ANY-THING?
KORO (ROLL) コロ
LIKE WHAT?
KORO コロ
A SUDDEN FEELING OF RESPECT OR FEAR TOWARD ME, PER-HAPS?
WHAT A HORRIBLE DISEASE THAT'D BE.
SCARY TO IMAGINE.

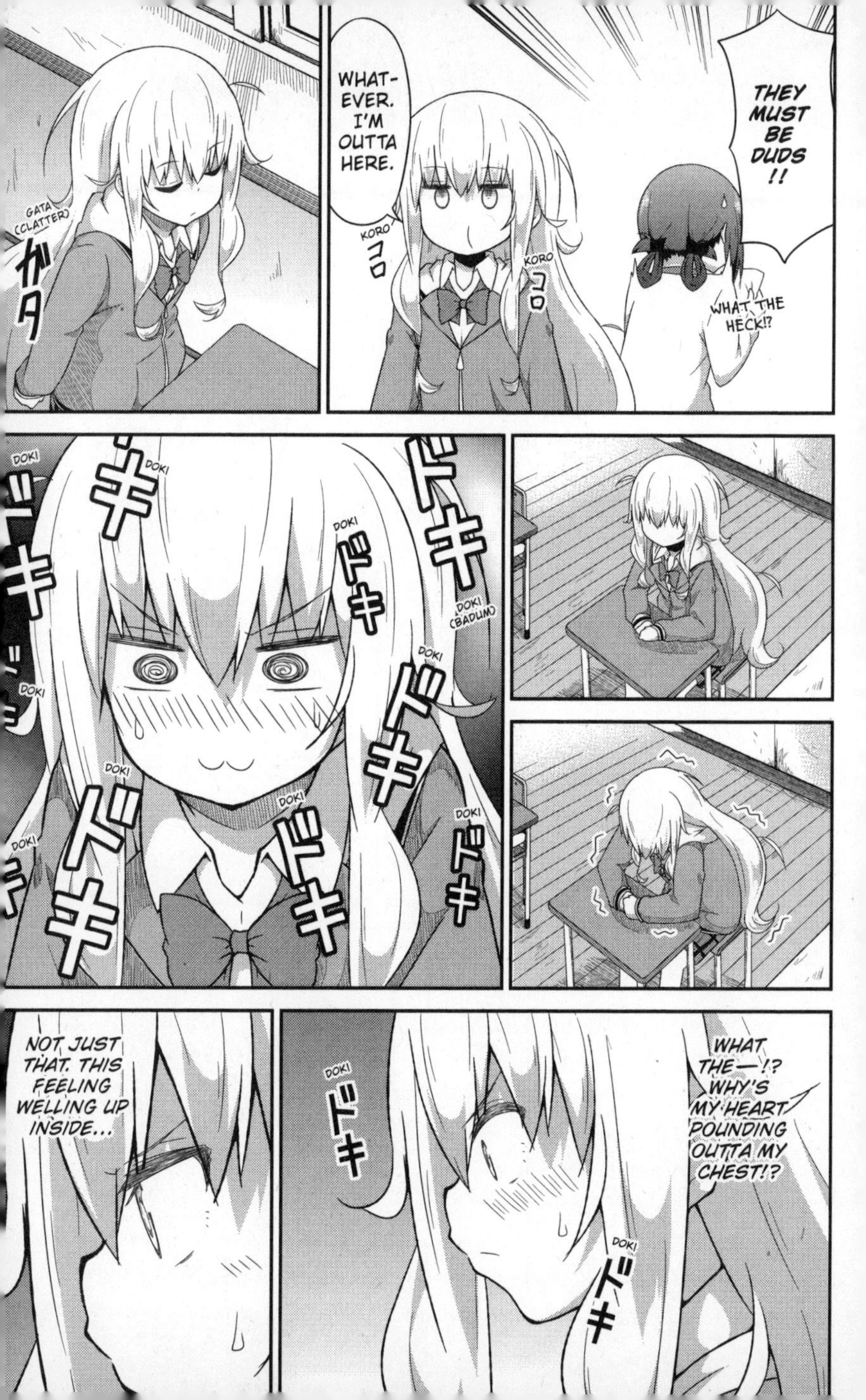

THEY MUST BE DUDS!!
WHAT-EVER. I'M OUTTA HERE.
KORO コロ
KORO コロ
WHAT THE HECK!?
GATA (CLATTER) ガタ
DOKI ドキ
DOKI ドキ
DOKI (BADUM) ドキ
DOKI ドキ
DOKI ドキ
DOKI ドキ
DOKI ドキ
DOKI ドキ
DOKI ドキ
DOKI ドキ
WHAT THE—!? WHY'S MY HEART POUNDING OUTTA MY CHEST!?
DOKI ドキ
DOKI ドキ
NOT JUST THAT. THIS FEELING WELLING UP INSIDE...

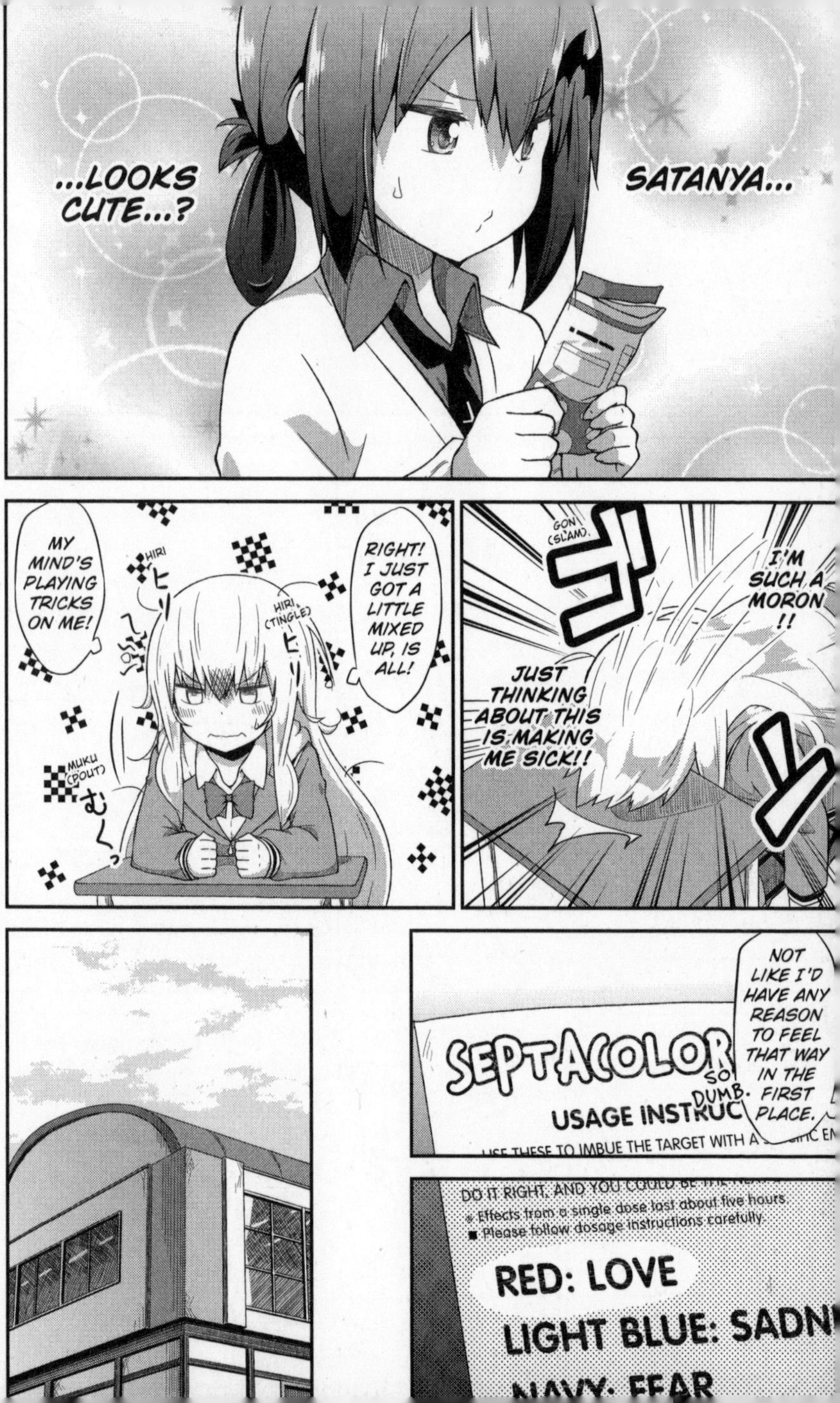
SATANYA...
...LOOKS CUTE...?
GON (SLAM)
I'M SUCH A MORON!!
JUST THINKING ABOUT THIS IS MAKING ME SICK!!
HIRI
HIRI (TINGLE)
RIGHT! I JUST GOT A LITTLE MIXED UP, IS ALL!
MY MIND'S PLAYING TRICKS ON ME!
MUKU (POUT)
SEPTACOLOR
USAGE INSTRUC
NOT LIKE I'D HAVE ANY REASON TO FEEL THAT WAY IN THE FIRST PLACE.
SO DUMB.
USE THESE TO IMBUE THE TARGET WITH A
DO IT RIGHT, AND YOU COULD BE THE
* Effects from a single dose last about five hours.
■ Please follow dosage instructions carefully.
RED: LOVE
LIGHT BLUE: SADN
NAVY: FEAR

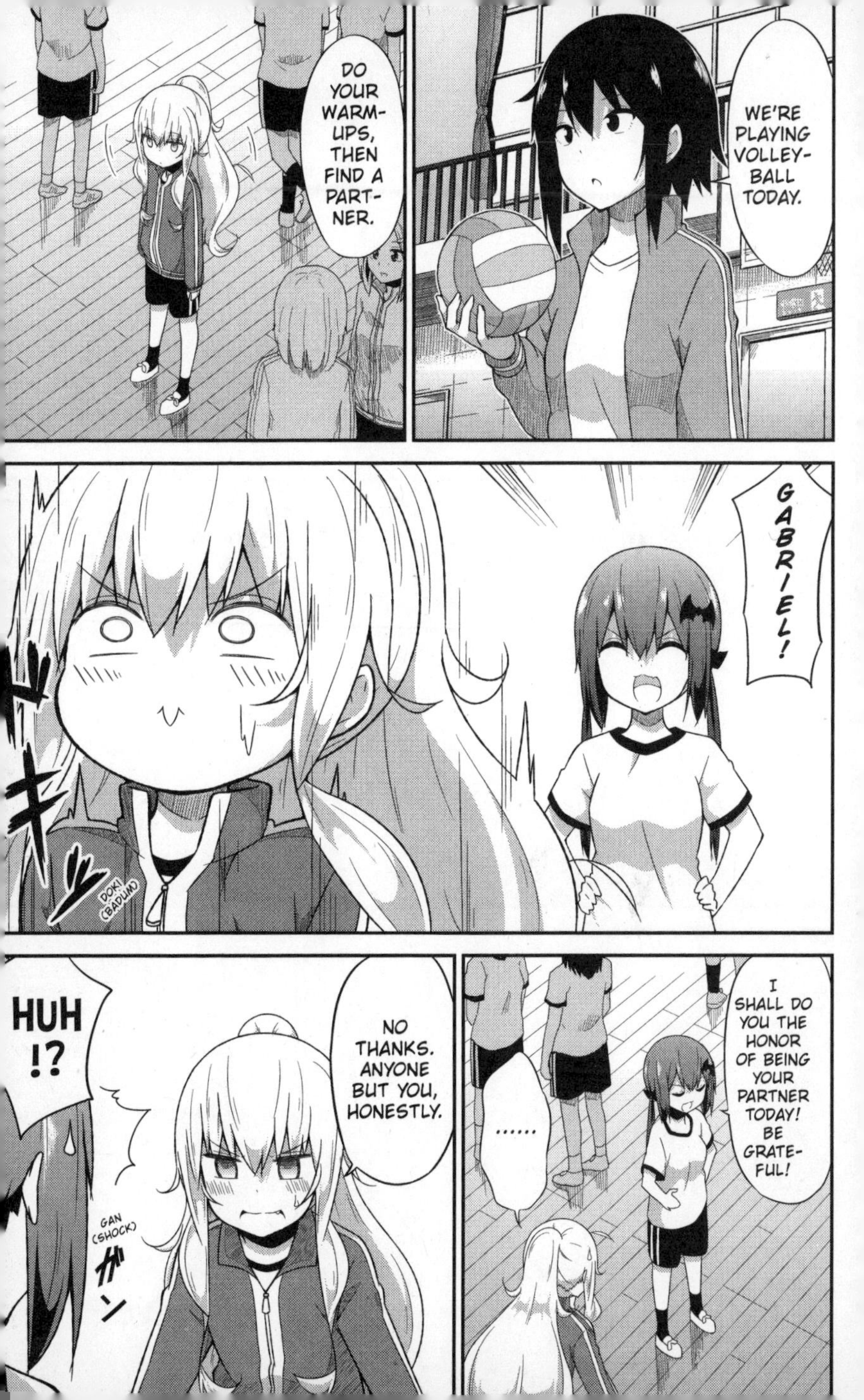
WE'RE PLAYING VOLLEY-BALL TODAY.
DO YOUR WARM-UPS, THEN FIND A PART-NER.
GABRIEL!
DOKI (BADUM)
I SHALL DO YOU THE HONOR OF BEING YOUR PARTNER TODAY! BE GRATE-FUL!
......
NO THANKS. ANYONE BUT YOU, HONESTLY.
HUH!?
GAN (SHOCK)
ガン

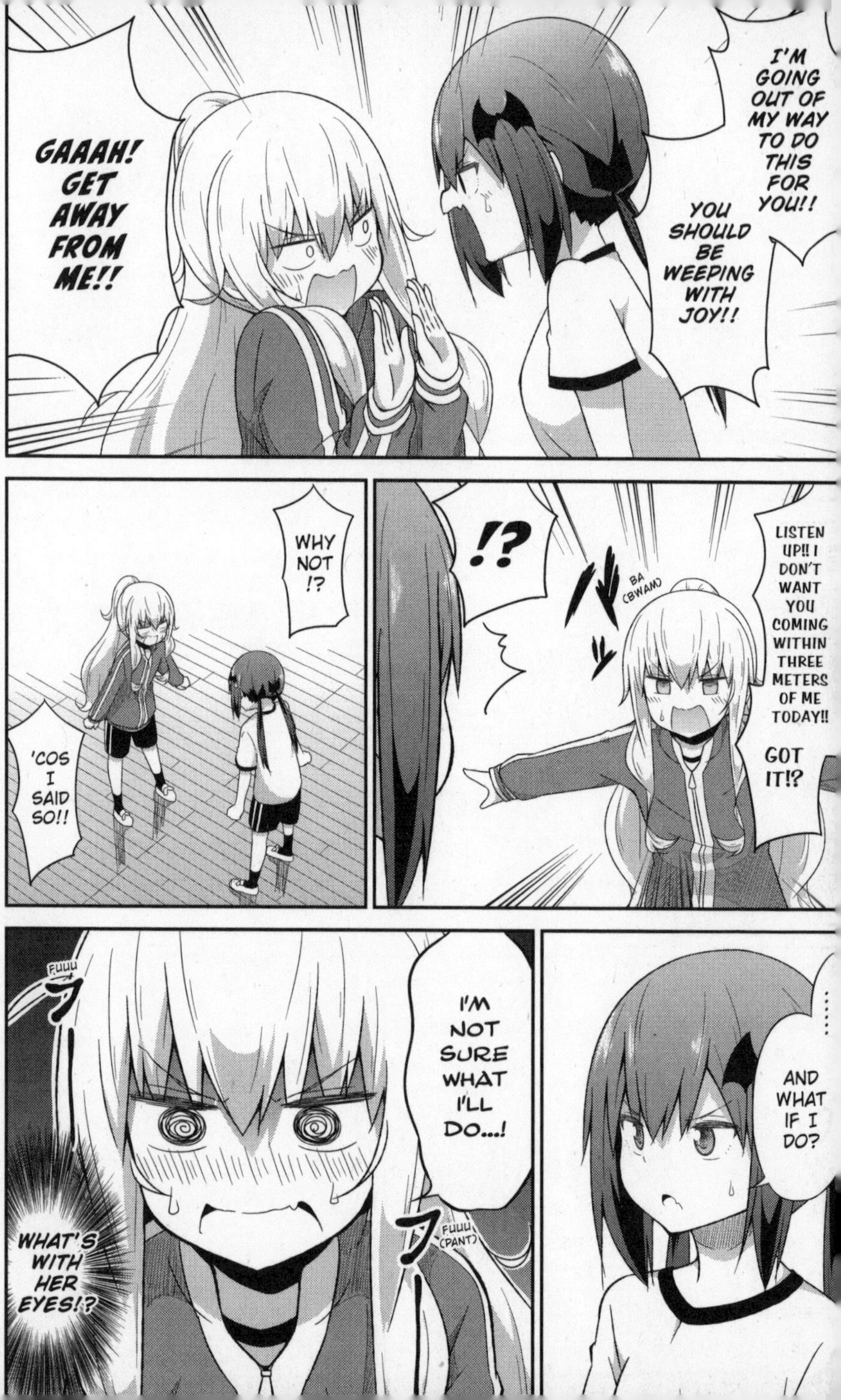
I'M GOING OUT OF MY WAY TO DO THIS FOR YOU!!
YOU SHOULD BE WEEPING WITH JOY!!
GAAAH! GET AWAY FROM ME!!
LISTEN UP!! I DON'T WANT YOU COMING WITHIN THREE METERS OF ME TODAY!!
!?
BA (BWAM)
GOT IT!?
WHY NOT!?
'COS I SAID SO!!
......
AND WHAT IF I DO?
FUUU
I'M NOT SURE WHAT I'LL DO...!
FUUU (PANT)
WHAT'S WITH HER EYES!?

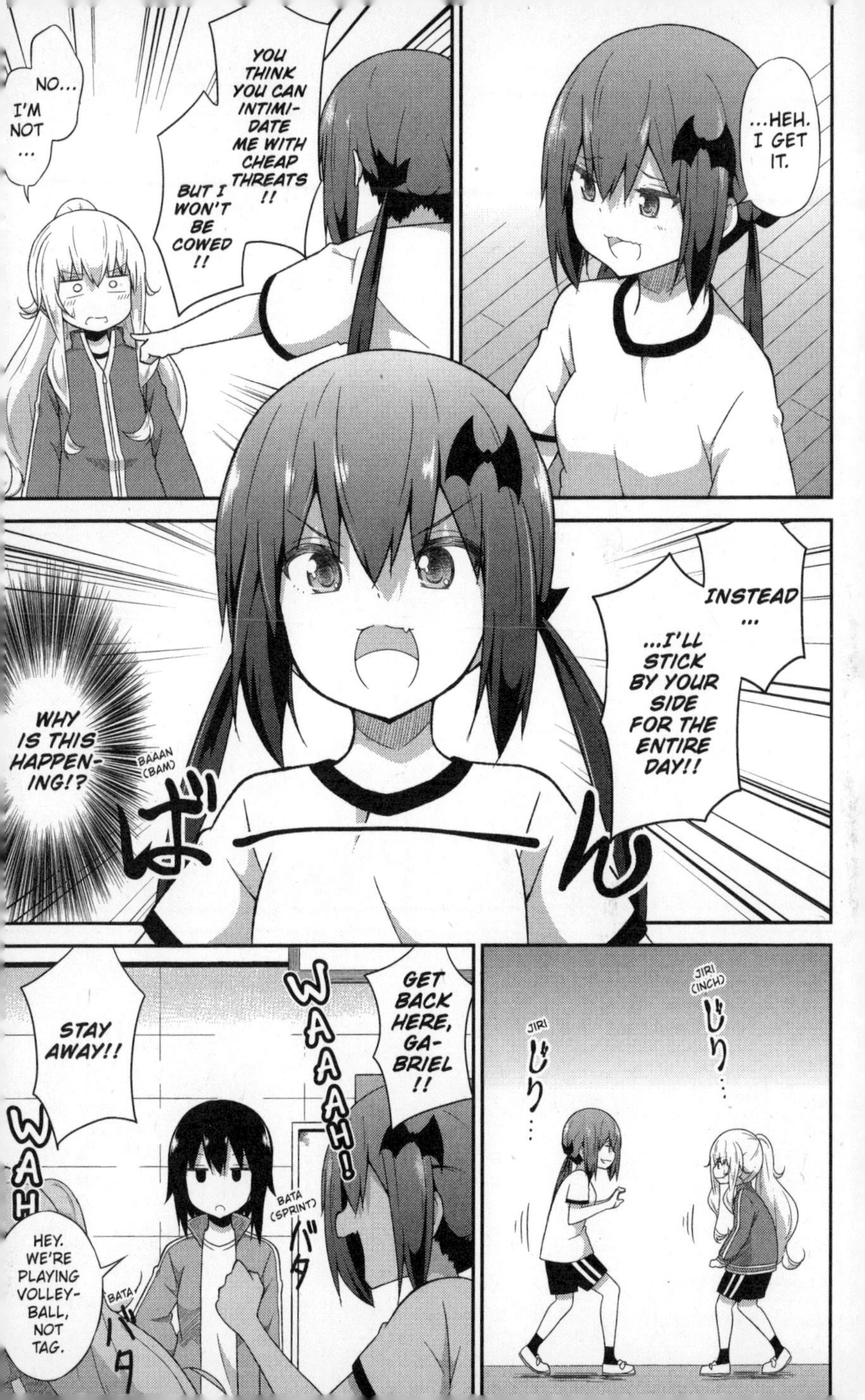
...HEH. I GET IT.
YOU THINK YOU CAN INTIMIDATE ME WITH CHEAP THREATS!!
BUT I WON'T BE COWED!!
NO... I'M NOT...
INSTEAD...
...I'LL STICK BY YOUR SIDE FOR THE ENTIRE DAY!!
ばーん
BAAAN (BAM)
WHY IS THIS HAPPENING!?
じり
JIRI (INCH)
じり
JIRI
GET BACK HERE, GABRIEL!!
WAAAAH!
STAY AWAY!!
WAH
BATA (SPRINT)
バタ
BATA
バタ
HEY. WE'RE PLAYING VOLLEYBALL, NOT TAG.

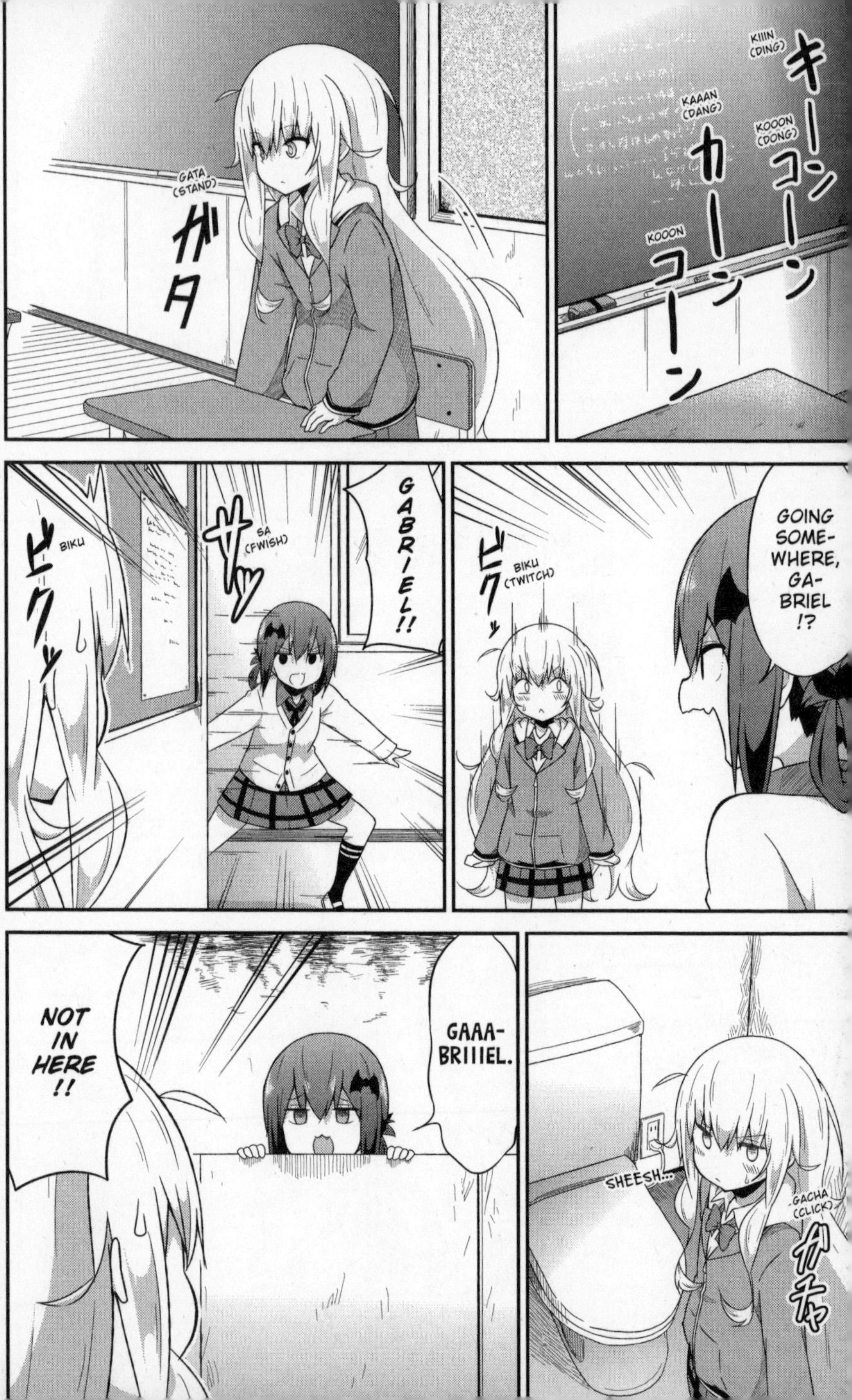

KIIN (DING)
キーンコーン
KOOON (DONG)
KAAAN (DANG)
カーン
KOOON
コーン
GATA (STAND)
ガタ
GOING SOME-WHERE, GA-BRIEL!?
BIKU (TWITCH)
ビクッ
GABRIEL!!
SA (FWISH)
サッ
BIKU
ビクッ
GACHA (CLICK)
ガチャ
SHEESH...
GAAA-BRIIIEL.
NOT IN HERE!!

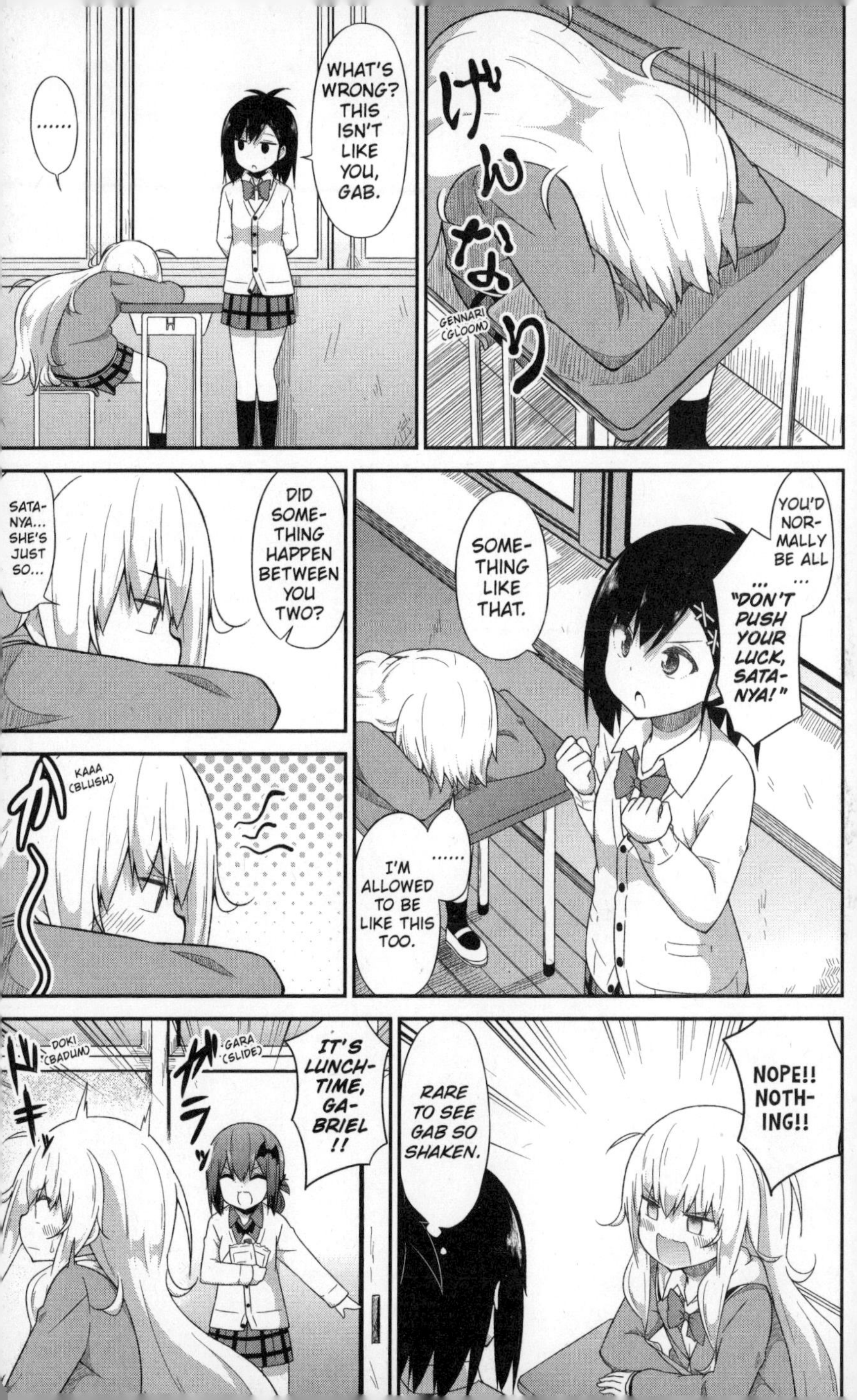
げんなり
GENNARI (GLOOM)
WHAT'S WRONG? THIS ISN'T LIKE YOU, GAB.
......
YOU'D NORMALLY BE ALL... "DON'T PUSH YOUR LUCK, SATANYA!"
SOMETHING LIKE THAT.
......
I'M ALLOWED TO BE LIKE THIS TOO.
DID SOMETHING HAPPEN BETWEEN YOU TWO?
SATANYA... SHE'S JUST SO...
か
KAAA (BLUSH)
NOPE!! NOTHING!!
RARE TO SEE GAB SO SHAKEN.
IT'S LUNCHTIME, GABRIEL!!
ガラッ
GARA (SLIDE)
ドキッ
DOKI (BADUM)

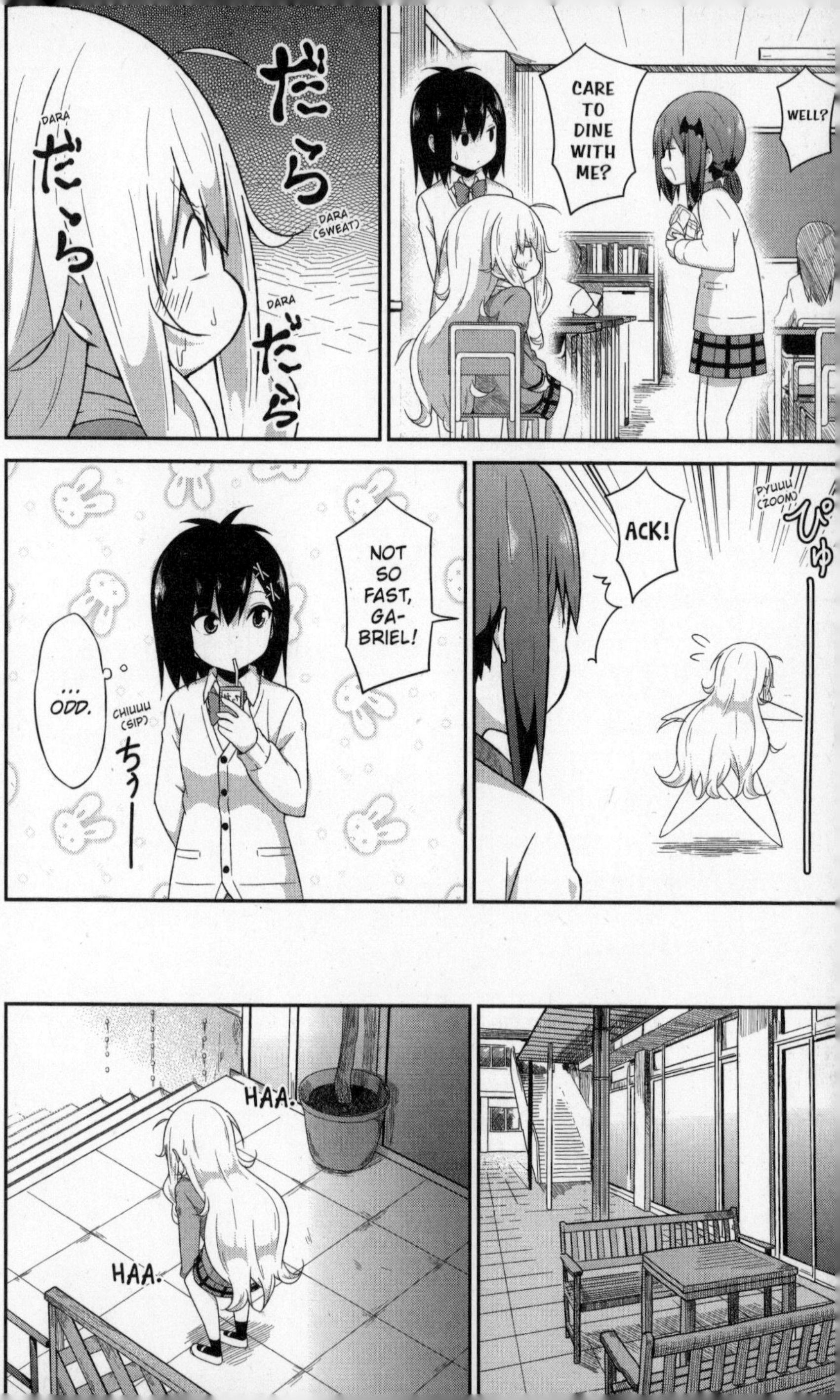
WELL?
CARE TO DINE WITH ME?
だら
DARA (SWEAT)
DARA
だら
DARA
だら
PYUUU (ZOOM)
ぴゅー
ACK!
NOT SO FAST, GA-BRIEL!
CHIUUU (SIP)
ちゅー
... ODD.
HAA.
HAA.

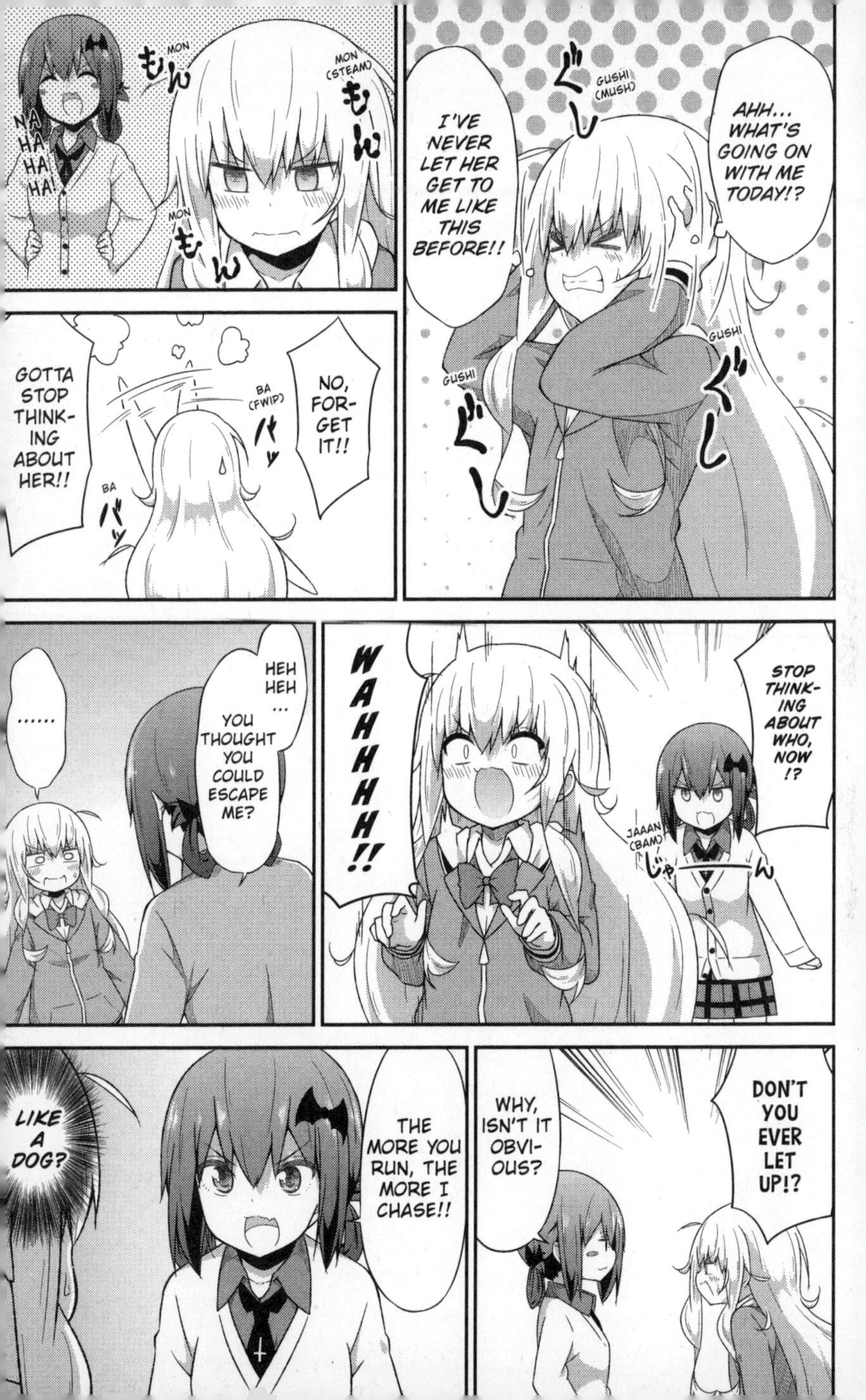
GUSHI (MUSH)
ぐし
AHH... WHAT'S GOING ON WITH ME TODAY!?
I'VE NEVER LET HER GET TO ME LIKE THIS BEFORE!!
GUSHI
ぐし
GUSHI
ぐし
MON (STEAM)
もん
MON
もん
MON
もん
NA HA HA HA HA HA!
NO, FOR-GET IT!!
BA (FWIP)
バッ
BA
バッ
GOTTA STOP THINK-ING ABOUT HER!!
STOP THINK-ING ABOUT WHO, NOW!?
JAAAN (BAM)
じゃーん
WAHHHHHH!!
HEH HEH... YOU THOUGHT YOU COULD ESCAPE ME?
......
DON'T YOU EVER LET UP!?
WHY, ISN'T IT OBVI-OUS?
THE MORE YOU RUN, THE MORE I CHASE!!
LIKE A DOG?

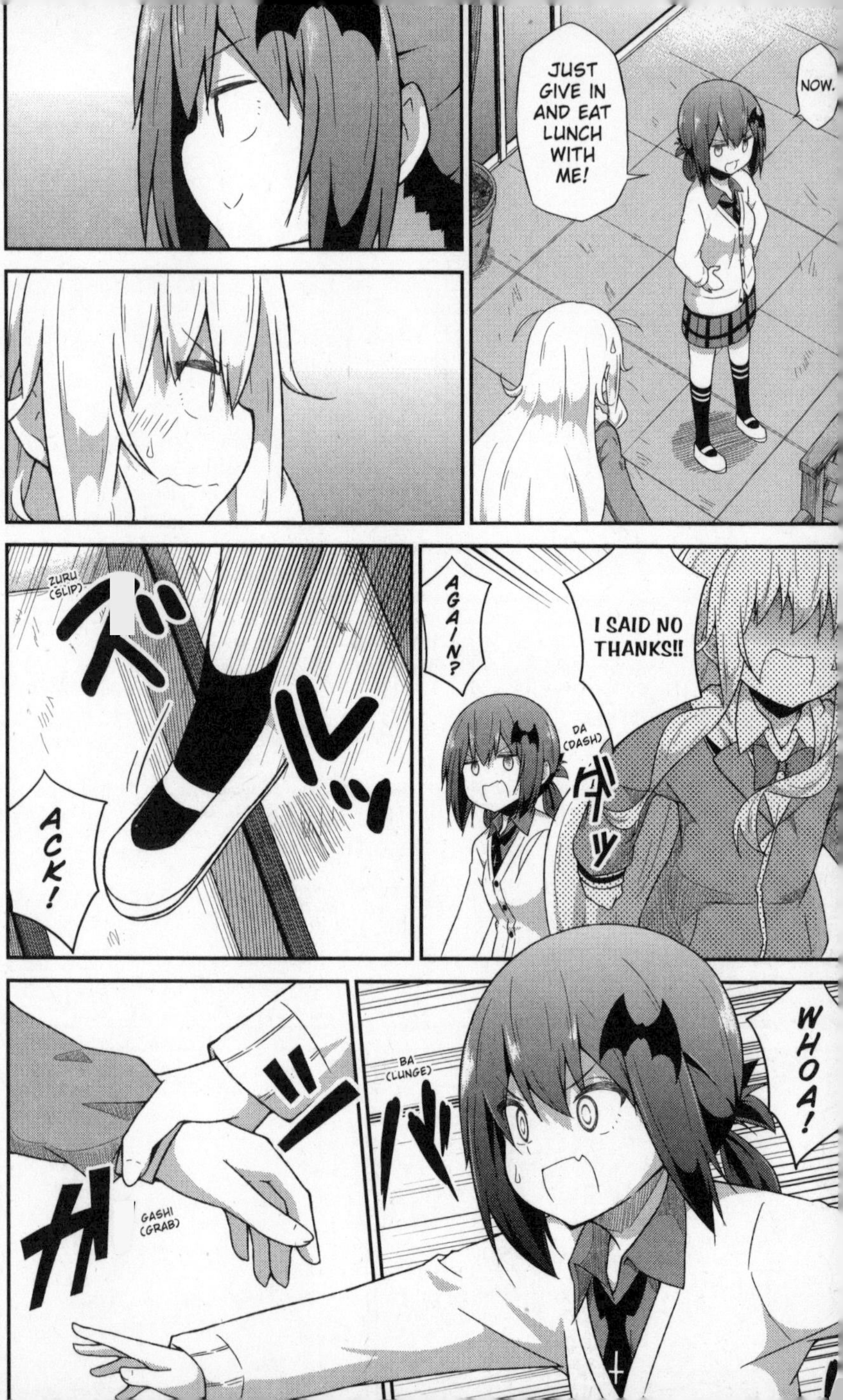
NOW.
JUST GIVE IN AND EAT LUNCH WITH ME!
I SAID NO THANKS!!
AGAIN?
DA (DASH)
ZURU (SLIP)
ACK!
WHOA!
BA (LUNGE)
GASHI (GRAB)

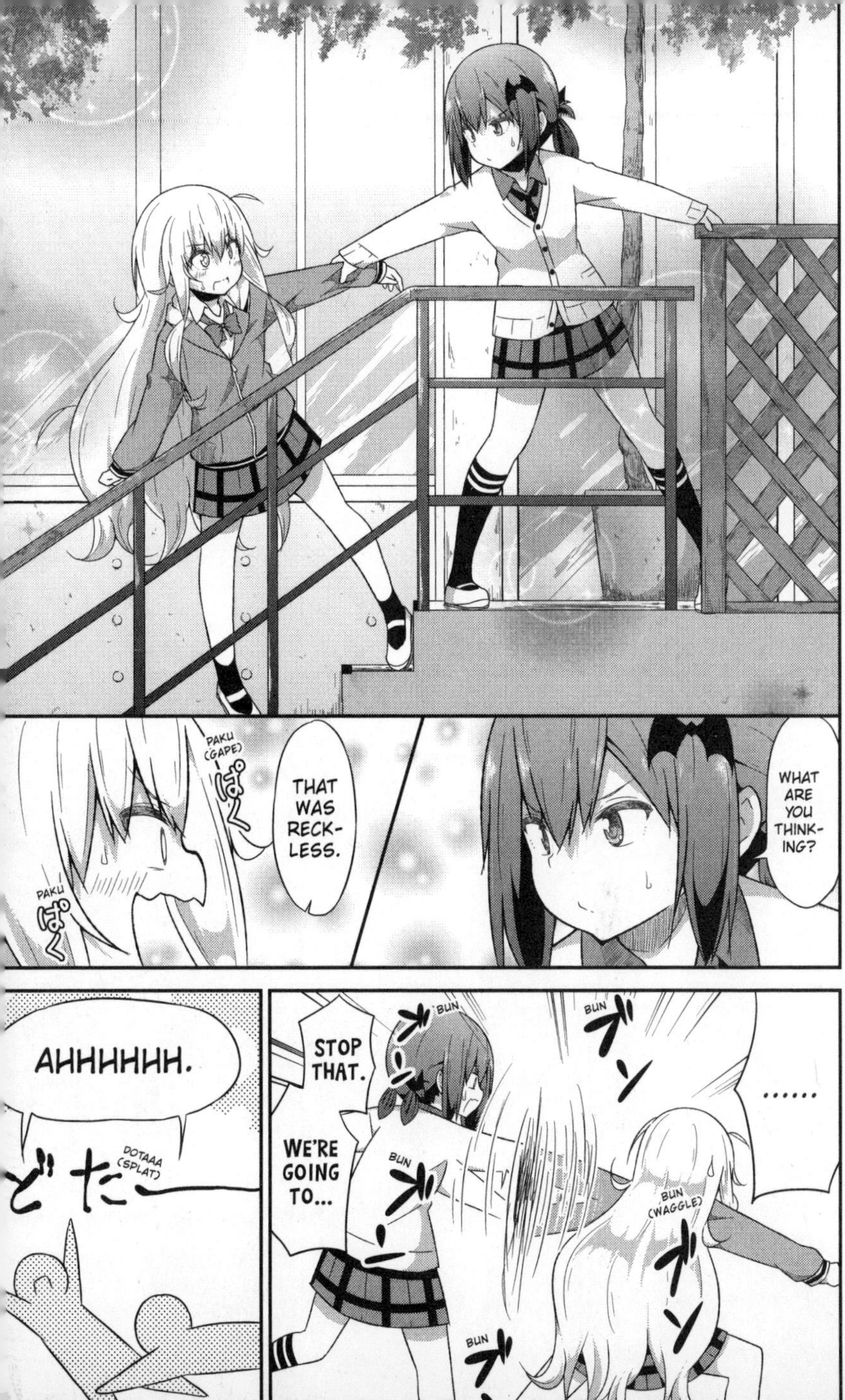
WHAT ARE YOU THINKING?
THAT WAS RECKLESS.
PAKU (GAPE) ぱく
PAKU ぱく
BUN ブン
......
BUN ブン
STOP THAT.
BUN (WAGGLE) ブン
BUN ブン
WE'RE GOING TO...
BUN ブ
AHHHHHH.
DOTAAA (SPLAT) どたー

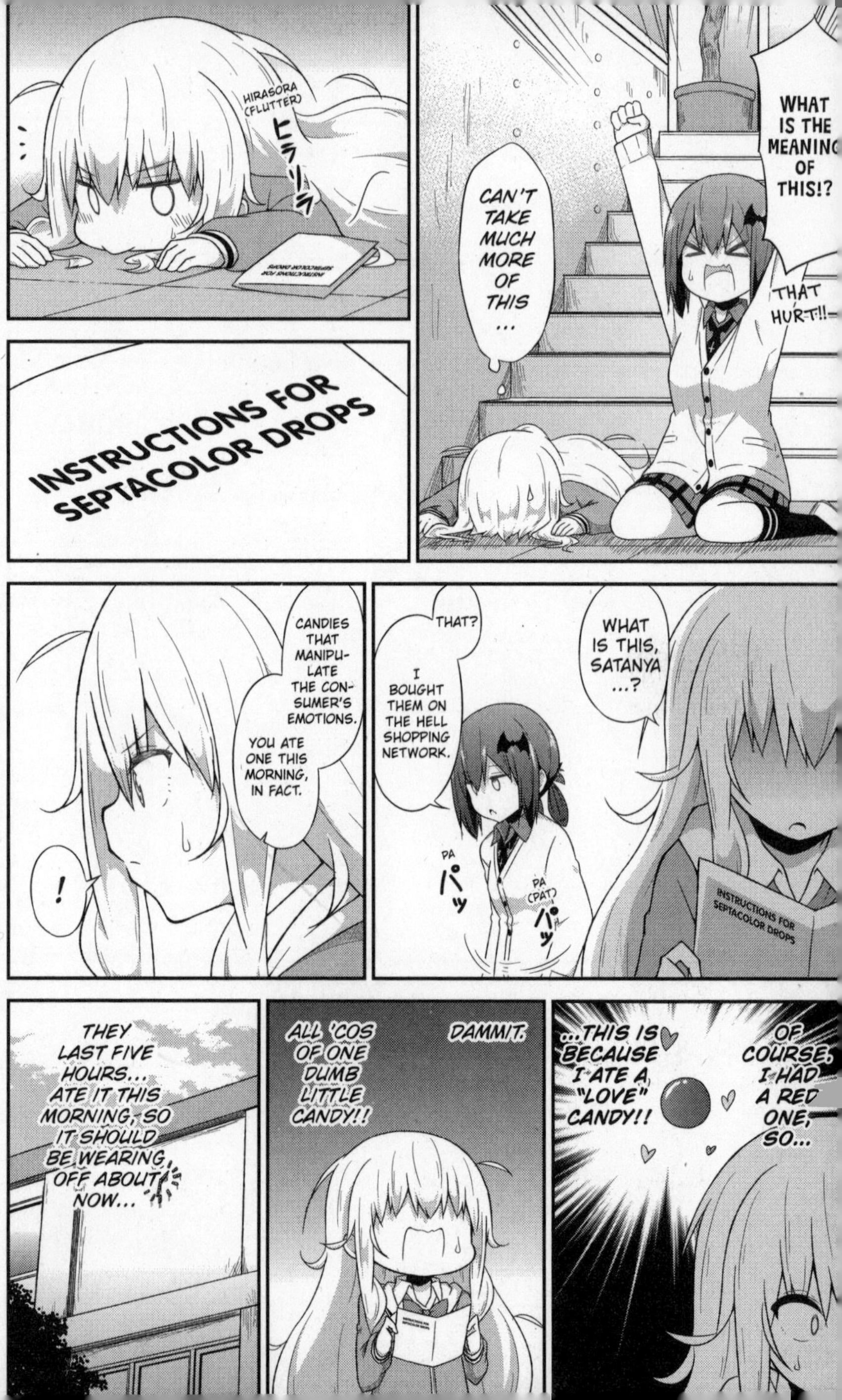
WHAT IS THE MEANING OF THIS!?
THAT HURT!!
CAN'T TAKE MUCH MORE OF THIS...
HIRASORA (FLUTTER)
ヒラリラ
INSTRUCTIONS FOR SEPTACOLOR DROPS
INSTRUCTIONS FOR SEPTACOLOR DROPS
WHAT IS THIS, SATANYA...?
INSTRUCTIONS FOR SEPTACOLOR DROPS
THAT?
I BOUGHT THEM ON THE HELL SHOPPING NETWORK.
PA (PAT)
パッ
PA
パッ
CANDIES THAT MANIPU-LATE THE CON-SUMER'S EMOTIONS.
YOU ATE ONE THIS MORNING, IN FACT.
!
OF COURSE, I HAD A RED ONE, SO...
...THIS IS BECAUSE I ATE A "LOVE" CANDY!!
DAMMIT.
ALL 'COS OF ONE DUMB LITTLE CANDY!!
THEY LAST FIVE HOURS... ATE IT THIS MORNING, SO IT SHOULD BE WEARING OFF ABOUT NOW...

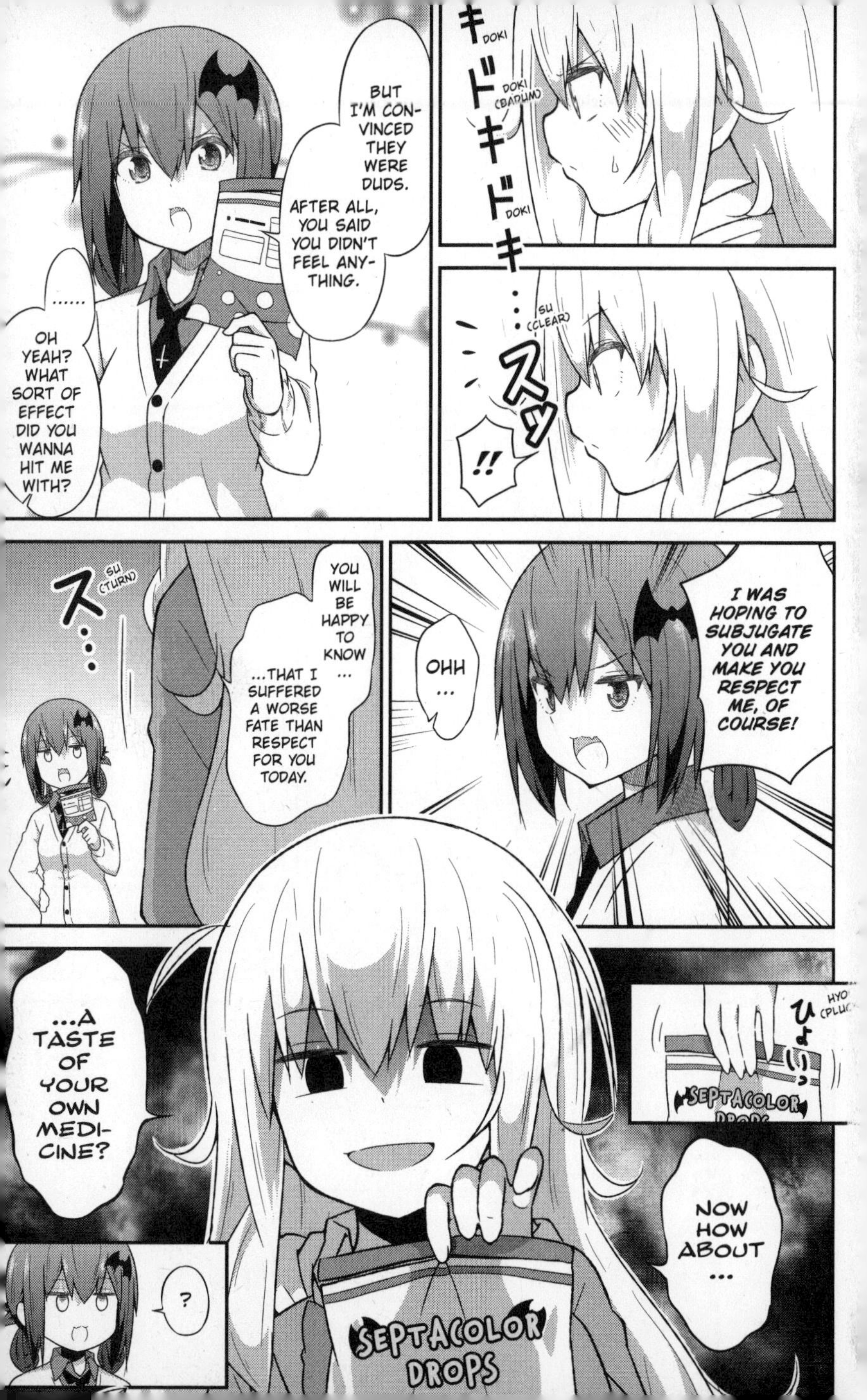

ドキドキドキ…
DOKI DOKI (BADUM) DOKI
SU (CLEAR)
スッ
!!
BUT I'M CON-VINCED THEY WERE DUDS.
AFTER ALL, YOU SAID YOU DIDN'T FEEL ANY-THING.
......
OH YEAH? WHAT SORT OF EFFECT DID YOU WANNA HIT ME WITH?
I WAS HOPING TO SUBJUGATE YOU AND MAKE YOU RESPECT ME, OF COURSE!
OHH...
ス…
SU (TURN)
YOU WILL BE HAPPY TO KNOW...
...THAT I SUFFERED A WORSE FATE THAN RESPECT FOR YOU TODAY.
ひょいっ
HYOI (PLUCK)
SEPTACOLOR DROPS
NOW HOW ABOUT...
...A TASTE OF YOUR OWN MEDI-CINE?
?
SEPTACOLOR DROPS

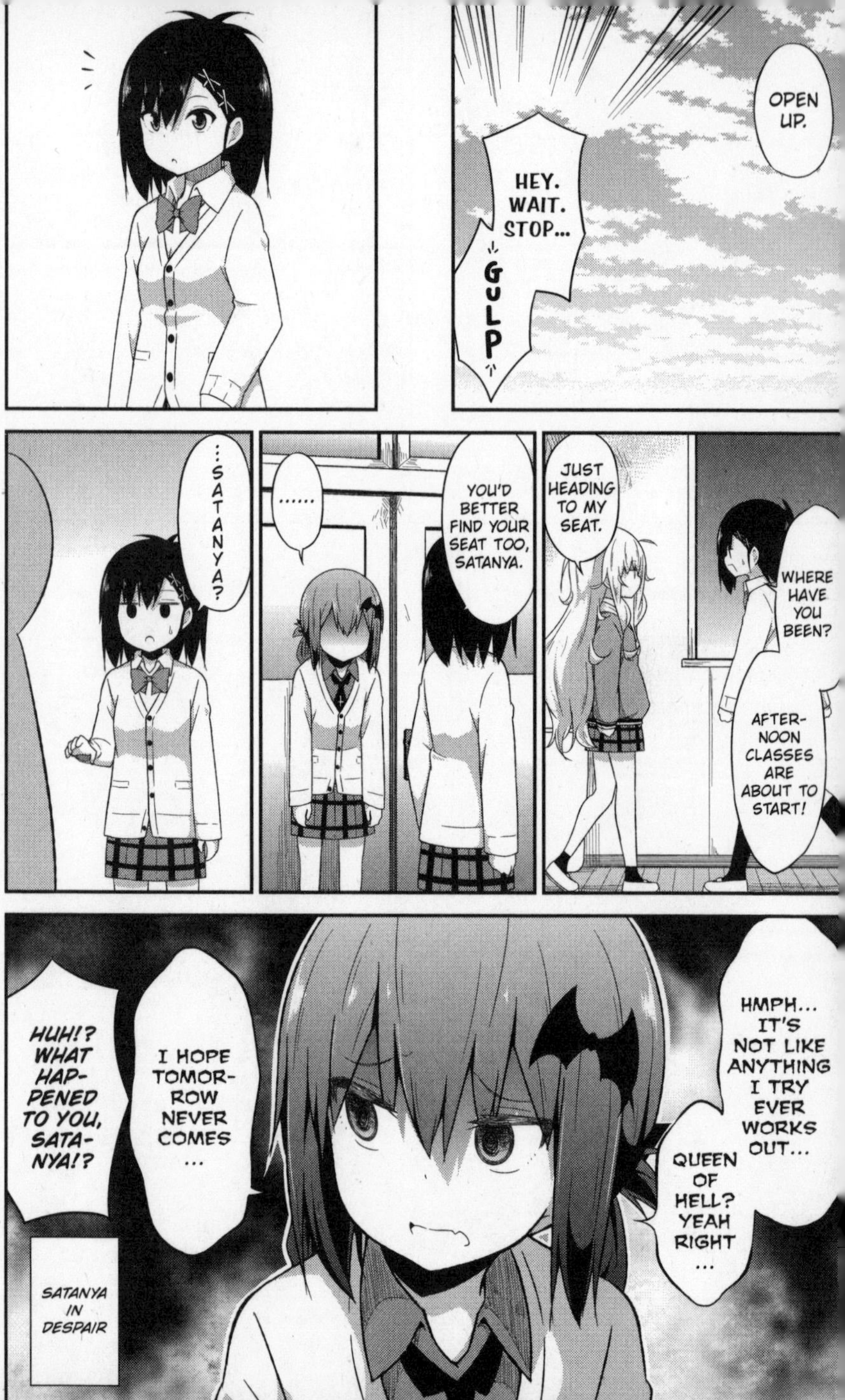
OPEN UP.
HEY. WAIT. STOP...
GULP
WHERE HAVE YOU BEEN?
AFTERNOON CLASSES ARE ABOUT TO START!
JUST HEADING TO MY SEAT.
YOU'D BETTER FIND YOUR SEAT TOO, SATANYA.
......
...SATANYA?
HMPH... IT'S NOT LIKE ANYTHING I TRY EVER WORKS OUT...
QUEEN OF HELL? YEAH RIGHT...
I HOPE TOMORROW NEVER COMES...
HUH!? WHAT HAPPENED TO YOU, SATANYA!?
SATANYA IN DESPAIR

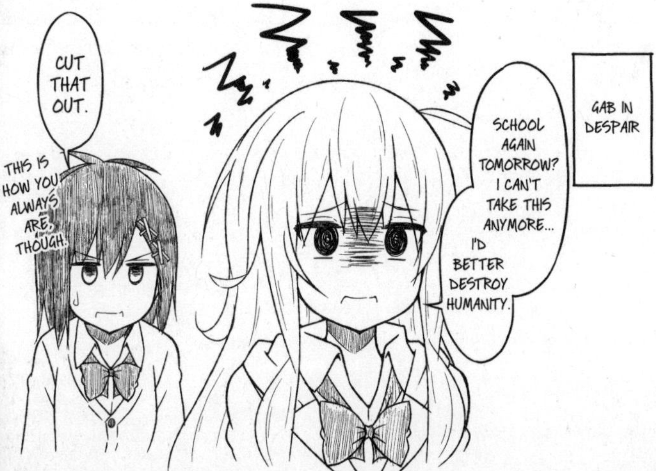
GAB IN DESPAIR
SCHOOL AGAIN TOMORROW? I CAN'T TAKE THIS ANYMORE...
I'D BETTER DESTROY HUMANITY.
CUT THAT OUT.
THIS IS HOW YOU ALWAYS ARE, THOUGH.

Gabriel Dropout

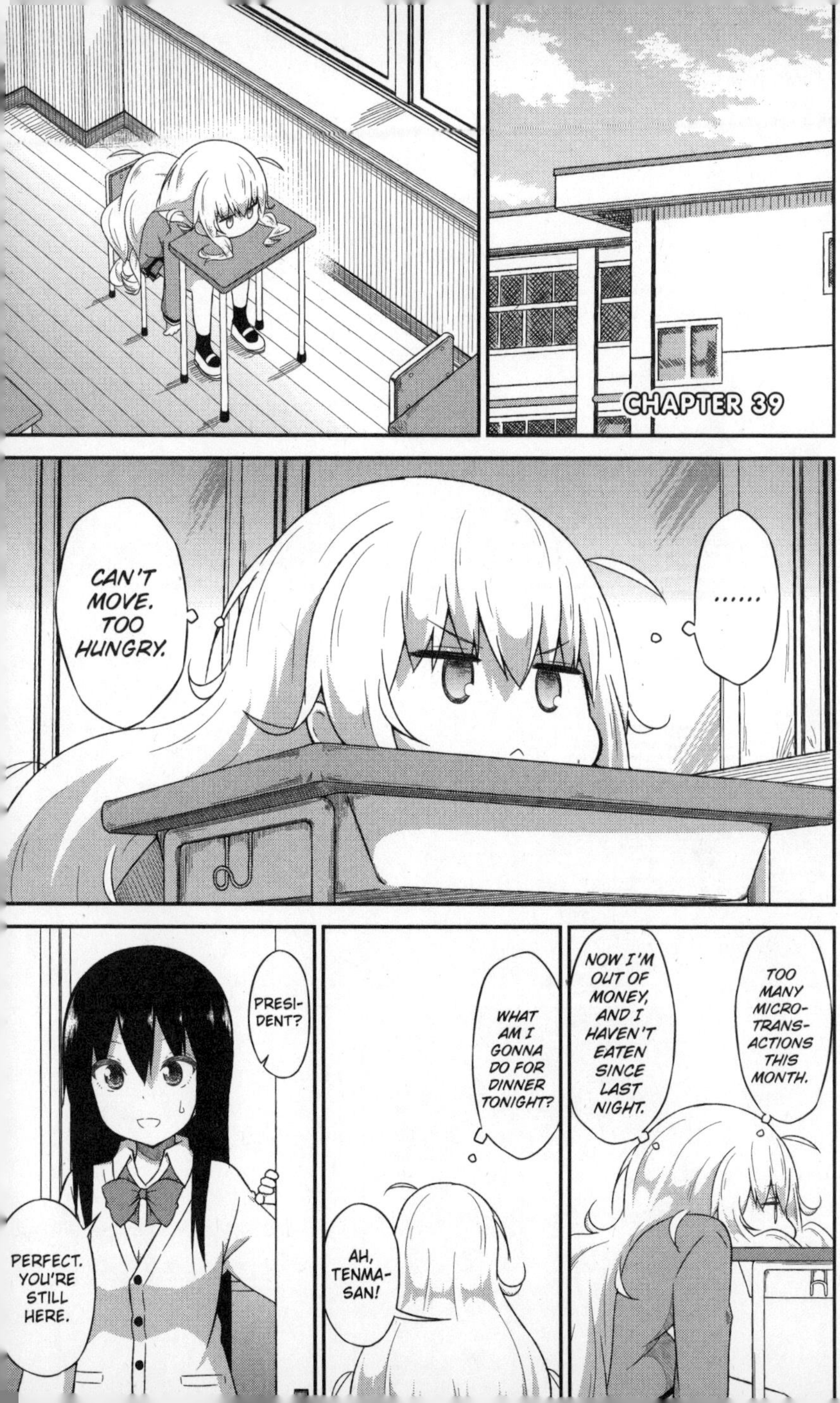
CHAPTER 39
......
CAN'T MOVE. TOO HUNGRY.
TOO MANY MICRO-TRANSACTIONS THIS MONTH.
NOW I'M OUT OF MONEY, AND I HAVEN'T EATEN SINCE LAST NIGHT.
WHAT AM I GONNA DO FOR DINNER TONIGHT?
AH, TENMA-SAN!
PRESIDENT?
PERFECT. YOU'RE STILL HERE.

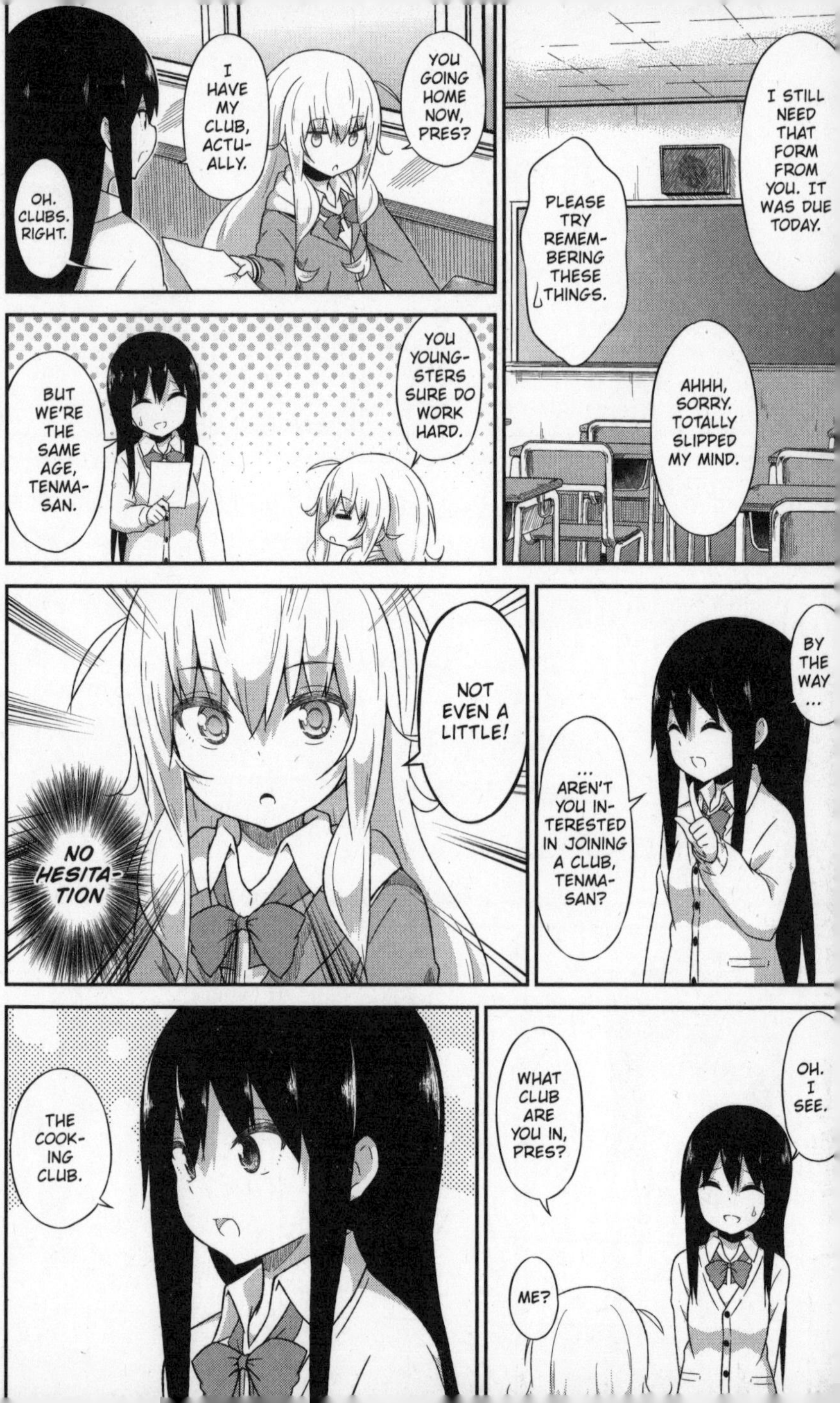
I STILL NEED THAT FORM FROM YOU. IT WAS DUE TODAY.
PLEASE TRY REMEMBERING THESE THINGS.
AHHH, SORRY. TOTALLY SLIPPED MY MIND.
YOU GOING HOME NOW, PRES?
I HAVE MY CLUB, ACTUALLY.
OH. CLUBS. RIGHT.
YOU YOUNGSTERS SURE DO WORK HARD.
BUT WE'RE THE SAME AGE, TENMA-SAN.
BY THE WAY...
...AREN'T YOU INTERESTED IN JOINING A CLUB, TENMA-SAN?
NOT EVEN A LITTLE!
NO HESITATION
OH. I SEE.
WHAT CLUB ARE YOU IN, PRES?
ME?
THE COOKING CLUB.

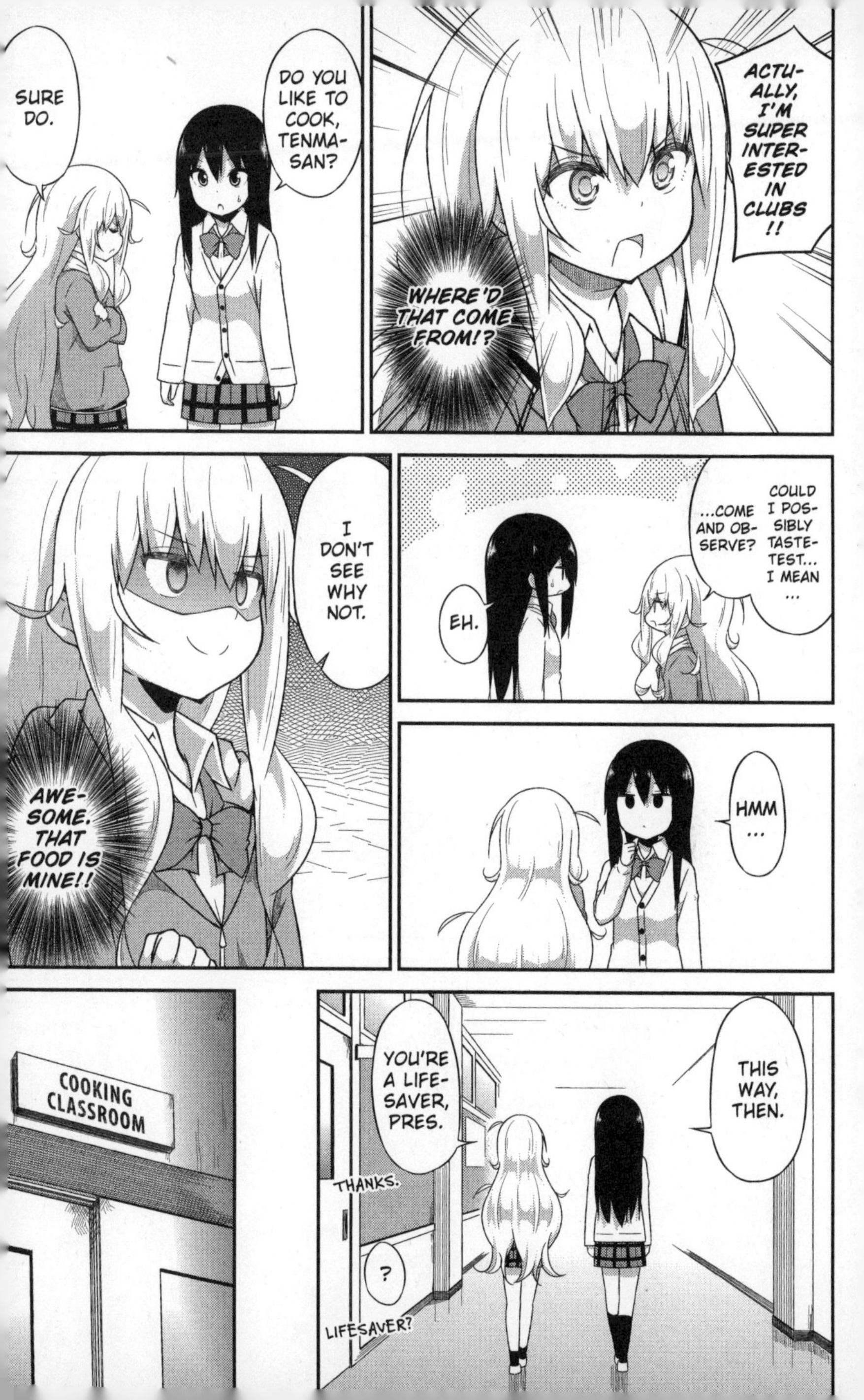
ACTUALLY, I'M SUPER INTERESTED IN CLUBS!!
WHERE'D THAT COME FROM!?
DO YOU LIKE TO COOK, TENMA-SAN?
SURE DO.
COULD I POSSIBLY TASTE-TEST... I MEAN ...
...COME AND OBSERVE?
EH.
HMM...
I DON'T SEE WHY NOT.
AWESOME. THAT FOOD IS MINE!!
THIS WAY, THEN.
YOU'RE A LIFESAVER, PRES.
THANKS.
?
LIFESAVER?
COOKING CLASSROOM

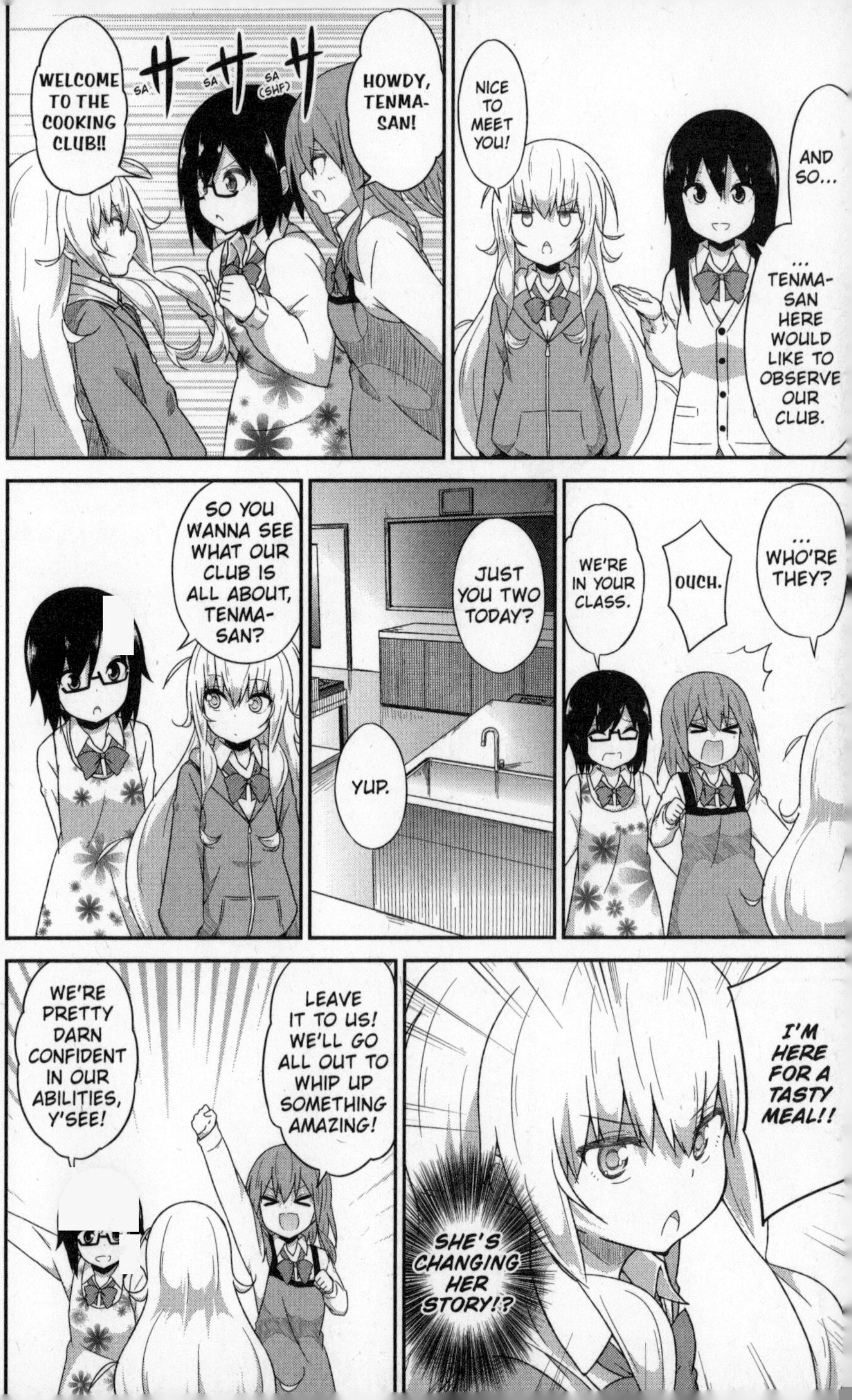
AND SO...
...TENMA-SAN HERE WOULD LIKE TO OBSERVE OUR CLUB.
NICE TO MEET YOU!
HOWDY, TENMA-SAN!
SA (SHF)
SA
SA
WELCOME TO THE COOKING CLUB!!
...WHO'RE THEY?
OUCH.
WE'RE IN YOUR CLASS.
JUST YOU TWO TODAY?
YUP.
SO YOU WANNA SEE WHAT OUR CLUB IS ALL ABOUT, TENMA-SAN?
I'M HERE FOR A TASTY MEAL!!
SHE'S CHANGING HER STORY!?
LEAVE IT TO US! WE'LL GO ALL OUT TO WHIP UP SOMETHING AMAZING!
WE'RE PRETTY DARN CONFIDENT IN OUR ABILITIES, Y'SEE!

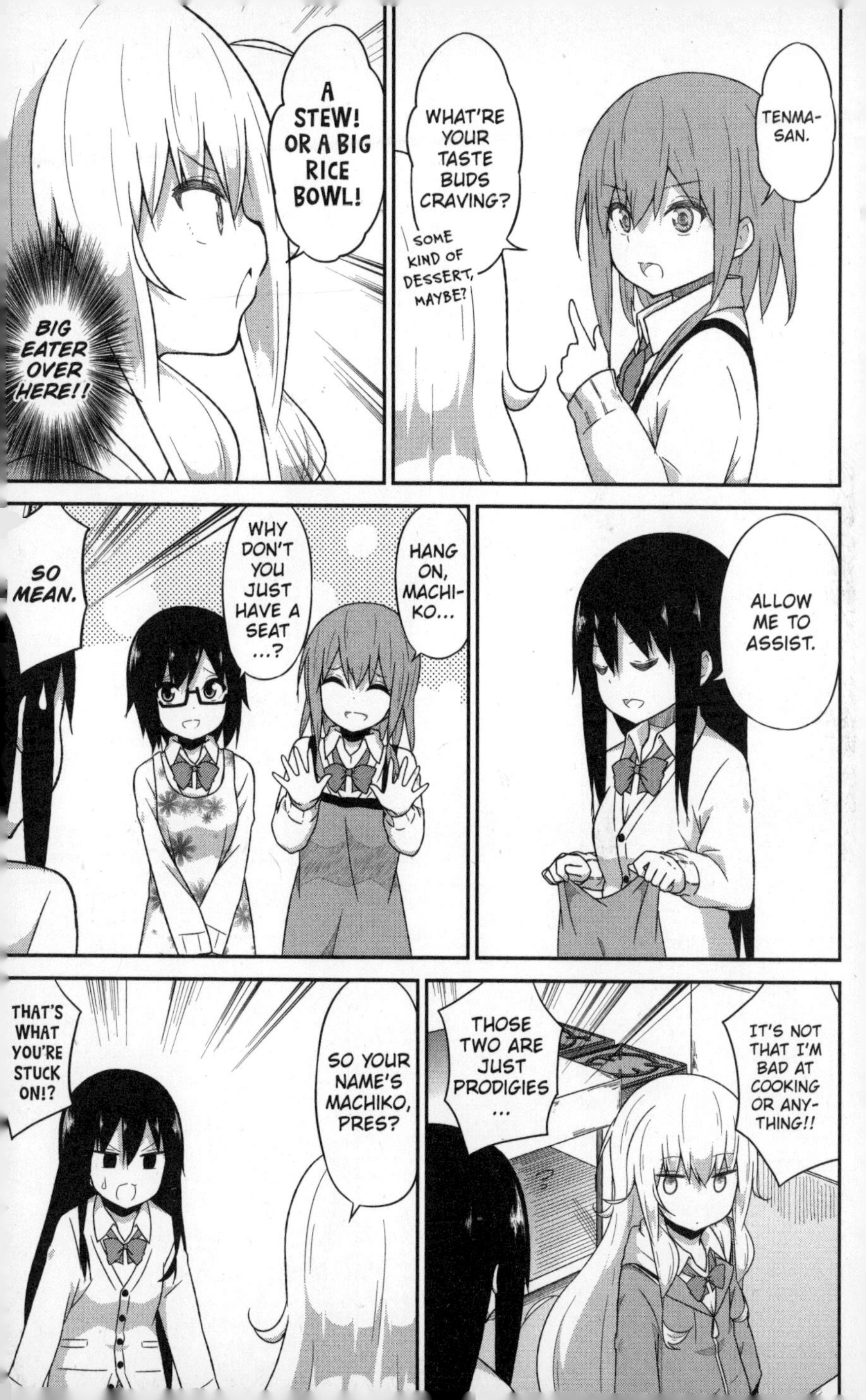
TENMA-SAN.
WHAT'RE YOUR TASTE BUDS CRAVING?
SOME KIND OF DESSERT, MAYBE?
A STEW! OR A BIG RICE BOWL!
BIG EATER OVER HERE!!
ALLOW ME TO ASSIST.
HANG ON, MACHIKO...
WHY DON'T YOU JUST HAVE A SEAT ...?
SO MEAN.
IT'S NOT THAT I'M BAD AT COOKING OR ANYTHING!!
THOSE TWO ARE JUST PRODIGIES ...
SO YOUR NAME'S MACHIKO, PRES?
THAT'S WHAT YOU'RE STUCK ON!?

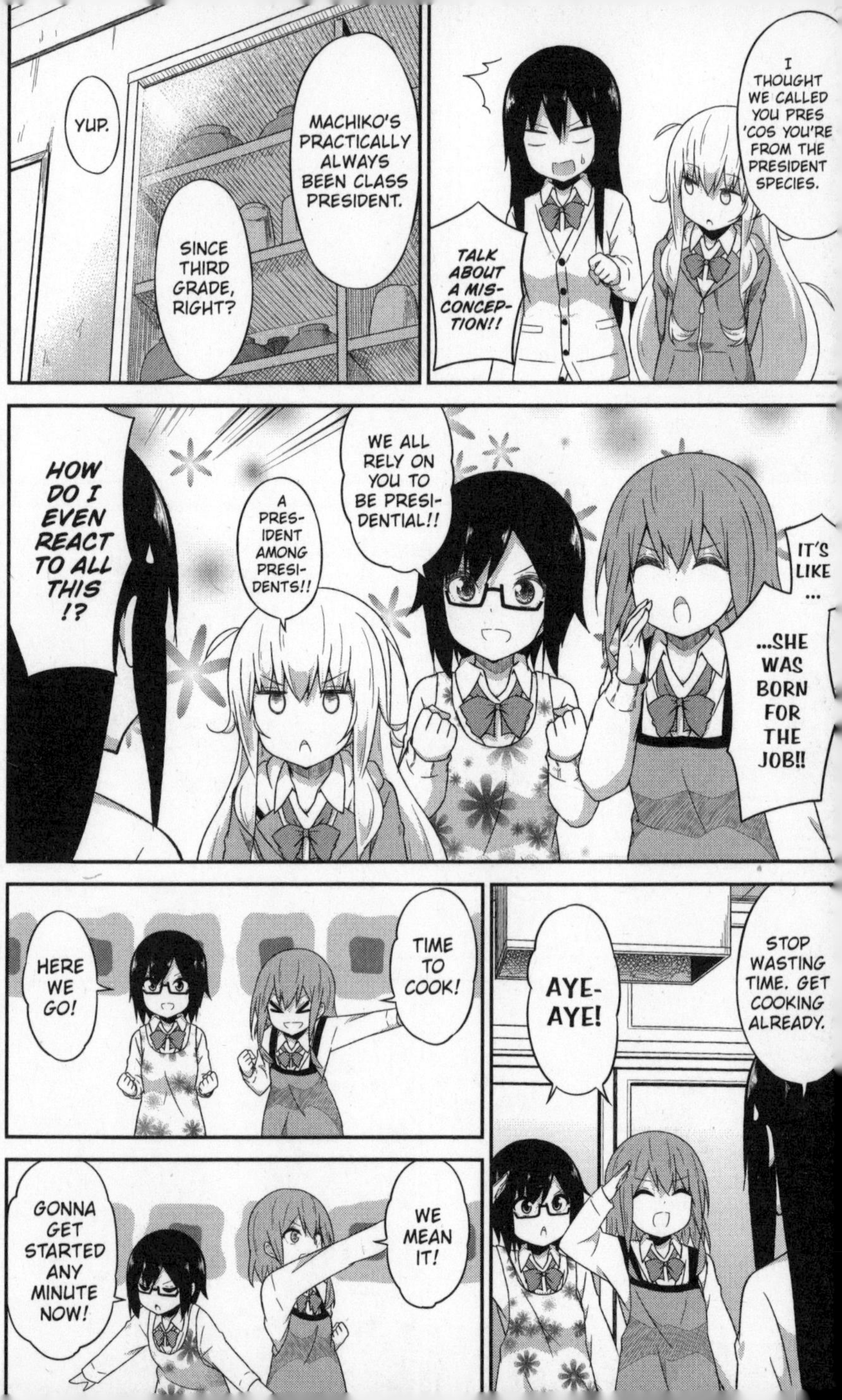

I THOUGHT WE CALLED YOU PRES 'COS YOU'RE FROM THE PRESIDENT SPECIES.
TALK ABOUT A MISCONCEPTION!!
MACHIKO'S PRACTICALLY ALWAYS BEEN CLASS PRESIDENT.
YUP.
SINCE THIRD GRADE, RIGHT?
IT'S LIKE ...
...SHE WAS BORN FOR THE JOB!!
WE ALL RELY ON YOU TO BE PRESIDENTIAL!!
A PRESIDENT AMONG PRESIDENTS!!
HOW DO I EVEN REACT TO ALL THIS!?
STOP WASTING TIME. GET COOKING ALREADY.
AYE-AYE!
TIME TO COOK!
HERE WE GO!
WE MEAN IT!
GONNA GET STARTED ANY MINUTE NOW!

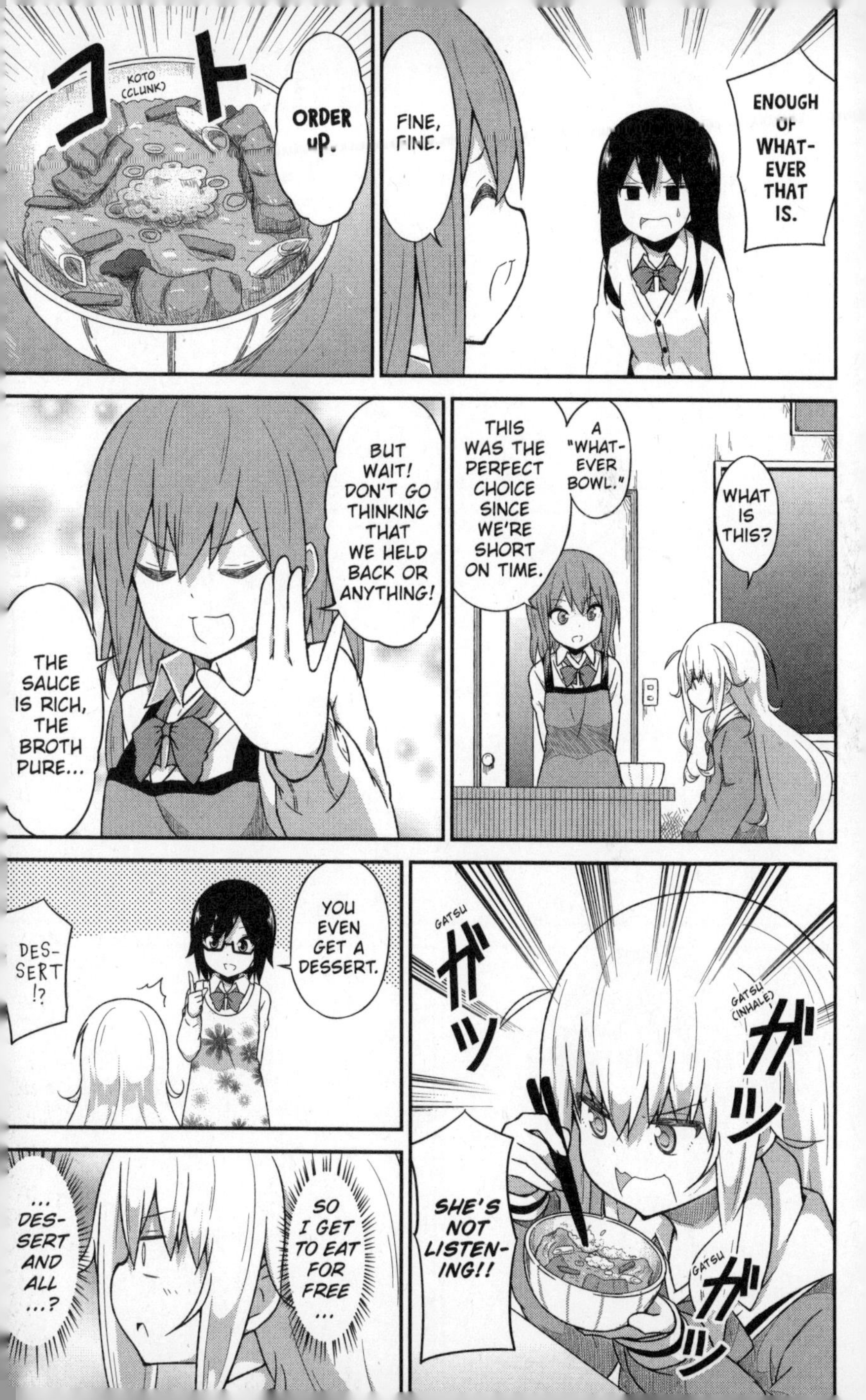
ENOUGH OF WHAT-EVER THAT IS.
FINE, FINE.
ORDER UP.
KOTO (CLUNK)
WHAT IS THIS?
A "WHAT-EVER BOWL."
THIS WAS THE PERFECT CHOICE SINCE WE'RE SHORT ON TIME.
BUT WAIT! DON'T GO THINKING THAT WE HELD BACK OR ANYTHING!
THE SAUCE IS RICH, THE BROTH PURE...
GATSU (INHALE)
GATSU
GATSU
SHE'S NOT LISTEN-ING!!
YOU EVEN GET A DESSERT.
DES-SERT!?
SO I GET TO EAT FOR FREE...
...DES-SERT AND ALL...?

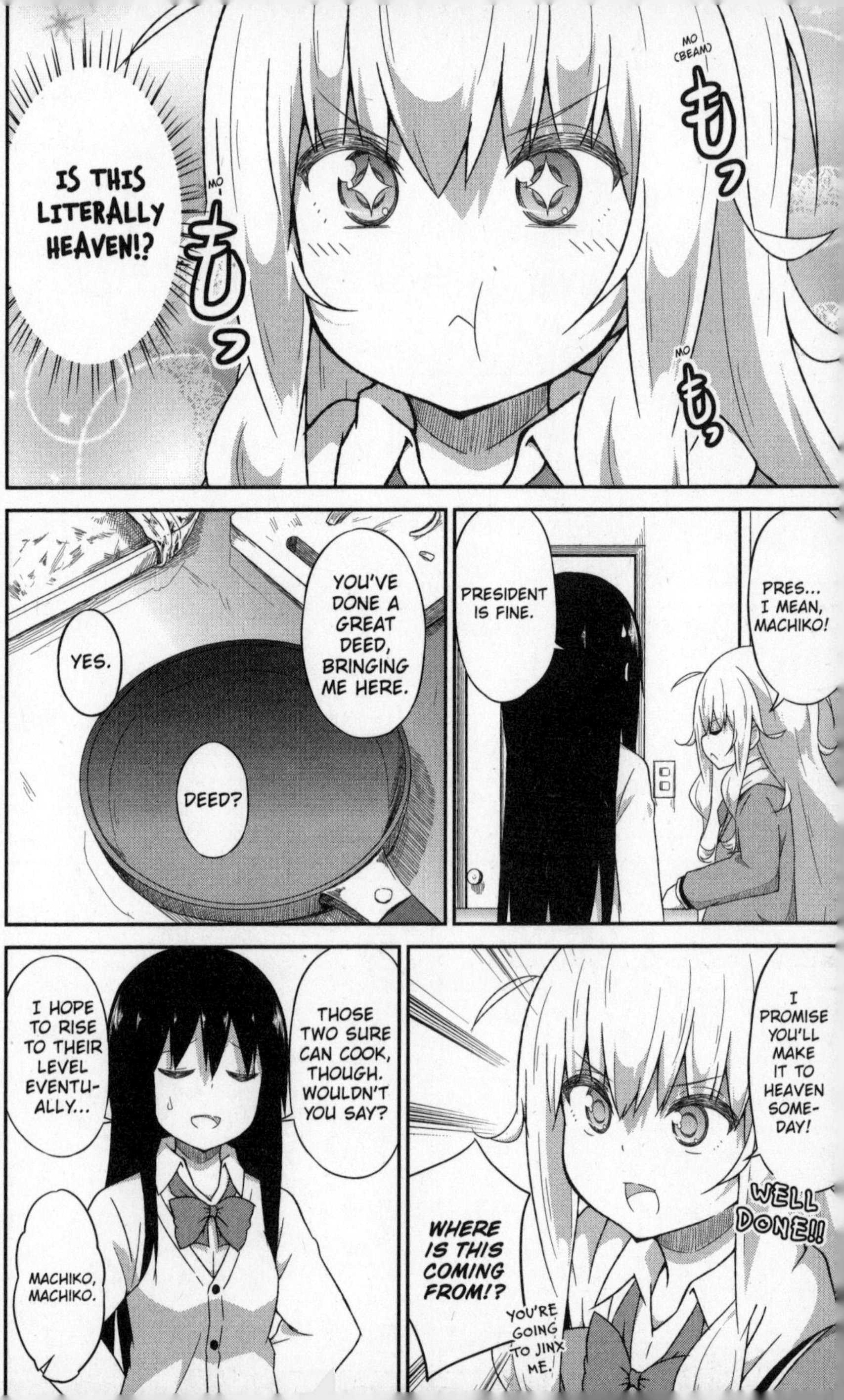

MO (BEAM)
もっ
IS THIS LITERALLY HEAVEN!?
MO
もっ
MO
もっ
PRES... I MEAN, MACHIKO!
PRESIDENT IS FINE.
YOU'VE DONE A GREAT DEED, BRINGING ME HERE.
YES.
DEED?
I PROMISE YOU'LL MAKE IT TO HEAVEN SOME-DAY!
WELL DONE!!
WHERE IS THIS COMING FROM!?
YOU'RE GOING TO JINX ME.
THOSE TWO SURE CAN COOK, THOUGH. WOULDN'T YOU SAY?
I HOPE TO RISE TO THEIR LEVEL EVENTU-ALLY...
MACHIKO, MACHIKO.

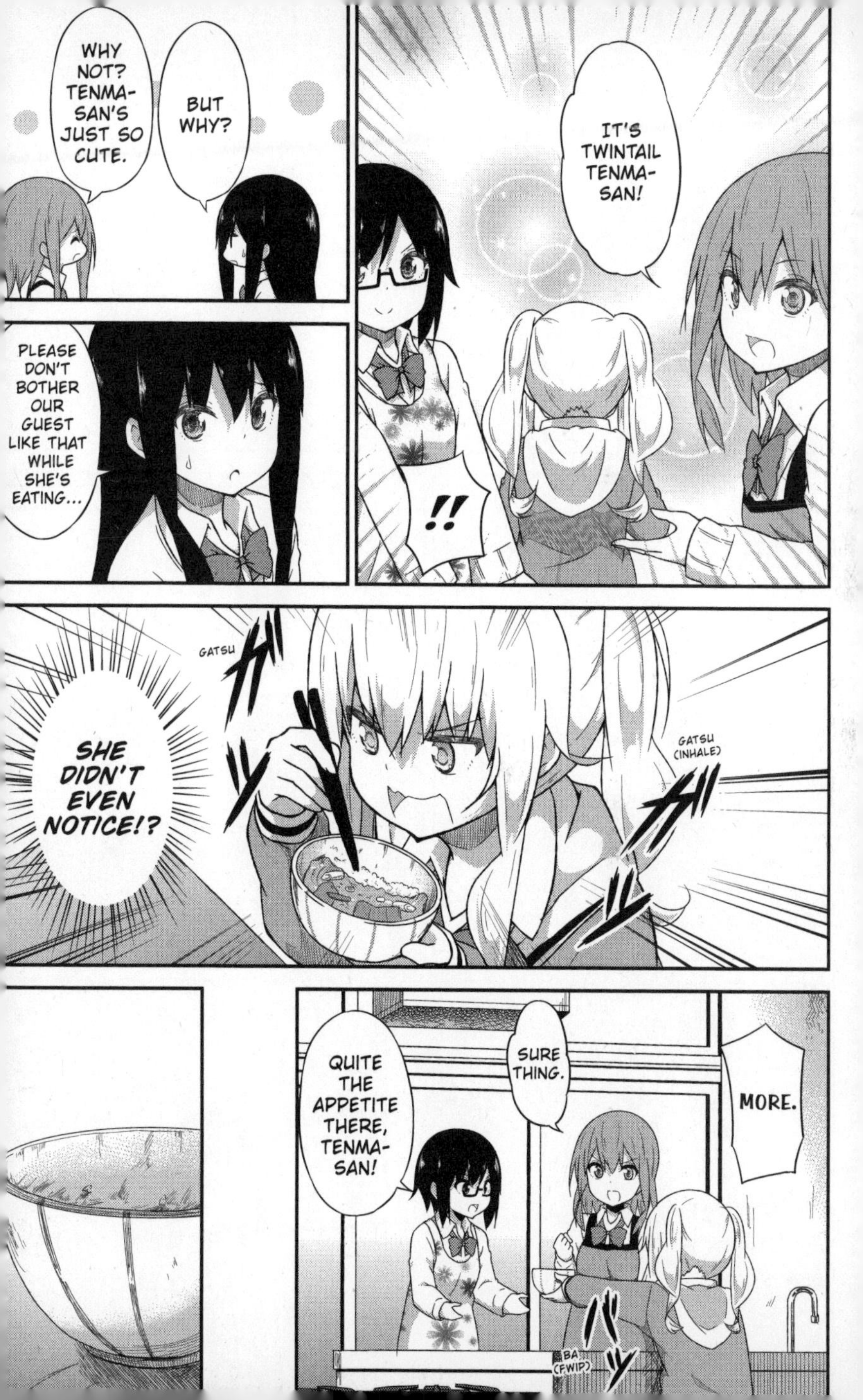
IT'S TWINTAIL TENMA-SAN!
!!
BUT WHY?
WHY NOT? TENMA-SAN'S JUST SO CUTE.
PLEASE DON'T BOTHER OUR GUEST LIKE THAT WHILE SHE'S EATING...
GATSU (INHALE)
GATSU
SHE DIDN'T EVEN NOTICE!?
MORE.
SURE THING.
QUITE THE APPETITE THERE, TENMA-SAN!
BA (FWIP)

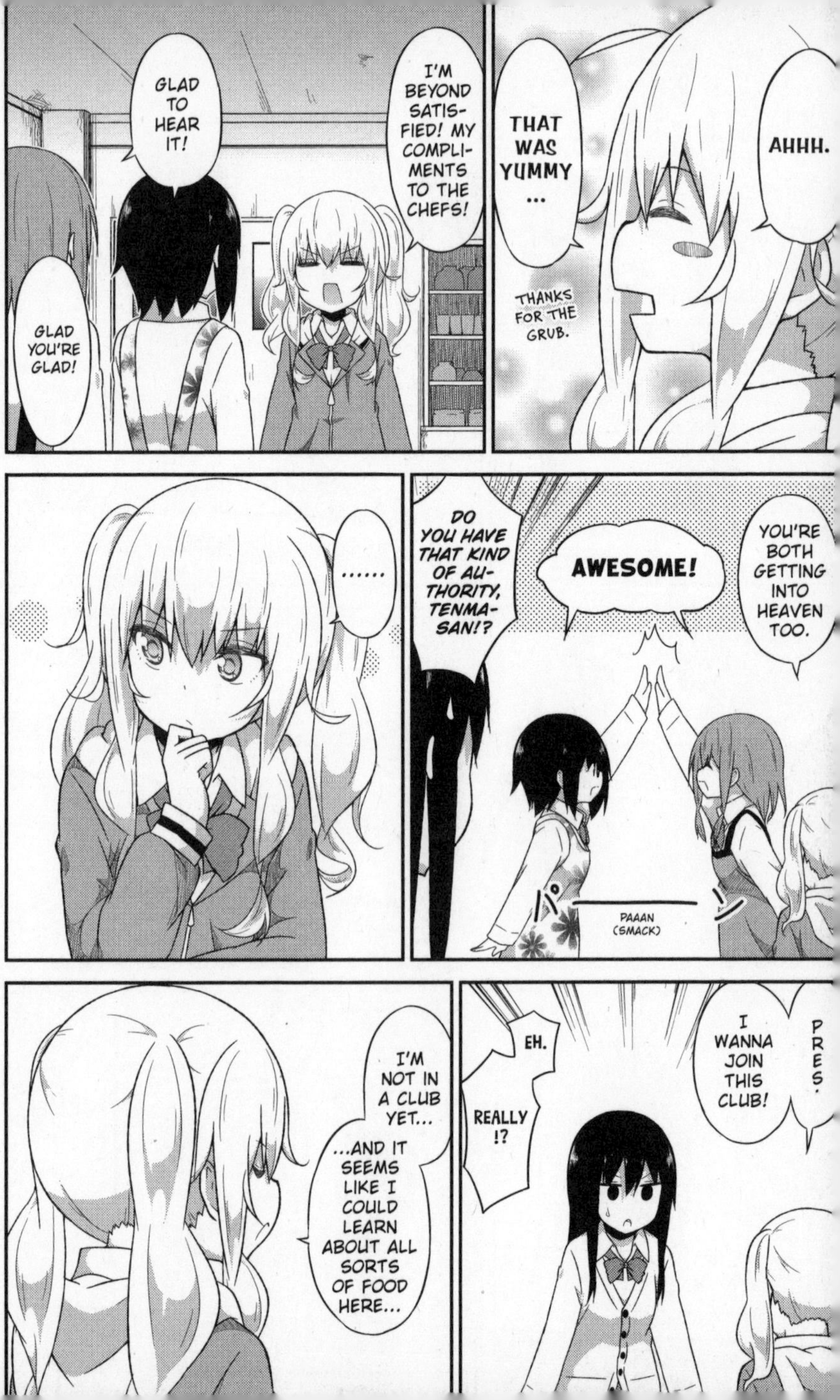
AHHH.
THAT WAS YUMMY...
THANKS FOR THE GRUB.
I'M BEYOND SATISFIED! MY COMPLIMENTS TO THE CHEFS!
GLAD TO HEAR IT!
GLAD YOU'RE GLAD!
YOU'RE BOTH GETTING INTO HEAVEN TOO.
AWESOME!
DO YOU HAVE THAT KIND OF AUTHORITY, TENMA-SAN!?
PAAAN (SMACK)
......
PRES.
I WANNA JOIN THIS CLUB!
EH.
REALLY!?
I'M NOT IN A CLUB YET...
...AND IT SEEMS LIKE I COULD LEARN ABOUT ALL SORTS OF FOOD HERE...

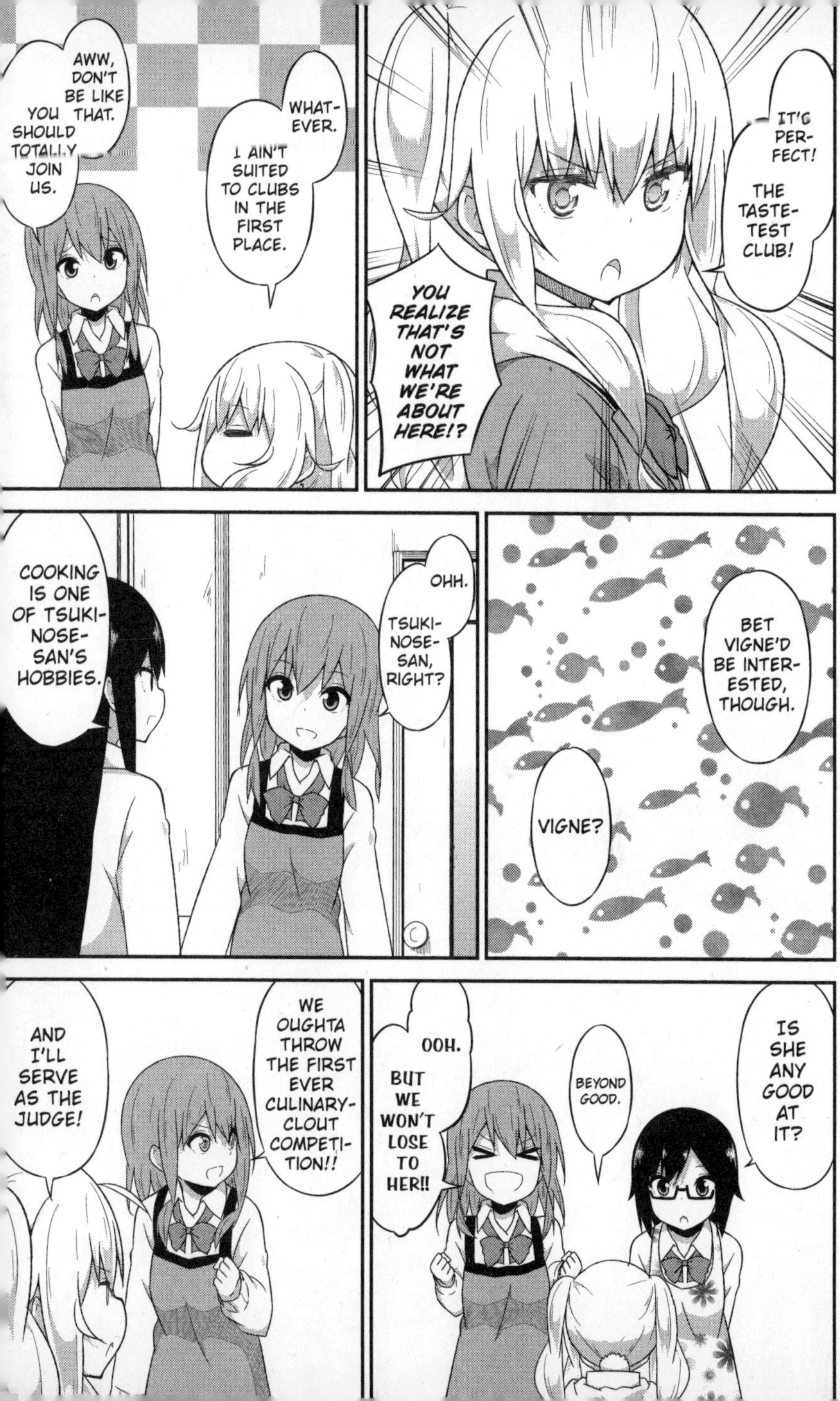
IT'S PERFECT! THE TASTE-TEST CLUB!
YOU REALIZE THAT'S NOT WHAT WE'RE ABOUT HERE!?
WHATEVER. I AIN'T SUITED TO CLUBS IN THE FIRST PLACE.
AWW, DON'T BE LIKE THAT. YOU SHOULD TOTALLY JOIN US.
BET VIGNE'D BE INTERESTED, THOUGH.
VIGNE?
OHH. TSUKINOSE-SAN, RIGHT?
COOKING IS ONE OF TSUKINOSE-SAN'S HOBBIES.
IS SHE ANY GOOD AT IT?
BEYOND GOOD.
OOH. BUT WE WON'T LOSE TO HER!!
WE OUGHTA THROW THE FIRST EVER CULINARY-CLOUT COMPETITION!!
AND I'LL SERVE AS THE JUDGE!

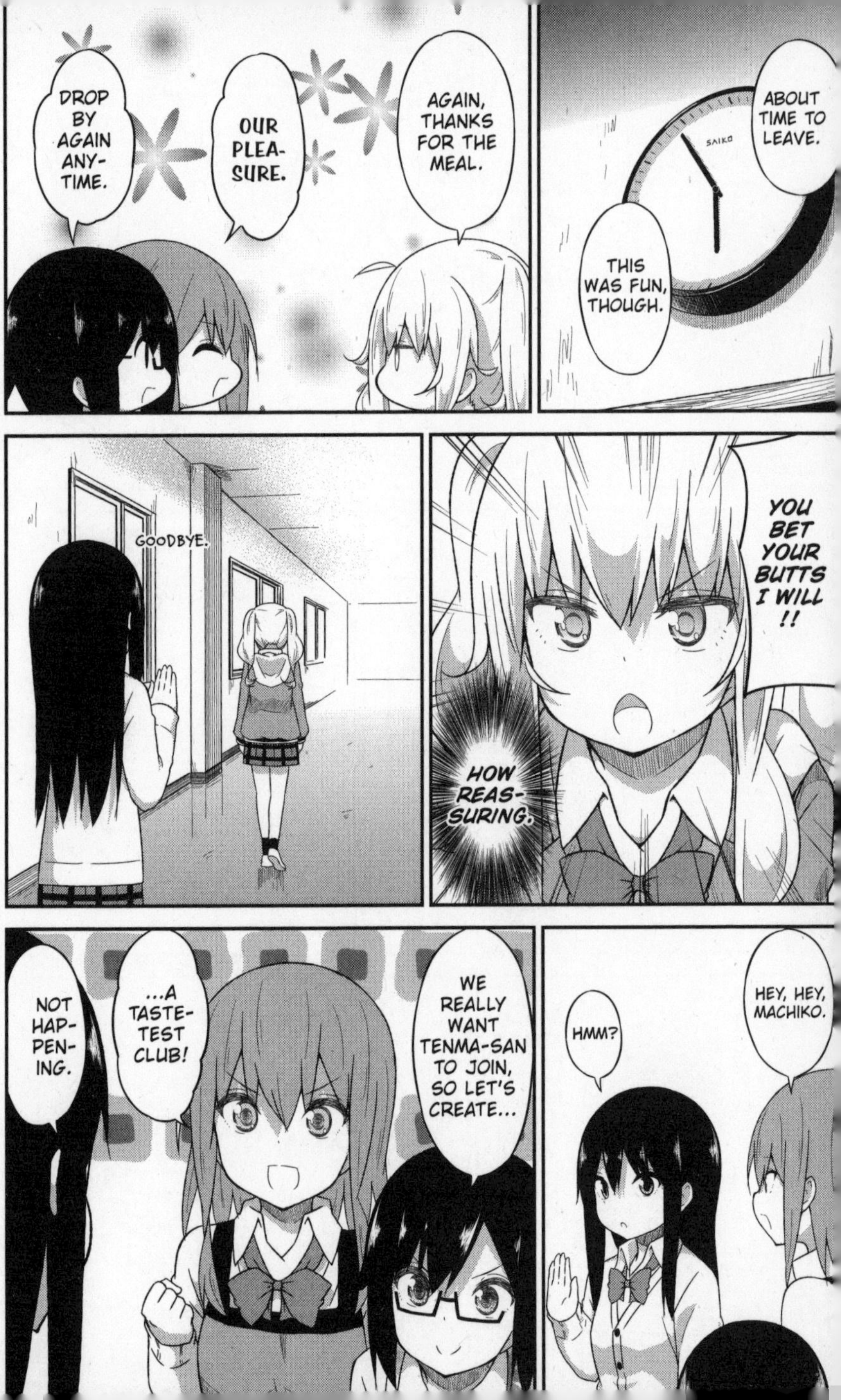
ABOUT TIME TO LEAVE.
THIS WAS FUN, THOUGH.
AGAIN, THANKS FOR THE MEAL.
OUR PLEA-SURE.
DROP BY AGAIN ANY-TIME.
YOU BET YOUR BUTTS I WILL !!
HOW REAS-SURING.
GOODBYE.
HEY, HEY, MACHIKO.
HMM?
WE REALLY WANT TENMA-SAN TO JOIN, SO LET'S CREATE...
...A TASTE-TEST CLUB!
NOT HAP-PEN-ING.

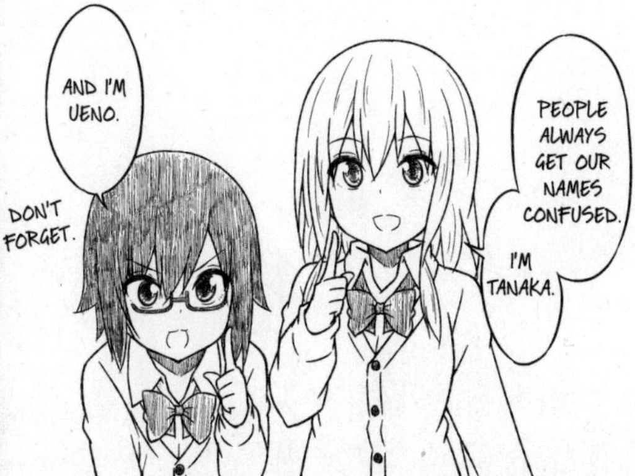
PEOPLE ALWAYS GET OUR NAMES CONFUSED.
I'M TANAKA.
AND I'M UENO.
DON'T FORGET.

Gabriel Dropout

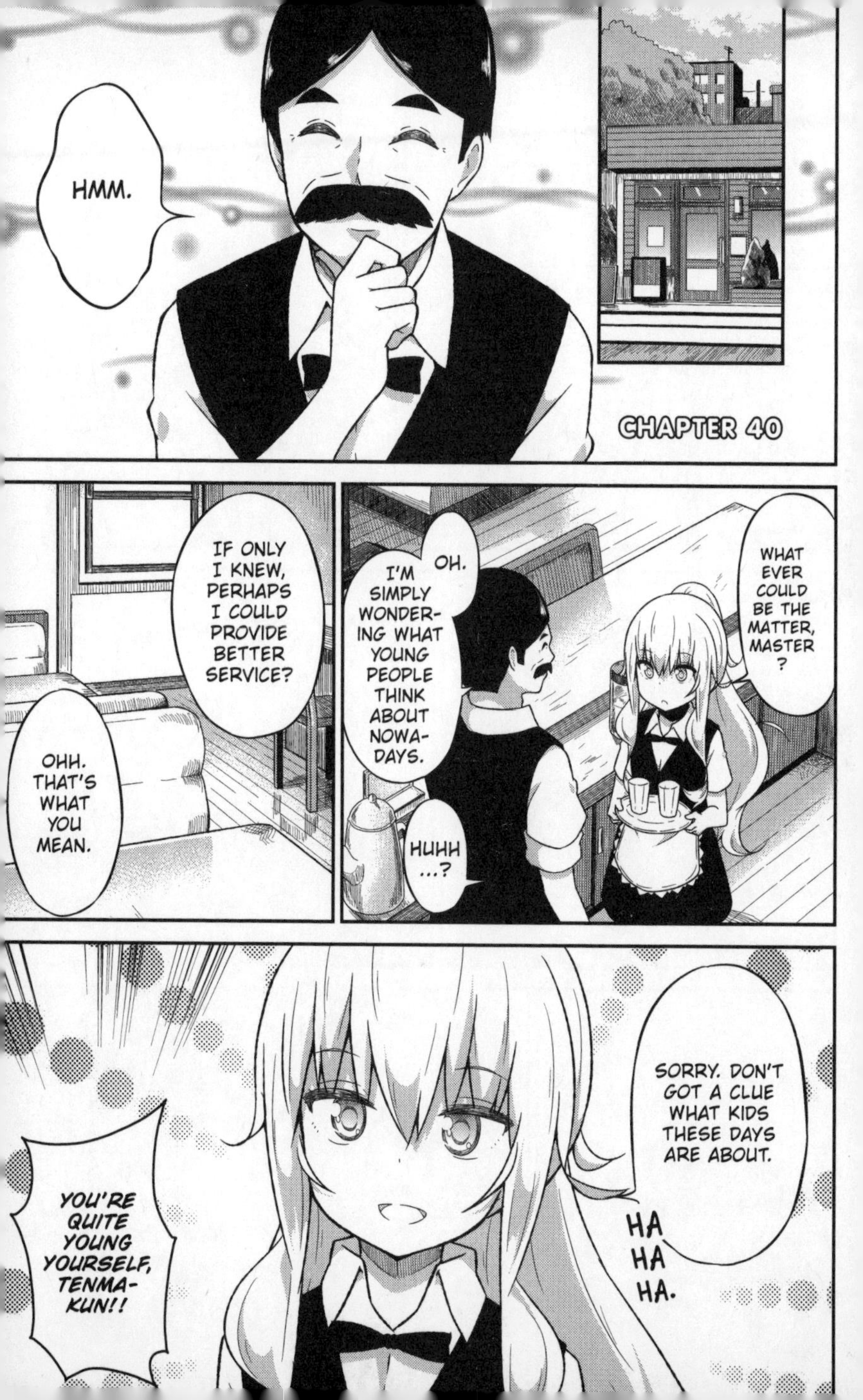
CHAPTER 40
HMM.
WHAT EVER COULD BE THE MATTER, MASTER?
OH.
I'M SIMPLY WONDERING WHAT YOUNG PEOPLE THINK ABOUT NOWADAYS.
HUHH...?
IF ONLY I KNEW, PERHAPS I COULD PROVIDE BETTER SERVICE?
OHH. THAT'S WHAT YOU MEAN.
SORRY. DON'T GOT A CLUE WHAT KIDS THESE DAYS ARE ABOUT.
HA HA HA.
YOU'RE QUITE YOUNG YOURSELF, TENMA-KUN!!

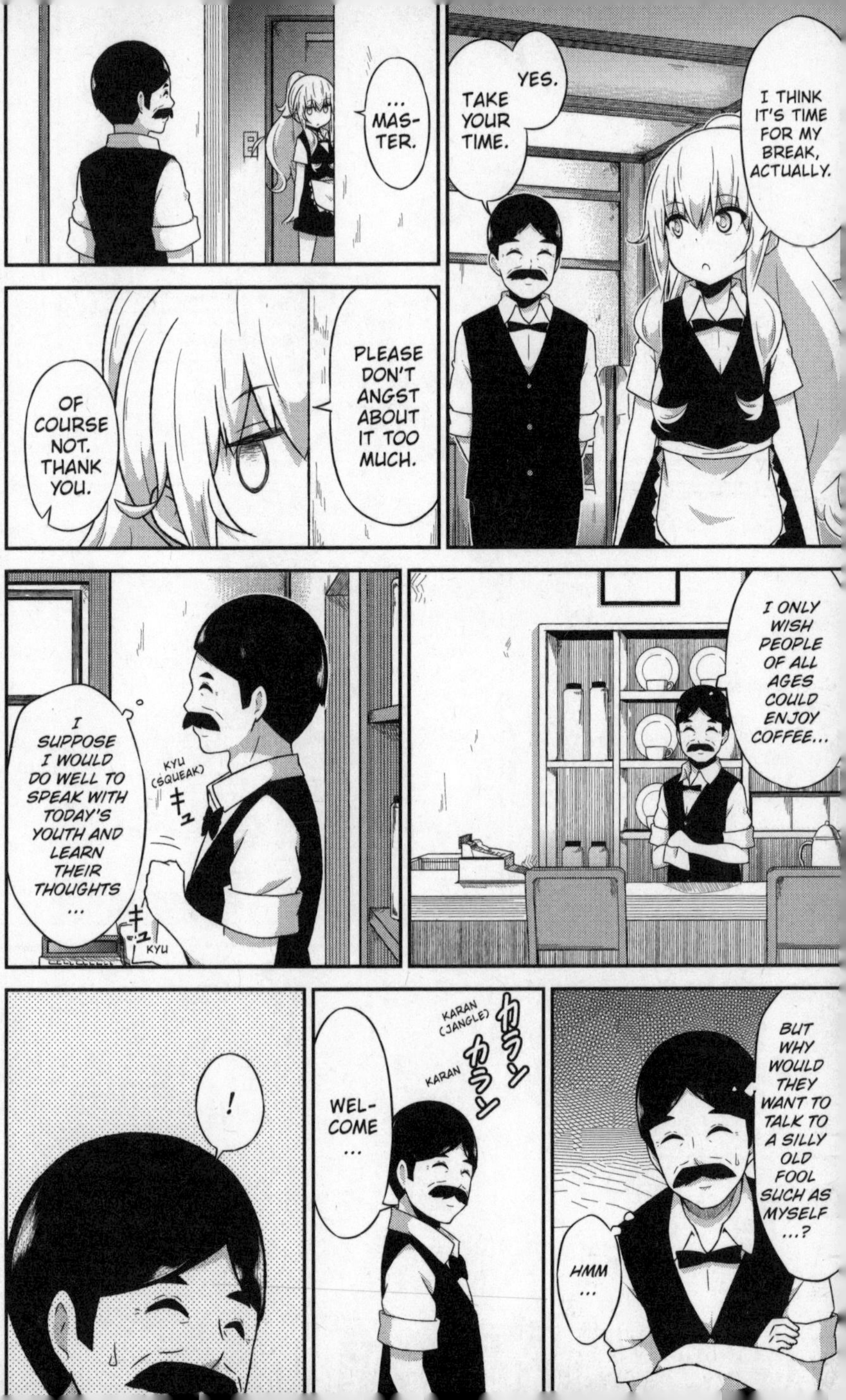
I THINK IT'S TIME FOR MY BREAK, ACTUALLY.
YES. TAKE YOUR TIME.
... MAS-TER.
PLEASE DON'T ANGST ABOUT IT TOO MUCH.
OF COURSE NOT. THANK YOU.
I ONLY WISH PEOPLE OF ALL AGES COULD ENJOY COFFEE...
I SUPPOSE I WOULD DO WELL TO SPEAK WITH TODAY'S YOUTH AND LEARN THEIR THOUGHTS ...
KYU (SQUEAK)
KYU
BUT WHY WOULD THEY WANT TO TALK TO A SILLY OLD FOOL SUCH AS MYSELF ...?
HMM ...
KARAN (JANGLE)
KARAN
WEL-COME ...
!

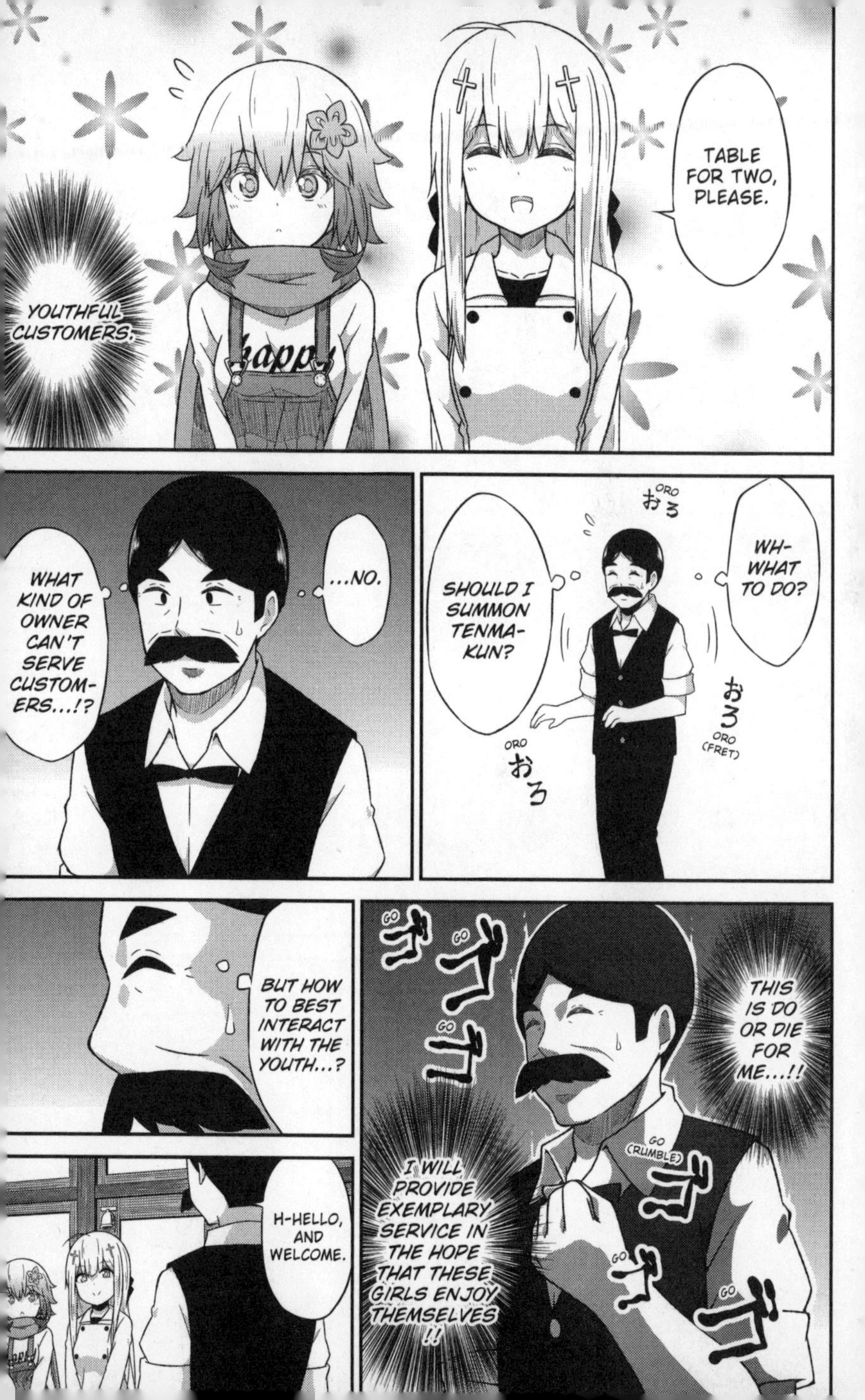
TABLE FOR TWO, PLEASE.
YOUTHFUL CUSTOMERS.
WH- WHAT TO DO?
ORO
おろ
SHOULD I SUMMON TENMA-KUN?
おろ
ORO (FRET)
ORO
おろ
...NO.
WHAT KIND OF OWNER CAN'T SERVE CUSTOMERS...!?
THIS IS DO OR DIE FOR ME...!!
GO
ゴ
GO
ゴ
GO
ゴ
GO (RUMBLE)
ゴ
GO
ゴ
GO
ゴ
I WILL PROVIDE EXEMPLARY SERVICE IN THE HOPE THAT THESE GIRLS ENJOY THEMSELVES!!
BUT HOW TO BEST INTERACT WITH THE YOUTH...?
H-HELLO, AND WELCOME.

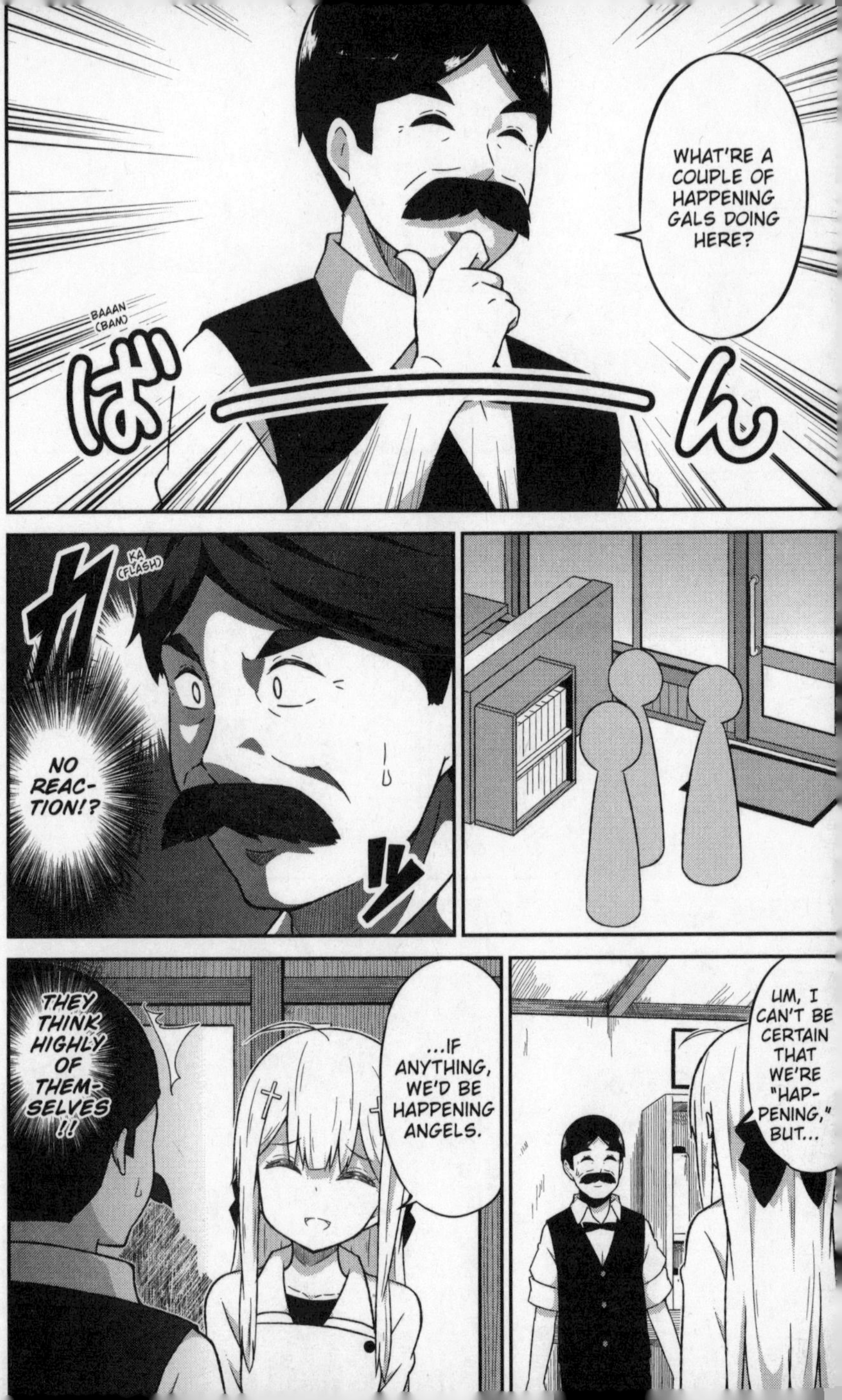
WHAT'RE A COUPLE OF HAPPENING GALS DOING HERE?
BAAAN (BAM)
KA (FLASH)
NO REACTION!?
UM, I CAN'T BE CERTAIN THAT WE'RE "HAPPENING," BUT...
...IF ANYTHING, WE'D BE HAPPENING ANGELS.
THEY THINK HIGHLY OF THEMSELVES!!

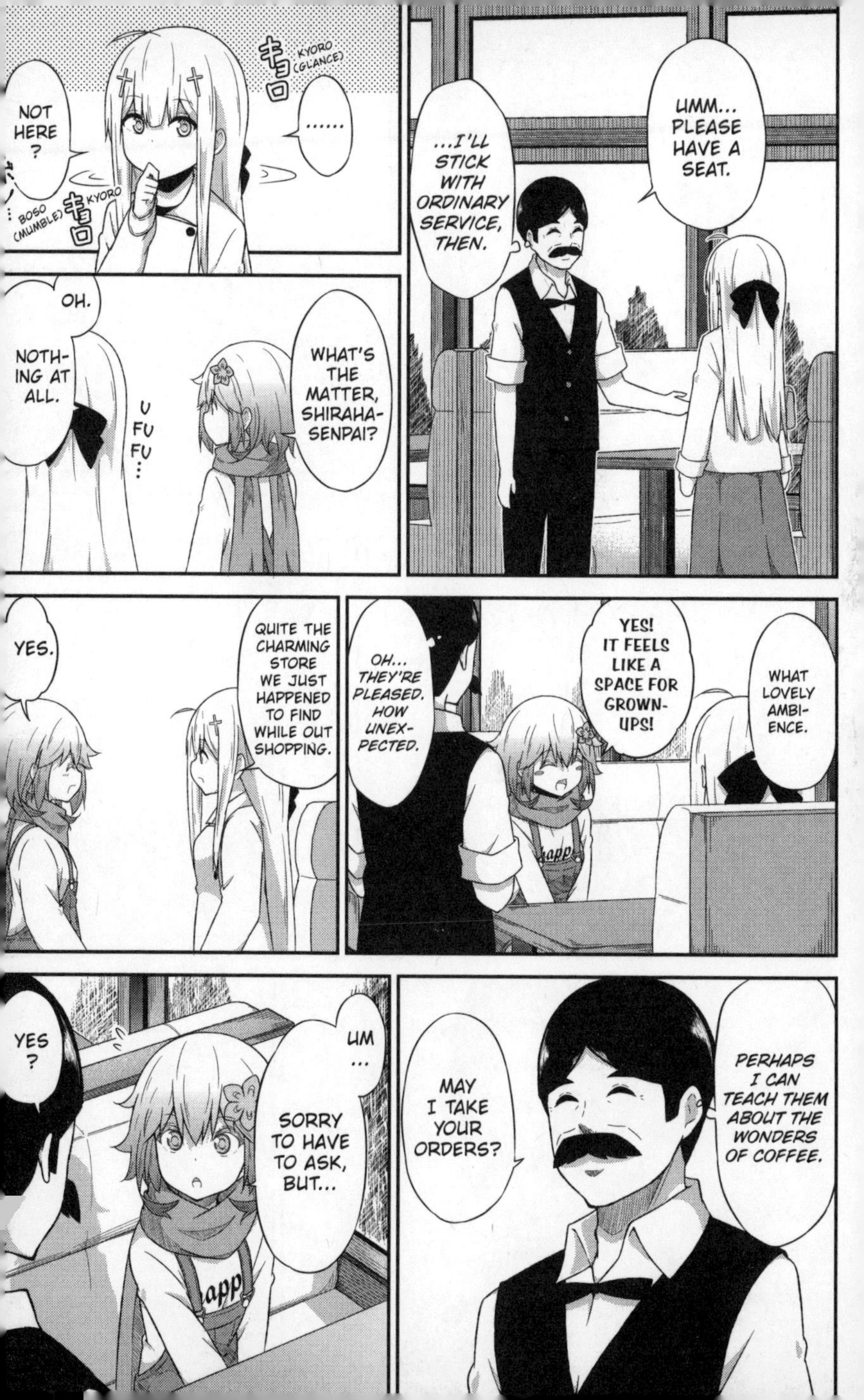
UMM... PLEASE HAVE A SEAT.
...I'LL STICK WITH ORDINARY SERVICE, THEN.
キョロ KYORO (GLANCE)
......
NOT HERE?
BOSO (MUMBLE)...
キョロ KYORO
WHAT'S THE MATTER, SHIRAHA-SENPAI?
UFUFU...
OH.
NOTHING AT ALL.
WHAT LOVELY AMBIENCE.
YES! IT FEELS LIKE A SPACE FOR GROWN-UPS!
OH... THEY'RE PLEASED. HOW UNEXPECTED.
QUITE THE CHARMING STORE WE JUST HAPPENED TO FIND WHILE OUT SHOPPING.
YES.
PERHAPS I CAN TEACH THEM ABOUT THE WONDERS OF COFFEE.
MAY I TAKE YOUR ORDERS?
UM...
SORRY TO HAVE TO ASK, BUT...
YES?

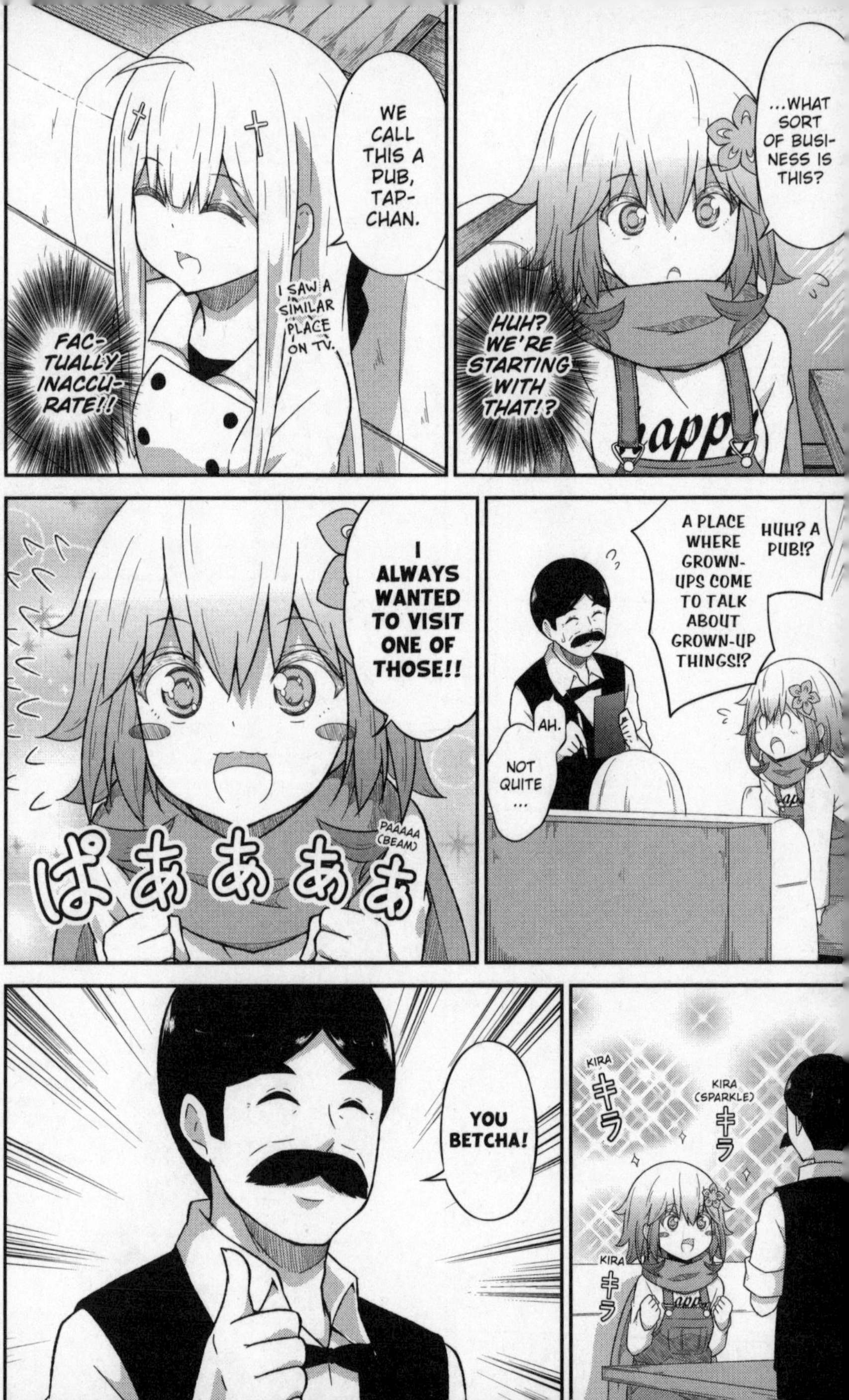
...WHAT SORT OF BUSI-NESS IS THIS?
HUH? WE'RE STARTING WITH THAT!?
WE CALL THIS A PUB, TAP-CHAN.
I SAW A SIMILAR PLACE ON TV.
FAC-TUALLY INACCU-RATE!!
HUH? A PUB!?
A PLACE WHERE GROWN-UPS COME TO TALK ABOUT GROWN-UP THINGS!?
AH.
NOT QUITE...
I ALWAYS WANTED TO VISIT ONE OF THOSE!!
ぱあああぁ
PAAAAA (BEAM)
KIRA
キラ
KIRA (SPARKLE)
キラ
KIRA
キラ
YOU BETCHA!

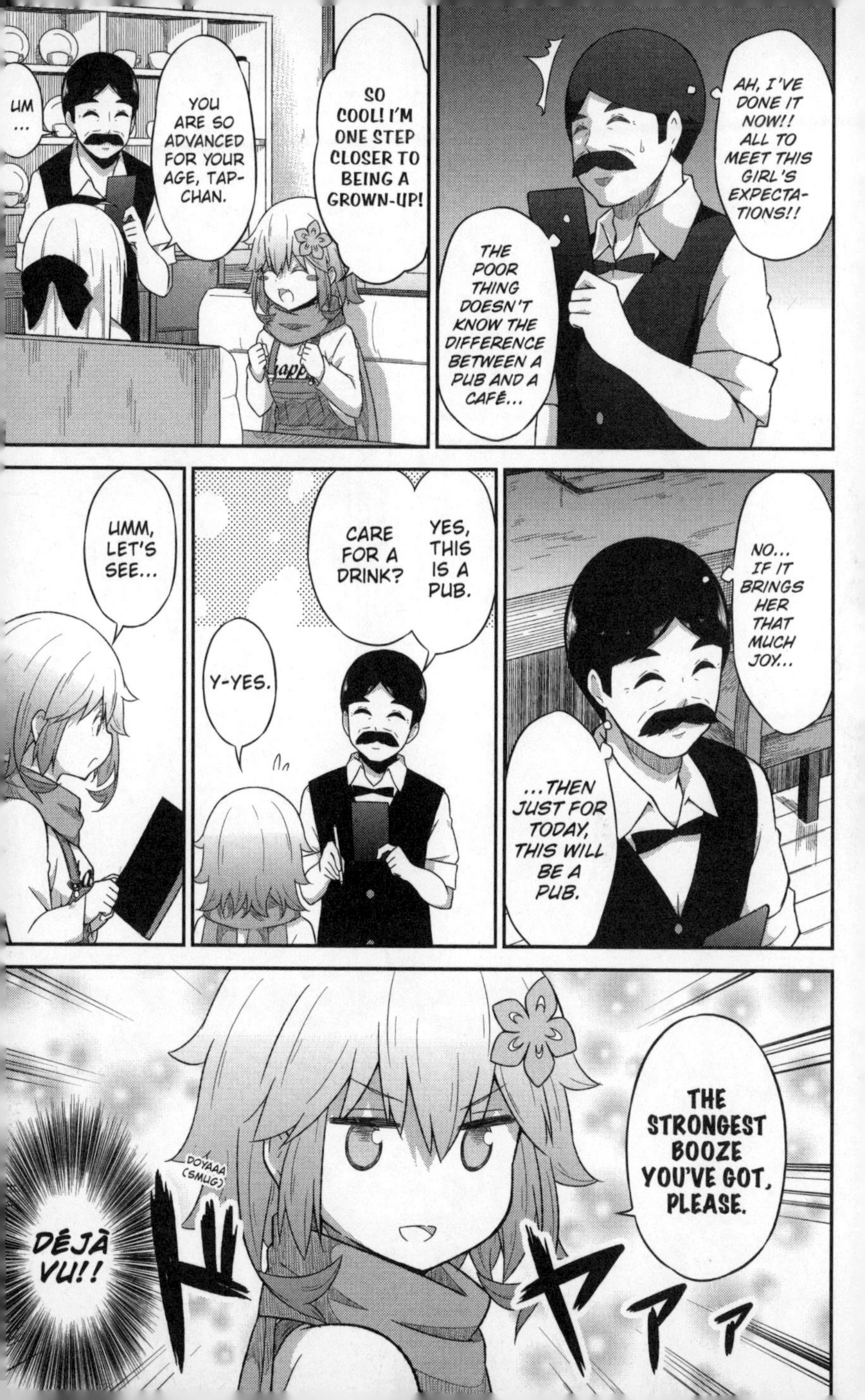
AH, I'VE DONE IT NOW!! ALL TO MEET THIS GIRL'S EXPECTATIONS!!
THE POOR THING DOESN'T KNOW THE DIFFERENCE BETWEEN A PUB AND A CAFÉ...
SO COOL! I'M ONE STEP CLOSER TO BEING A GROWN-UP!
YOU ARE SO ADVANCED FOR YOUR AGE, TAP-CHAN.
UM...
NO... IF IT BRINGS HER THAT MUCH JOY...
...THEN JUST FOR TODAY, THIS WILL BE A PUB.
YES, THIS IS A PUB.
CARE FOR A DRINK?
Y-YES.
UMM, LET'S SEE...
THE STRONGEST BOOZE YOU'VE GOT, PLEASE.
DOYAAA (SMUG)
DÉJÀ VU!!

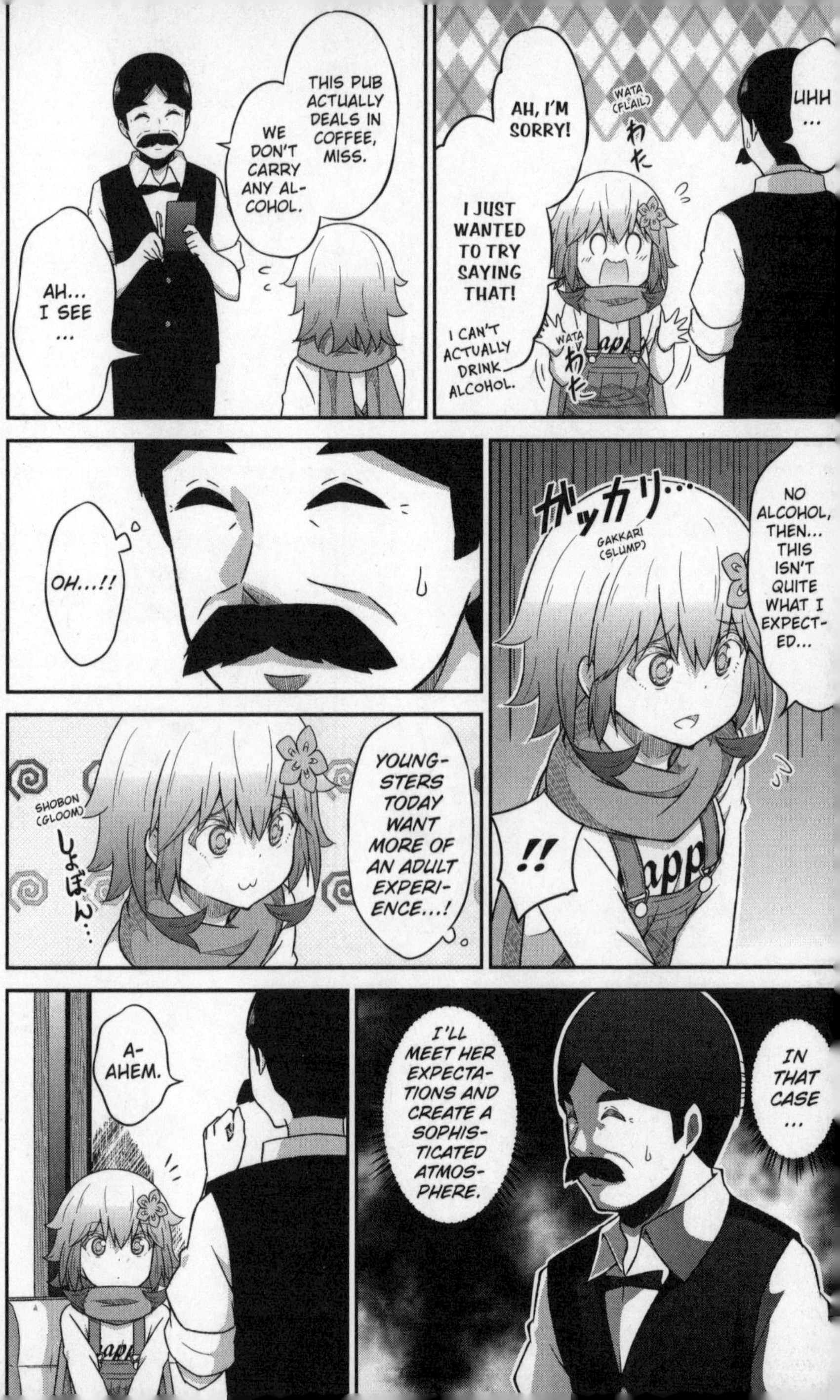
UHH...
AH, I'M SORRY!
WATA (FLAIL)
わた
I JUST WANTED TO TRY SAYING THAT!
I CAN'T ACTUALLY DRINK ALCOHOL.
WATA
わた
THIS PUB ACTUALLY DEALS IN COFFEE, MISS.
WE DON'T CARRY ANY ALCOHOL.
AH... I SEE...
NO ALCOHOL, THEN... THIS ISN'T QUITE WHAT I EXPECTED...
ガッカリ...
GAKKARI (SLUMP)
!!
OH...!!
YOUNGSTERS TODAY WANT MORE OF AN ADULT EXPERIENCE...!
SHOBON (GLOOM)
しょぼん...
IN THAT CASE...
I'LL MEET HER EXPECTATIONS AND CREATE A SOPHISTICATED ATMOSPHERE.
A-AHEM.

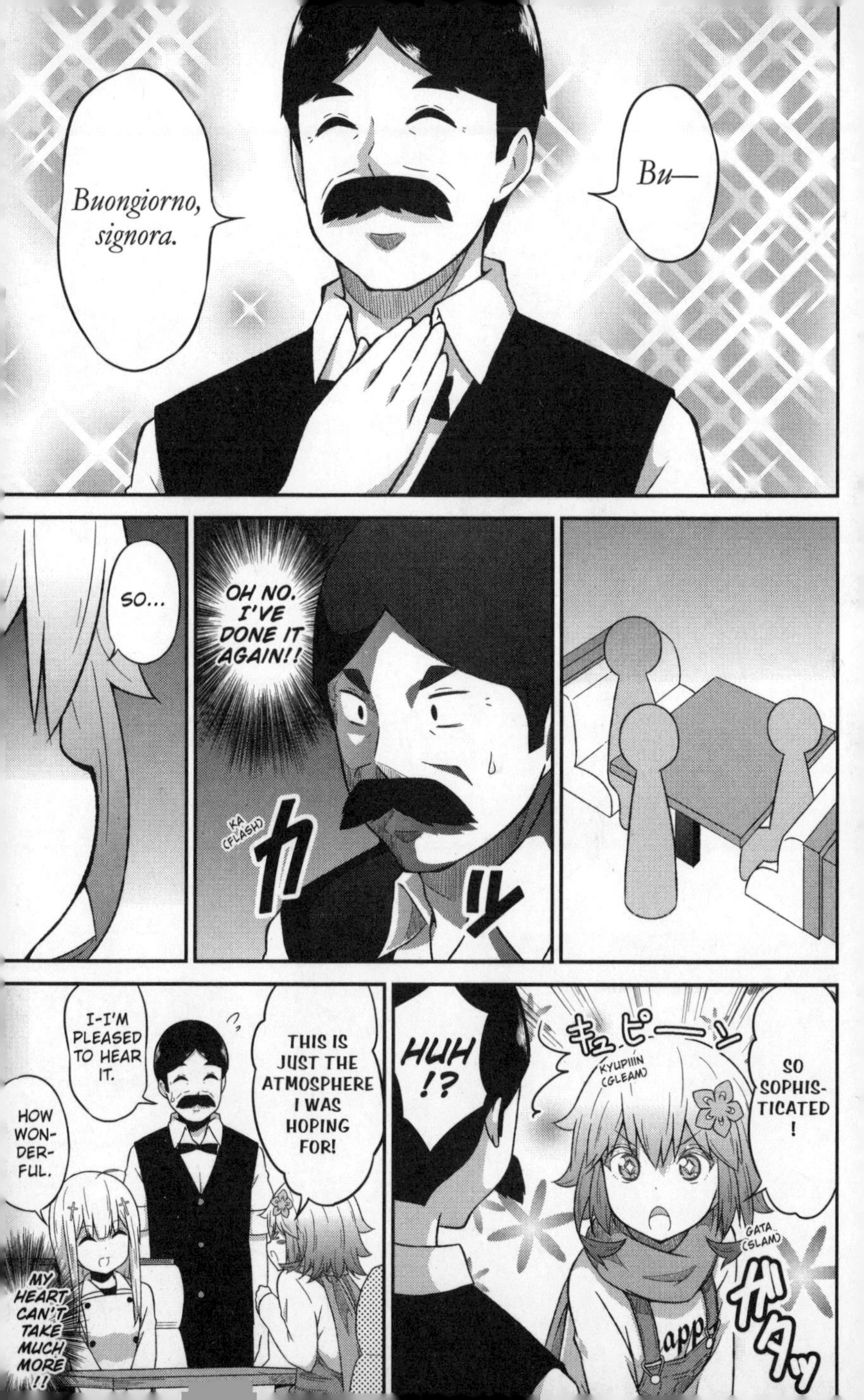
Bu—
Buongiorno, signora.
OH NO. I'VE DONE IT AGAIN!!
カッ
KA (FLASH)
SO...
キュピーン
KYUPIIN (GLEAM)
SO SOPHISTICATED!
GATA (SLAM)
HUH!?
THIS IS JUST THE ATMOSPHERE I WAS HOPING FOR!
I-I'M PLEASED TO HEAR IT.
HOW WONDERFUL.
MY HEART CAN'T TAKE MUCH MORE!!

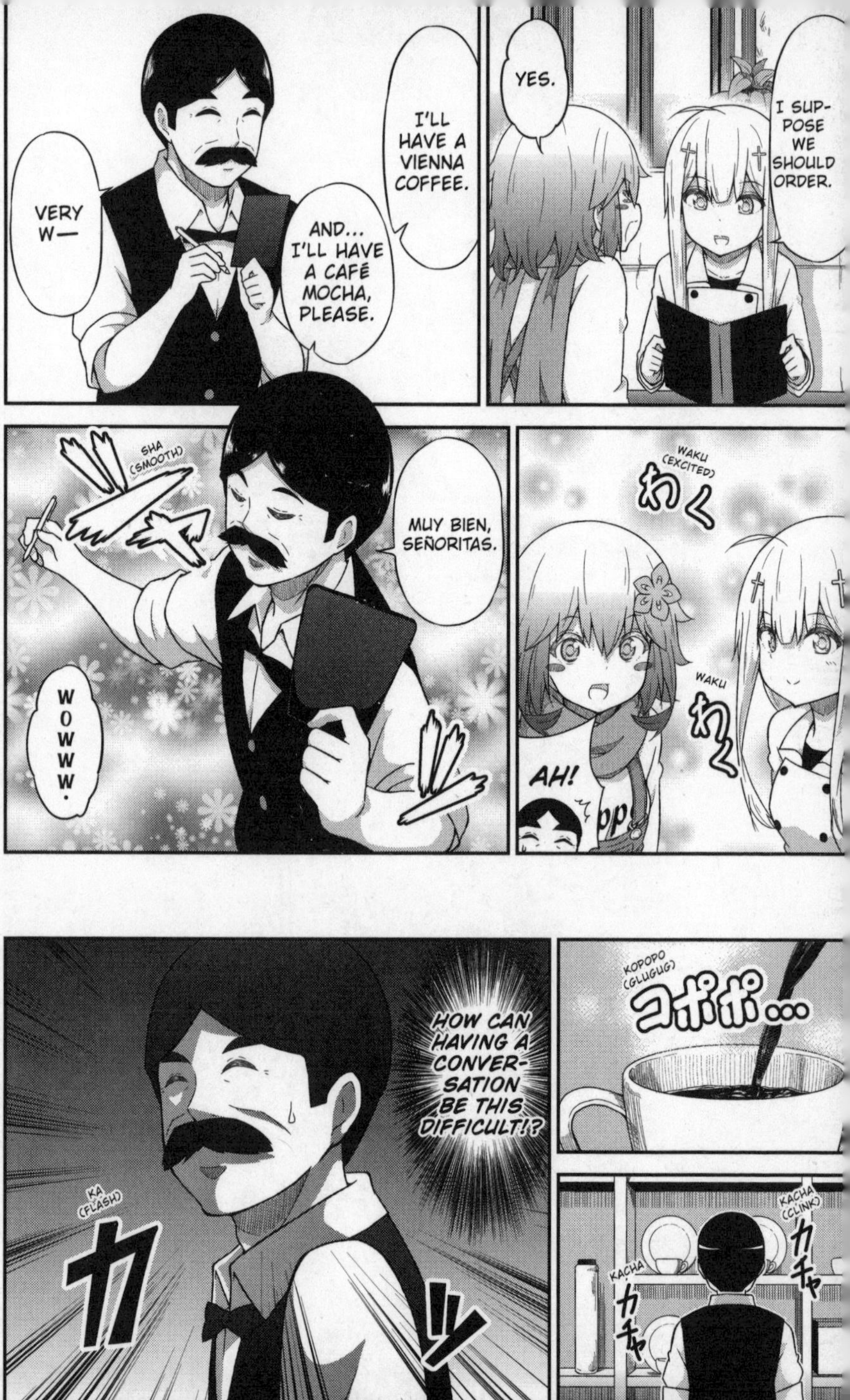
I SUPPOSE WE SHOULD ORDER.
YES.
I'LL HAVE A VIENNA COFFEE.
AND... I'LL HAVE A CAFÉ MOCHA, PLEASE.
VERY W—
WAKU (EXCITED)
わく
WAKU
わく
AH!
MUY BIEN, SEÑORITAS.
SHA (SMOOTH)
WOWWWW.
KOPOPO (GLUGUG)
コポポ…
KACHA (CLINK)
カチャ
KACHA
カチャ
HOW CAN HAVING A CONVERSATION BE THIS DIFFICULT!?
KA (FLASH)
カッ

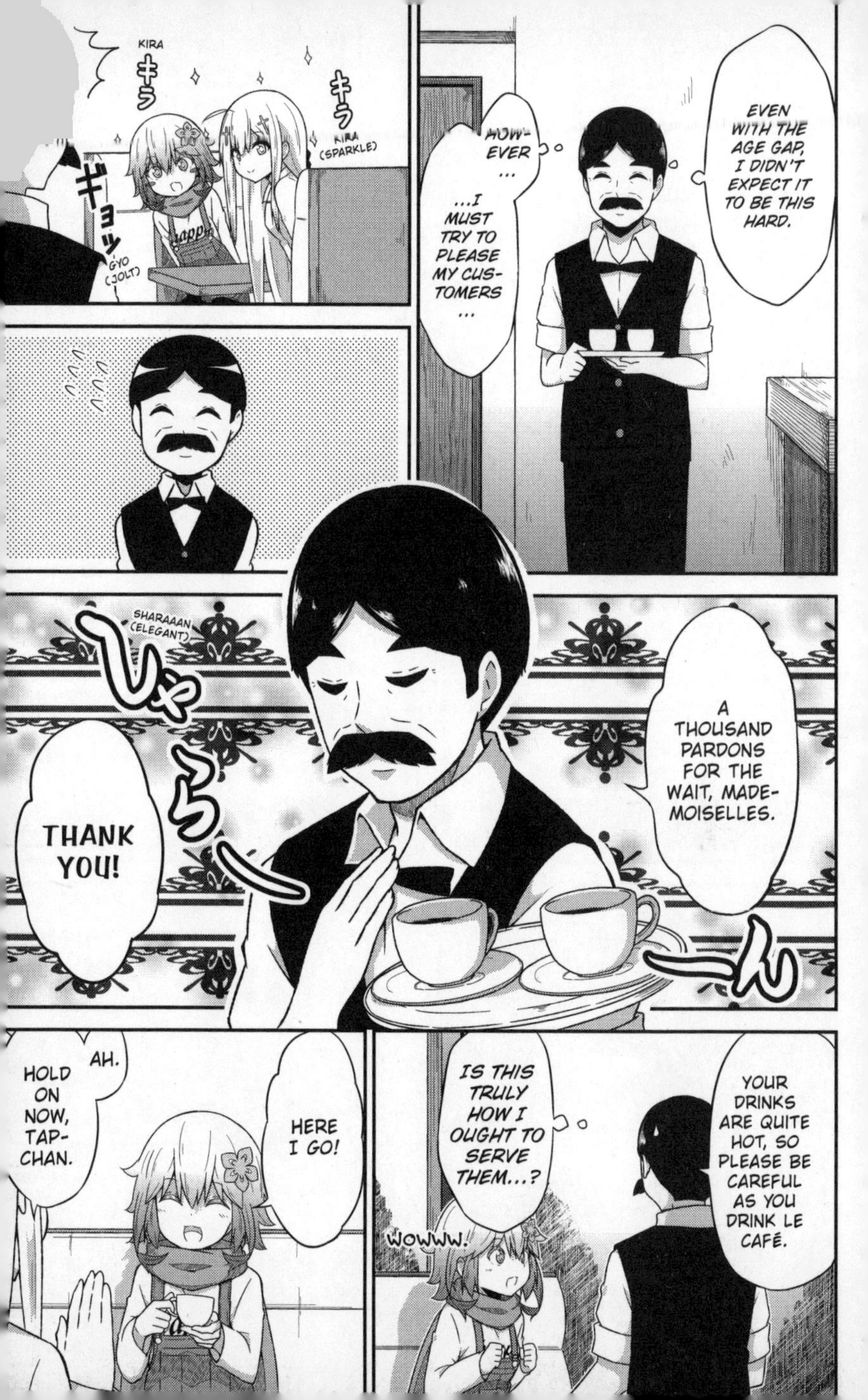
EVEN WITH THE AGE GAP, I DIDN'T EXPECT IT TO BE THIS HARD.
HOWEVER...
...I MUST TRY TO PLEASE MY CUSTOMERS...
キラ KIRA
キラ KIRA (SPARKLE)
ギョッ GYO (JOLT)
A THOUSAND PARDONS FOR THE WAIT, MADEMOISELLES.
SHARAAAN (ELEGANT)
THANK YOU!
YOUR DRINKS ARE QUITE HOT, SO PLEASE BE CAREFUL AS YOU DRINK LE CAFÉ.
IS THIS TRULY HOW I OUGHT TO SERVE THEM...?
WOWWW.
HERE I GO!
AH.
HOLD ON NOW, TAP-CHAN.

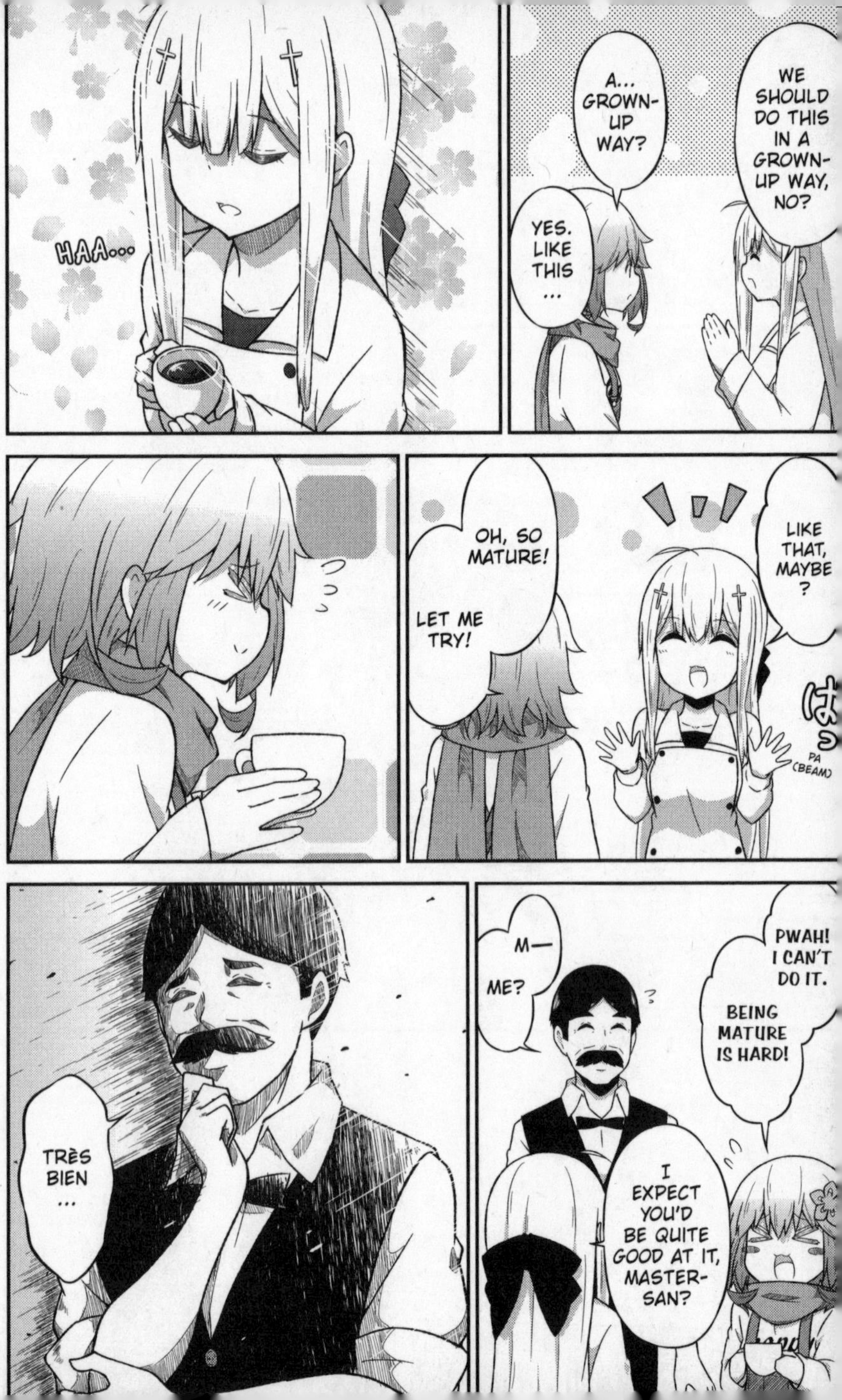

WE SHOULD DO THIS IN A GROWN-UP WAY, NO?
A... GROWN-UP WAY?
YES. LIKE THIS ...
HAA...
LIKE THAT, MAYBE?
はっ
PA (BEAM)
OH, SO MATURE!
LET ME TRY!
PWAH! I CAN'T DO IT.
BEING MATURE IS HARD!
I EXPECT YOU'D BE QUITE GOOD AT IT, MASTER-SAN?
M— ME?
TRÈS BIEN ...

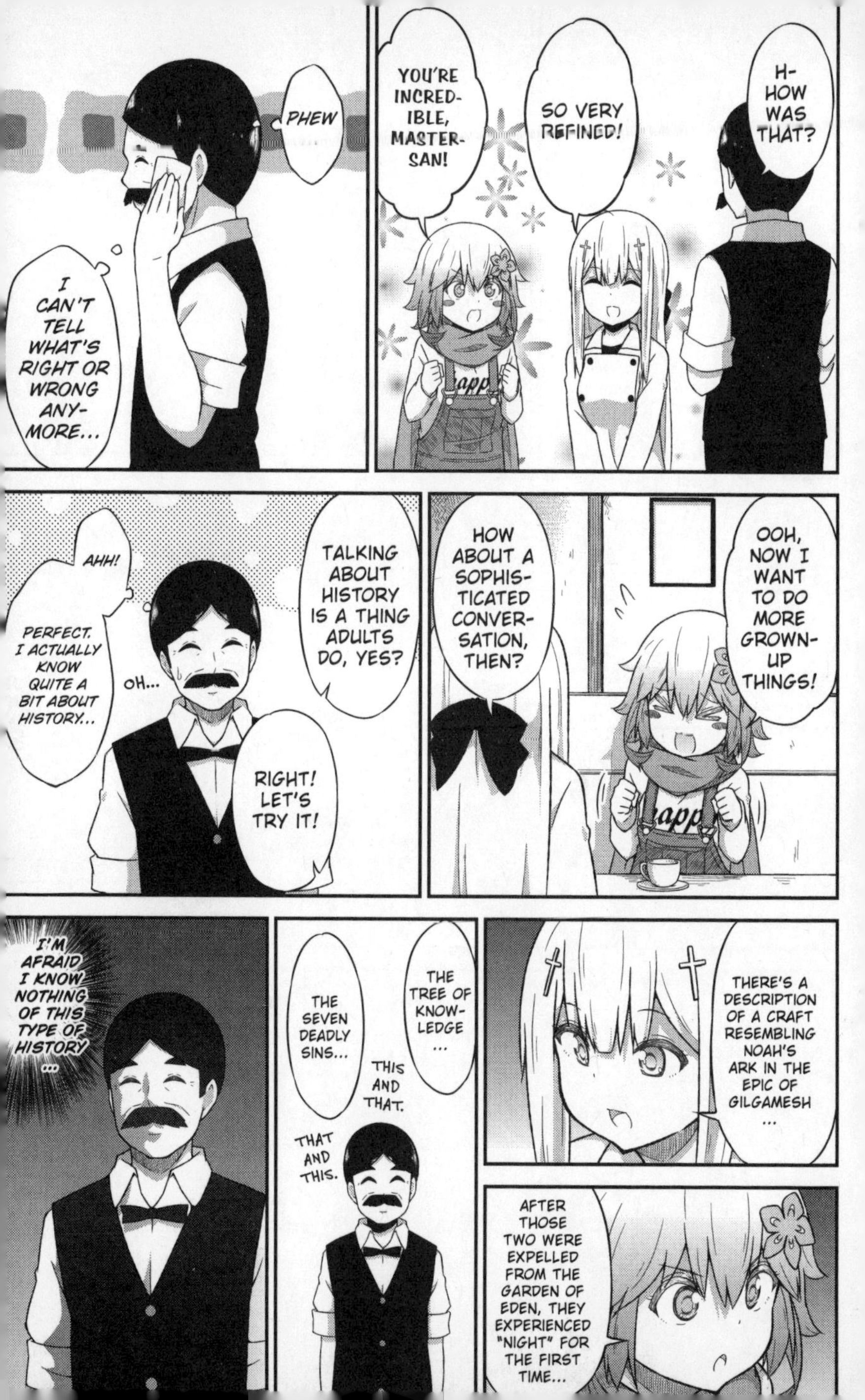
H-HOW WAS THAT?
SO VERY REFINED!
YOU'RE INCREDIBLE, MASTER-SAN!
PHEW
I CAN'T TELL WHAT'S RIGHT OR WRONG ANYMORE...
OOH, NOW I WANT TO DO MORE GROWN-UP THINGS!
HOW ABOUT A SOPHISTICATED CONVERSATION, THEN?
TALKING ABOUT HISTORY IS A THING ADULTS DO, YES?
AHH!
RIGHT! LET'S TRY IT!
OH...
PERFECT. I ACTUALLY KNOW QUITE A BIT ABOUT HISTORY...
THERE'S A DESCRIPTION OF A CRAFT RESEMBLING NOAH'S ARK IN THE EPIC OF GILGAMESH...
AFTER THOSE TWO WERE EXPELLED FROM THE GARDEN OF EDEN, THEY EXPERIENCED "NIGHT" FOR THE FIRST TIME...
THE TREE OF KNOWLEDGE...
THE SEVEN DEADLY SINS...
THIS AND THAT.
THAT AND THIS.
I'M AFRAID I KNOW NOTHING OF THIS TYPE OF HISTORY...

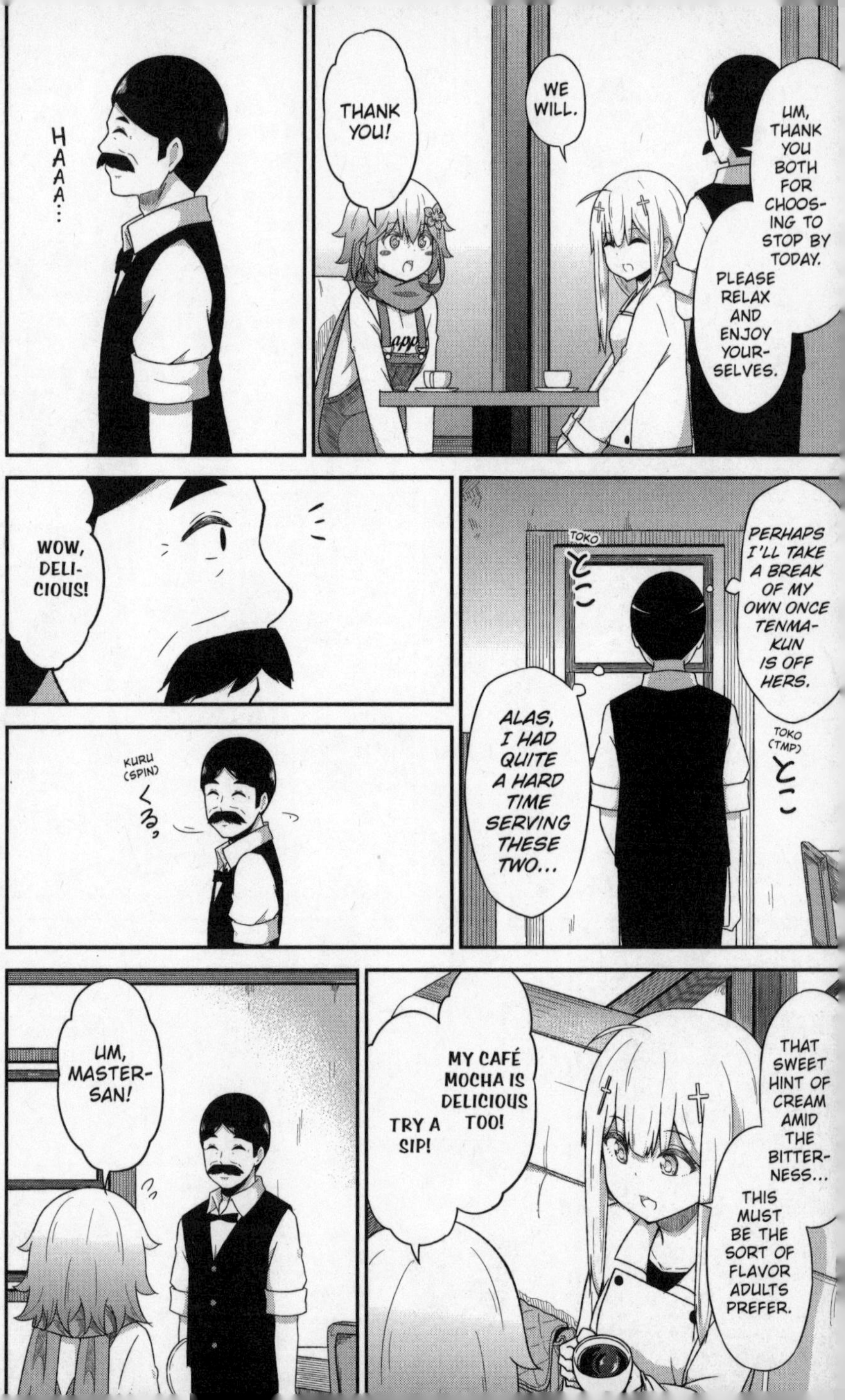
UM, THANK YOU BOTH FOR CHOOSING TO STOP BY TODAY.
PLEASE RELAX AND ENJOY YOURSELVES.
WE WILL.
THANK YOU!
HAAAA...
PERHAPS I'LL TAKE A BREAK OF MY OWN ONCE TENMA-KUN IS OFF HERS.
TOKO
とこ
ALAS, I HAD QUITE A HARD TIME SERVING THESE TWO...
TOKO (TMP)
とこ
WOW, DELICIOUS!
KURU (SPIN)
くるっ
THAT SWEET HINT OF CREAM AMID THE BITTERNESS...
THIS MUST BE THE SORT OF FLAVOR ADULTS PREFER.
MY CAFÉ MOCHA IS DELICIOUS TOO!
TRY A SIP!
UM, MASTER-SAN!

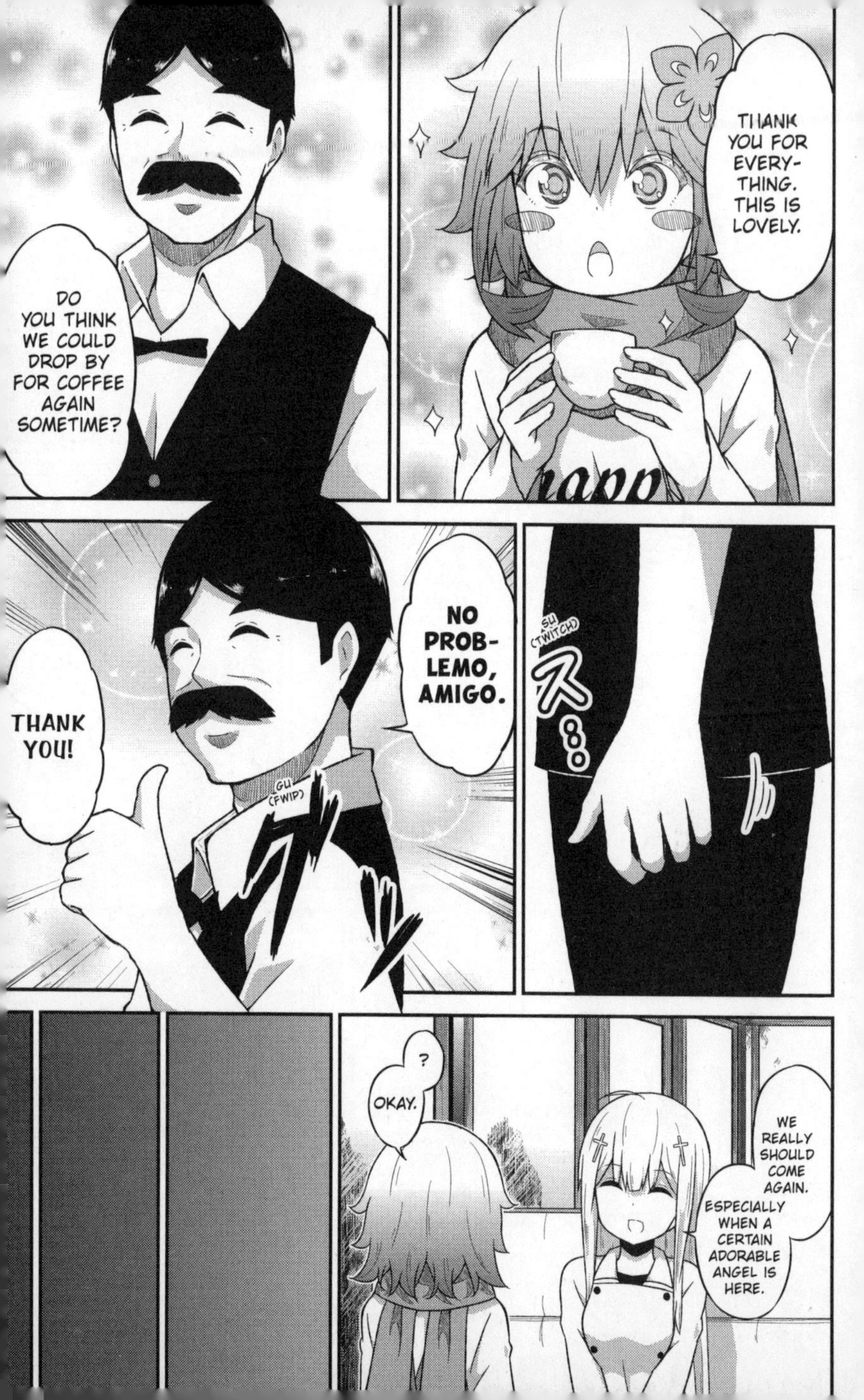
THANK YOU FOR EVERYTHING. THIS IS LOVELY.
DO YOU THINK WE COULD DROP BY FOR COFFEE AGAIN SOMETIME?
SU (TWITCH)
ス
NO PROBLEMO, AMIGO.
THANK YOU!
GU (FWIP)
WE REALLY SHOULD COME AGAIN.
ESPECIALLY WHEN A CERTAIN ADORABLE ANGEL IS HERE.
?
OKAY.

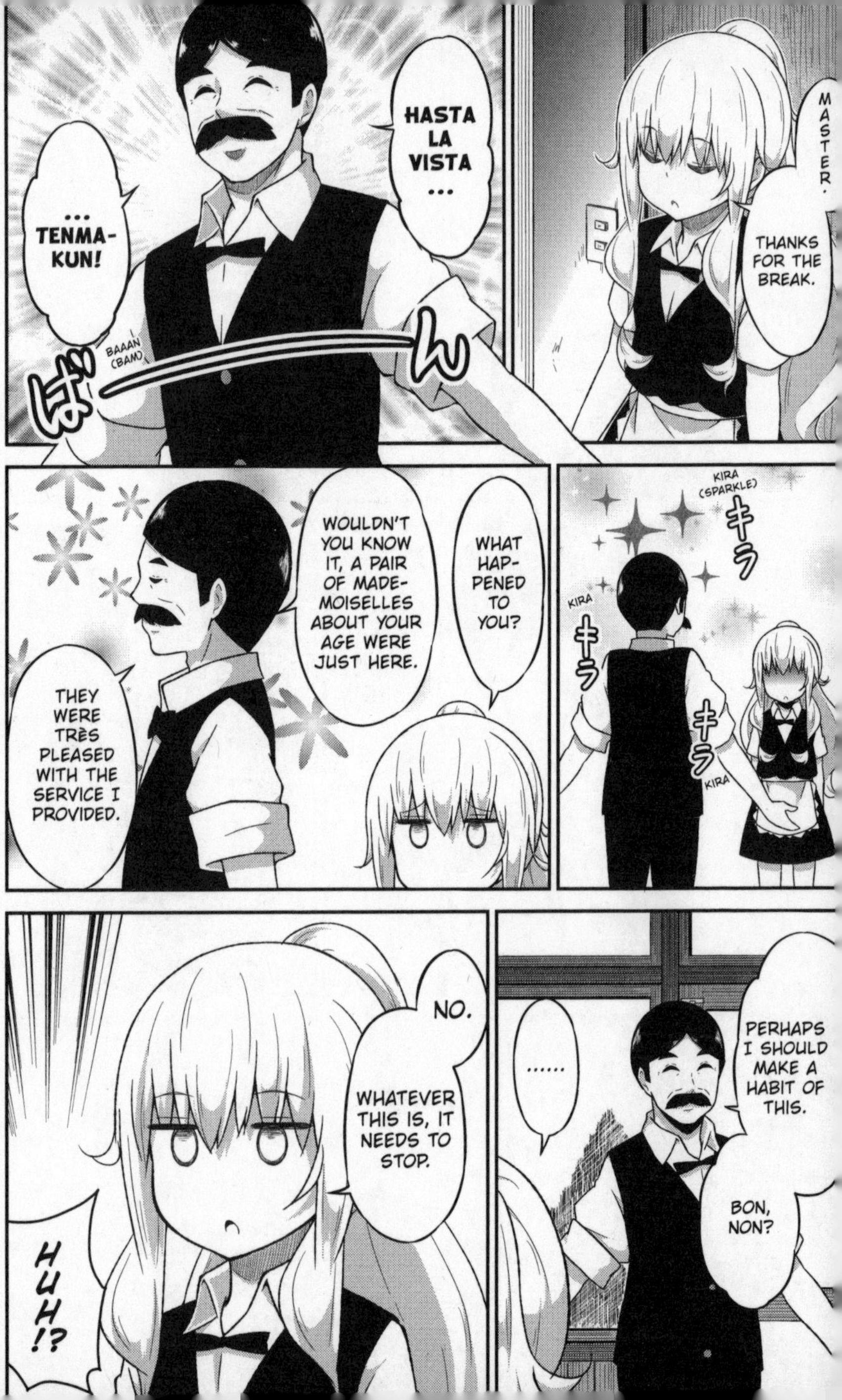
MASTER.
THANKS FOR THE BREAK.
HASTA LA VISTA ...
... TENMA-KUN!
BAAAN (BAM)
ばーん
KIRA (SPARKLE)
キラ
KIRA
キラ
KIRA
キラ
WHAT HAPPENED TO YOU?
WOULDN'T YOU KNOW IT, A PAIR OF MADEMOISELLES ABOUT YOUR AGE WERE JUST HERE.
THEY WERE TRÈS PLEASED WITH THE SERVICE I PROVIDED.
PERHAPS I SHOULD MAKE A HABIT OF THIS.
BON, NON?
......
NO.
WHATEVER THIS IS, IT NEEDS TO STOP.
HUH!?

OUT OF NOWHERE, A PORTRAIT OF MASTER...

...FROM HIS HIGH SCHOOL DAYS.

Gabriel Dropout

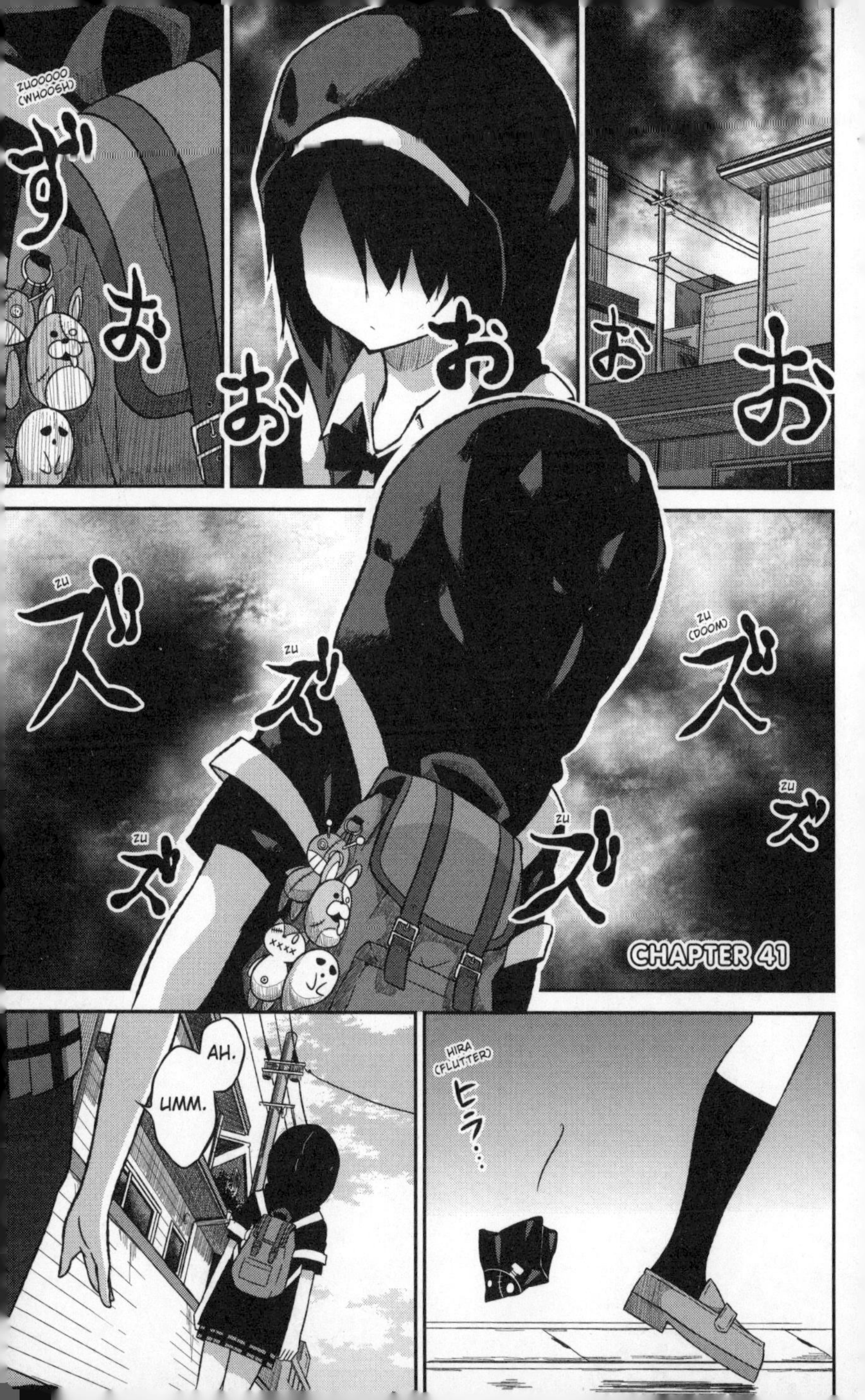
ZUOOOOO (WHOOSH)
ずおおおおお
ZU (DOOM)
ズ
ZU
ズ
ZU
ズ
ZU
ズ
ZU
ズ
ZU
ズ
CHAPTER 41
HIRA (FLUTTER)
ヒラ…
AH.
UMM.

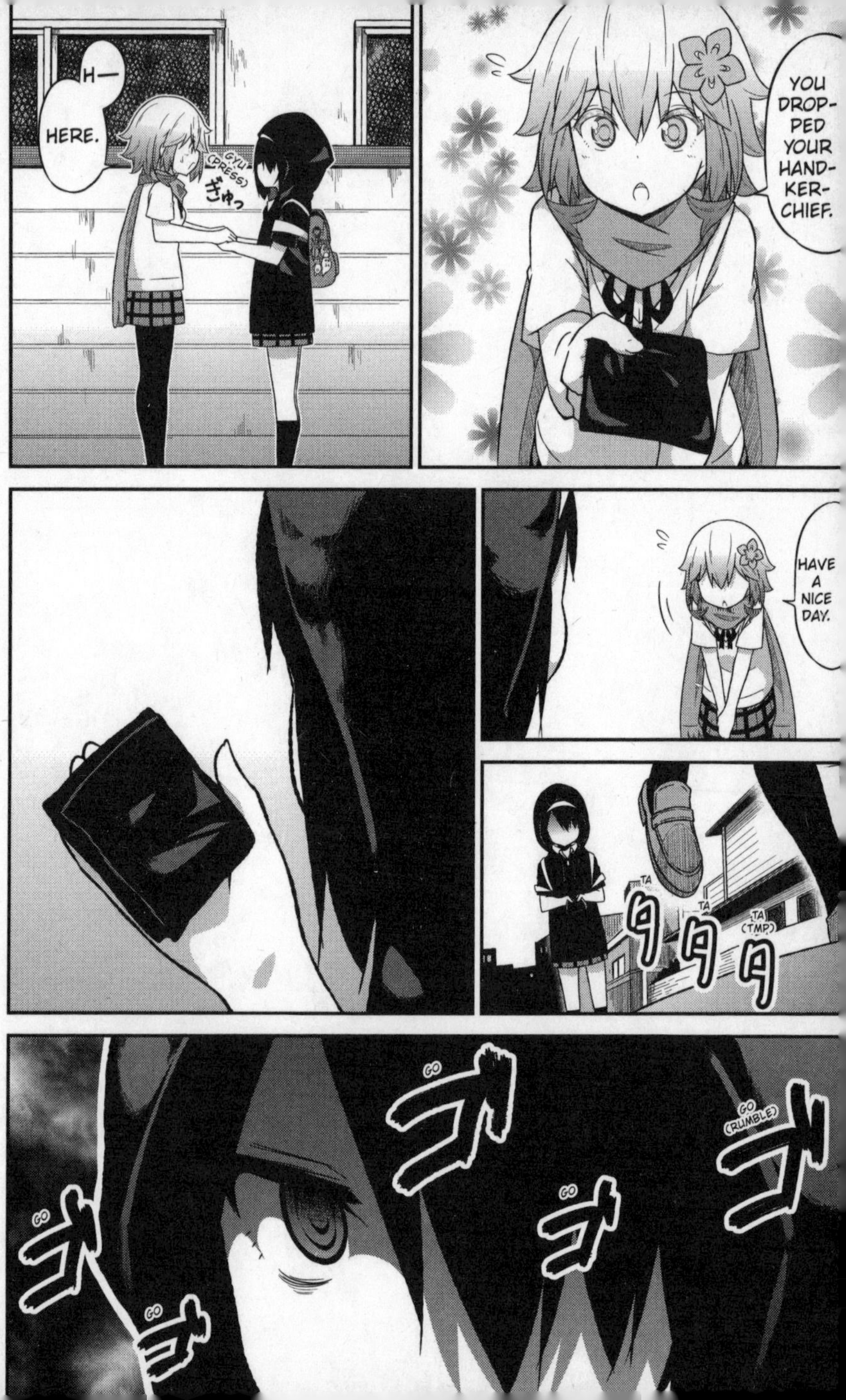
YOU DROPPED YOUR HANDKERCHIEF.
H— HERE.
GYU (PRESS)
ぎゅっ
HAVE A NICE DAY.
TA TA TA (TMP)
タタタ
GO GO GO (RUMBLE)
GO GO
ゴゴゴゴゴ

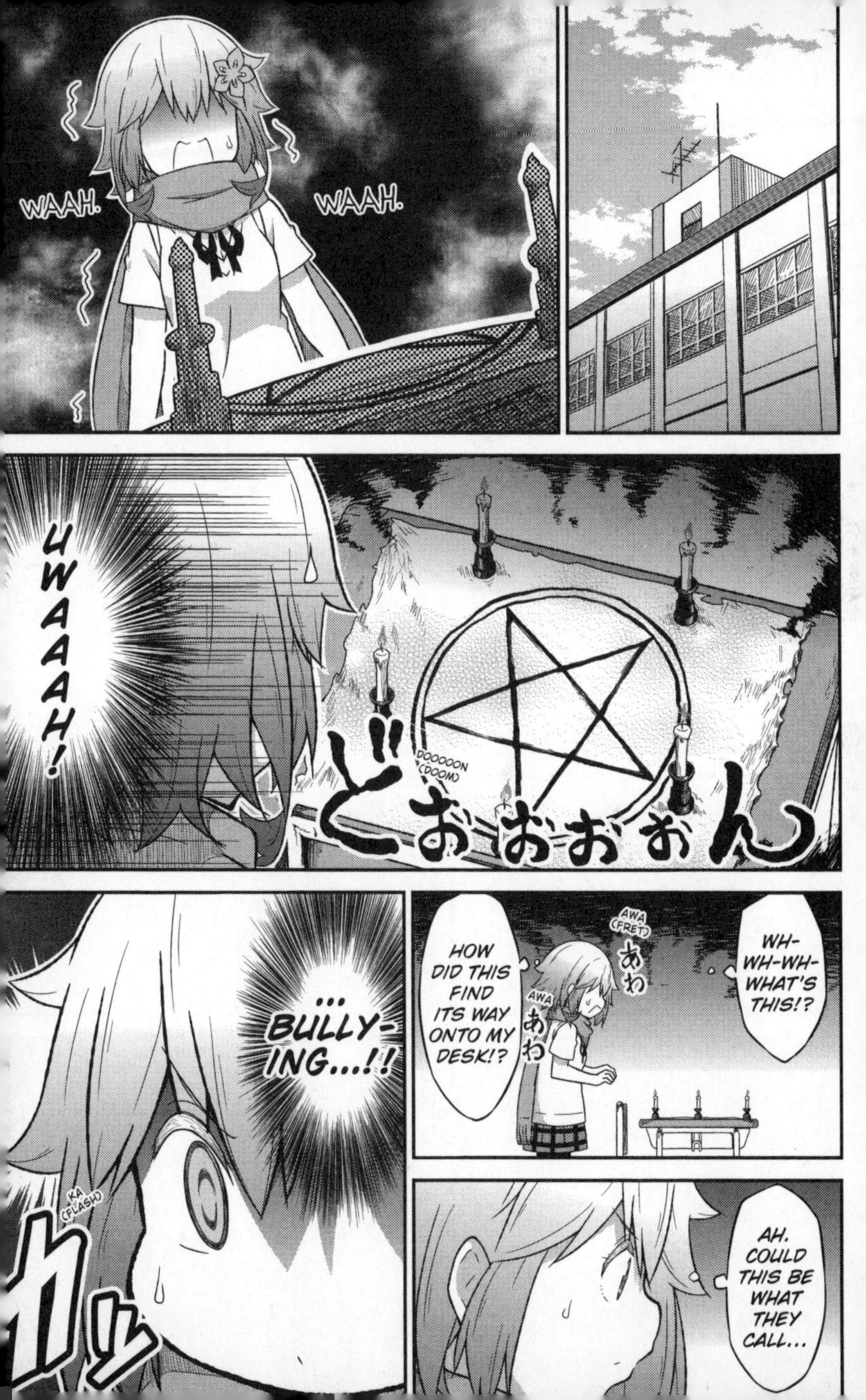
WAAH.
WAAH.
DOOOOON (DOOM)
どぉぉぉん
UWAAAAH!
WH-WH-WH-WHAT'S THIS!?
AWA (FRET)
あわ
AWA
あわ
HOW DID THIS FIND ITS WAY ONTO MY DESK!?
AH. COULD THIS BE WHAT THEY CALL...
...BULLYING...!!
KA (FLASH)
カッ

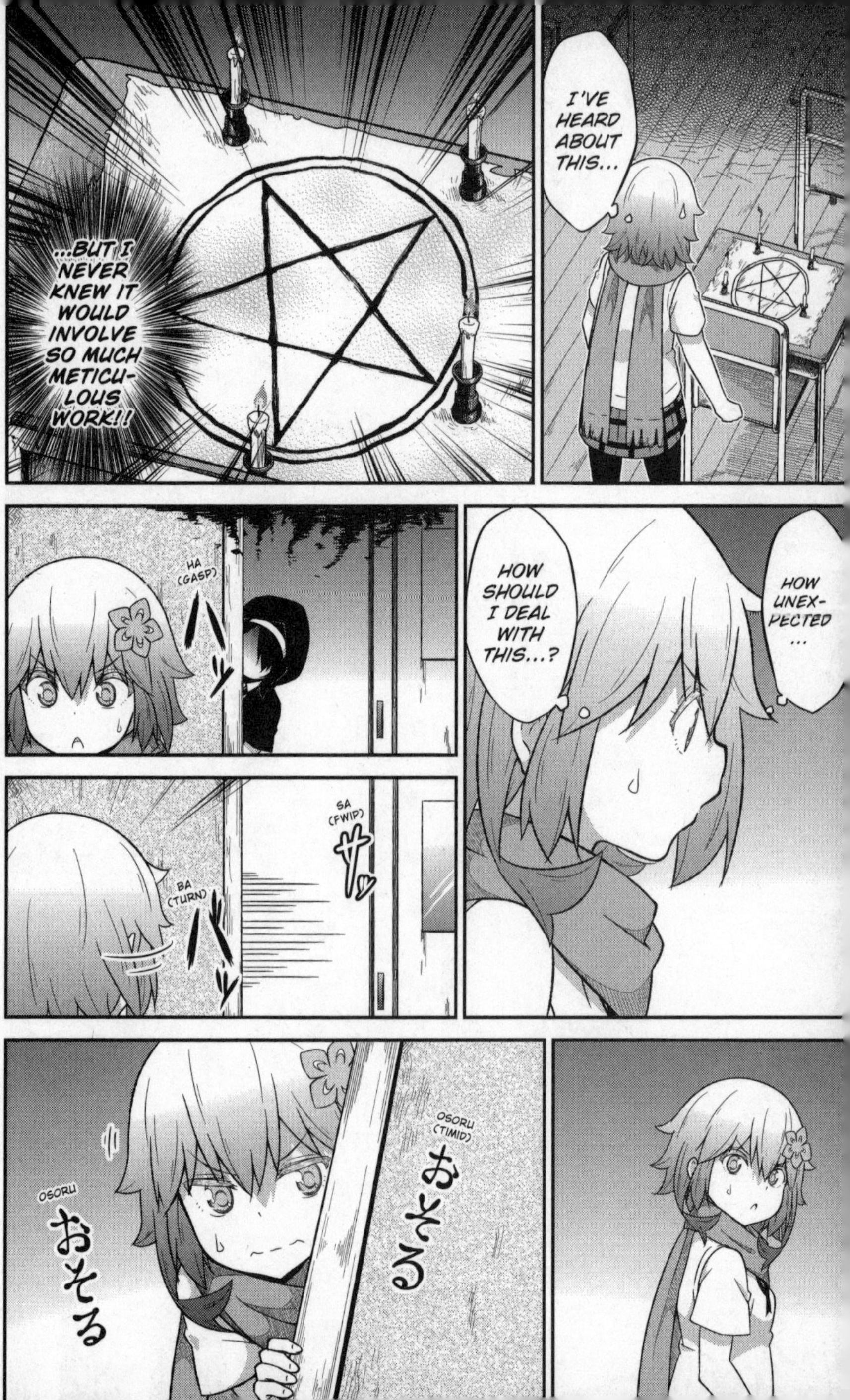
I'VE HEARD ABOUT THIS...
...BUT I NEVER KNEW IT WOULD INVOLVE SO MUCH METICULOUS WORK!!
HOW UNEXPECTED...
HOW SHOULD I DEAL WITH THIS...?
HA (GASP)
ハッ
SA (FWIP)
サッ
BA (TURN)
バッ
OSORU (TIMID)
おそる
OSORU
おそる

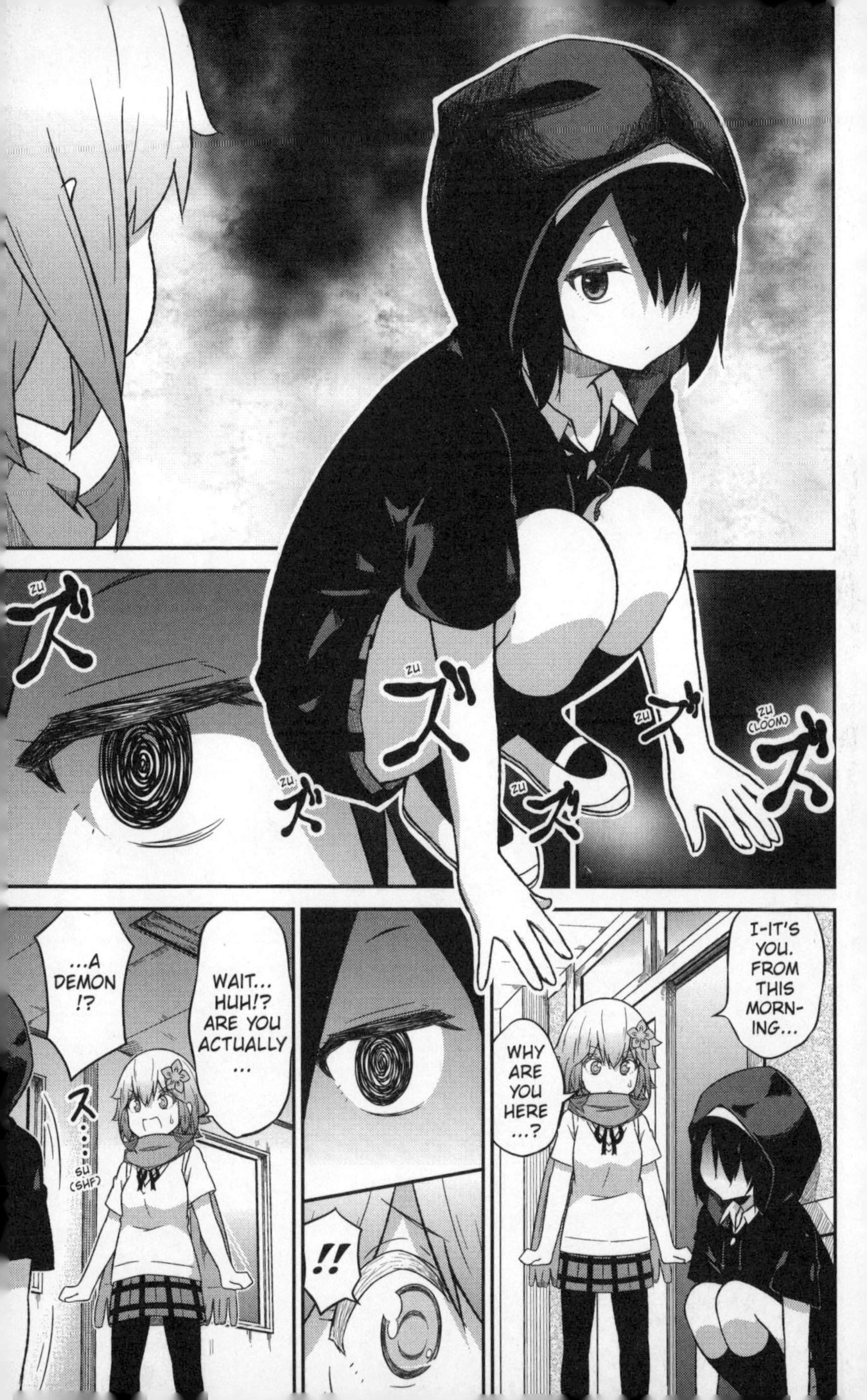

ズ
ZU (LOOM)
ズ
ZU
ズ
ZU
ズ
ZU
ズ
ZU
ズ
ZU
I-IT'S YOU. FROM THIS MORNING...
WHY ARE YOU HERE...?
!!
WAIT... HUH!? ARE YOU ACTUALLY...
...A DEMON!?
ス...
SU (SHF)

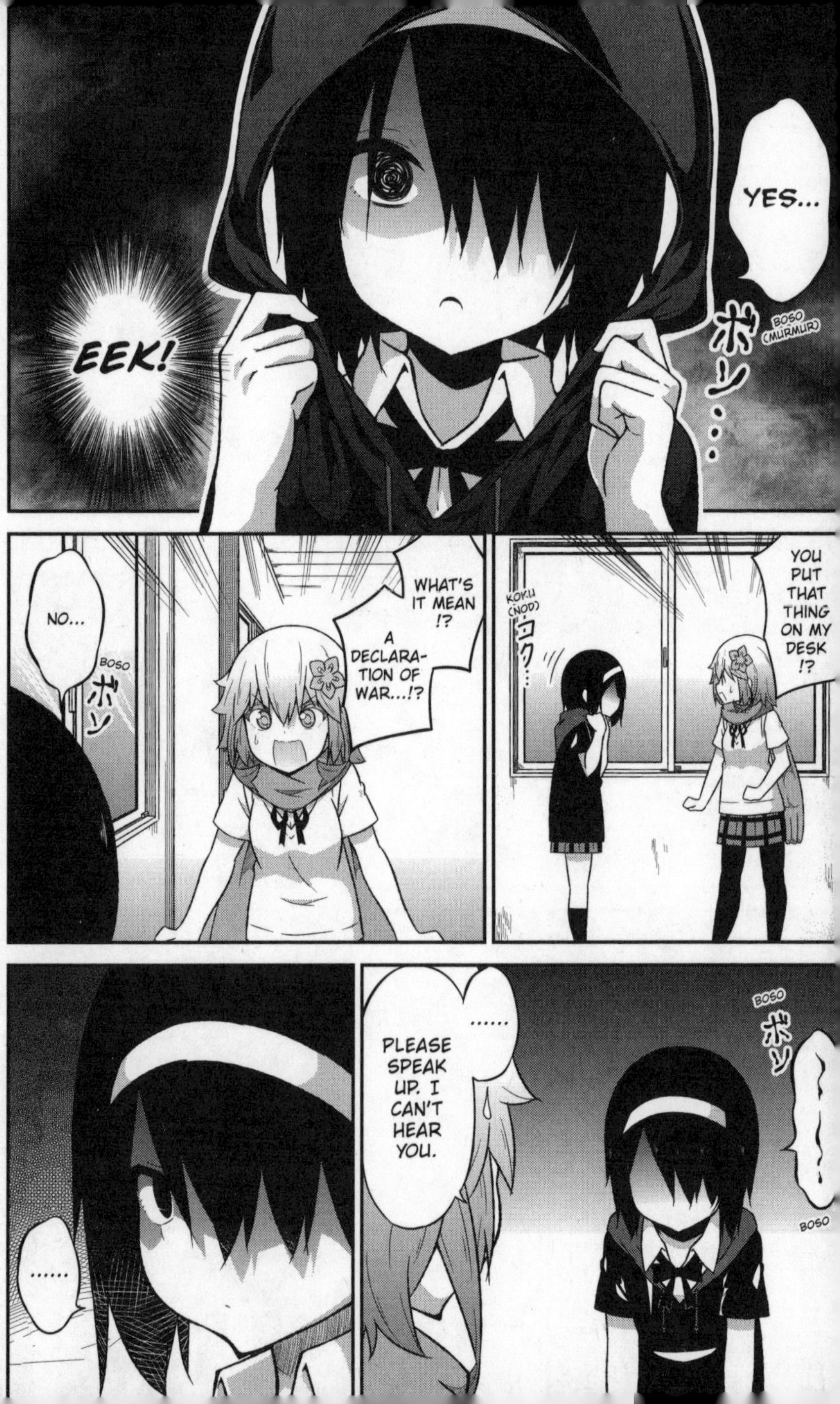
YES...
ボソ...
BOSO (MURMUR)
EEK!
YOU PUT THAT THING ON MY DESK !?
コク...
KOKU (NOD)
WHAT'S IT MEAN !?
A DECLARATION-OF WAR...!?
NO...
ボソ
BOSO
ボソ
BOSO
BOSO
......
PLEASE SPEAK UP. I CAN'T HEAR YOU.
......

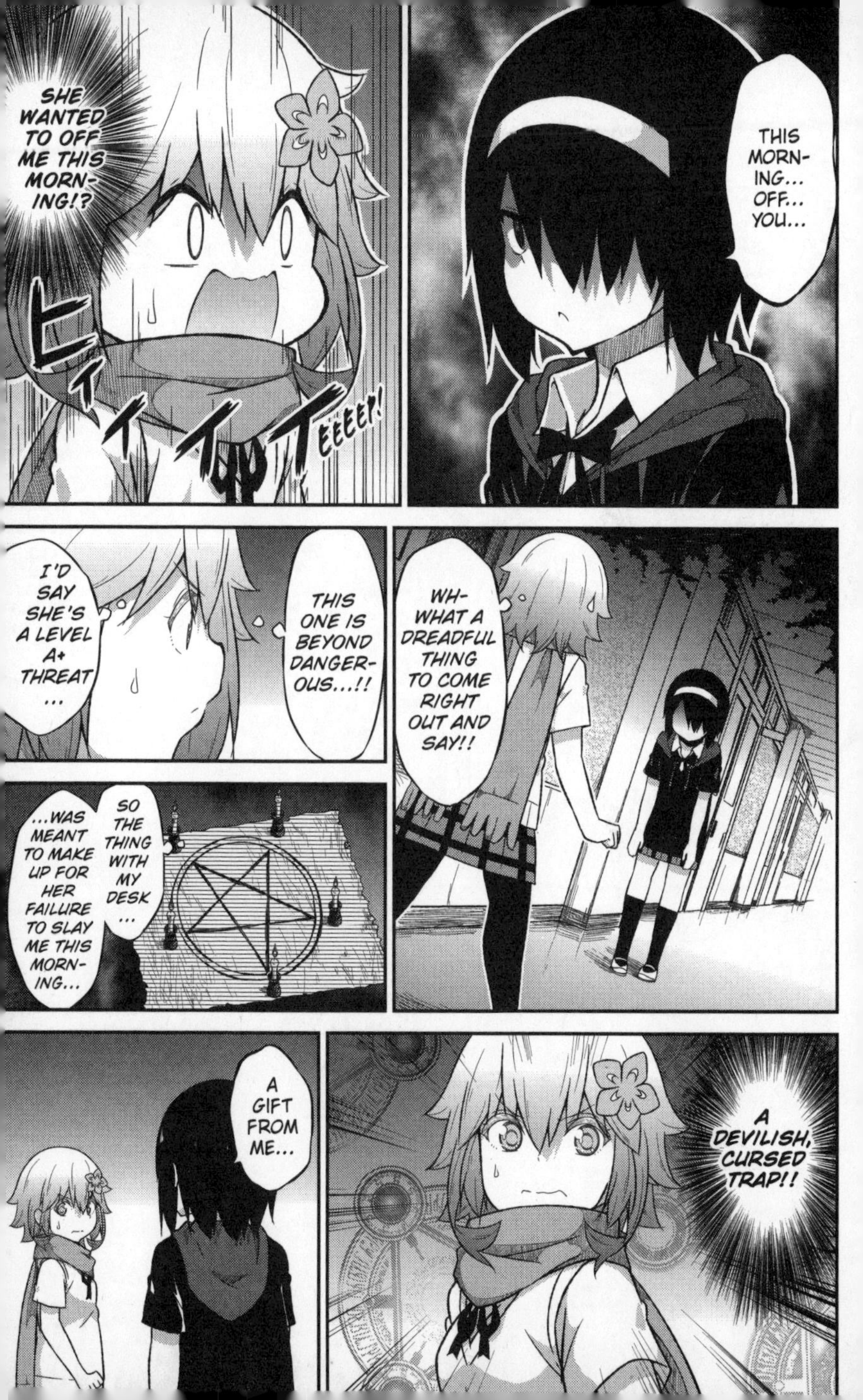
THIS MORNING... OFF... YOU...
SHE WANTED TO OFF ME THIS MORNING!?
EEEEEP!
WH-WHAT A DREADFUL THING TO COME RIGHT OUT AND SAY!!
THIS ONE IS BEYOND DANGEROUS...!!
I'D SAY SHE'S A LEVEL A+ THREAT...
SO THE THING WITH MY DESK...
...WAS MEANT TO MAKE UP FOR HER FAILURE TO SLAY ME THIS MORNING...
A DEVILISH, CURSED TRAP!!
A GIFT FROM ME...

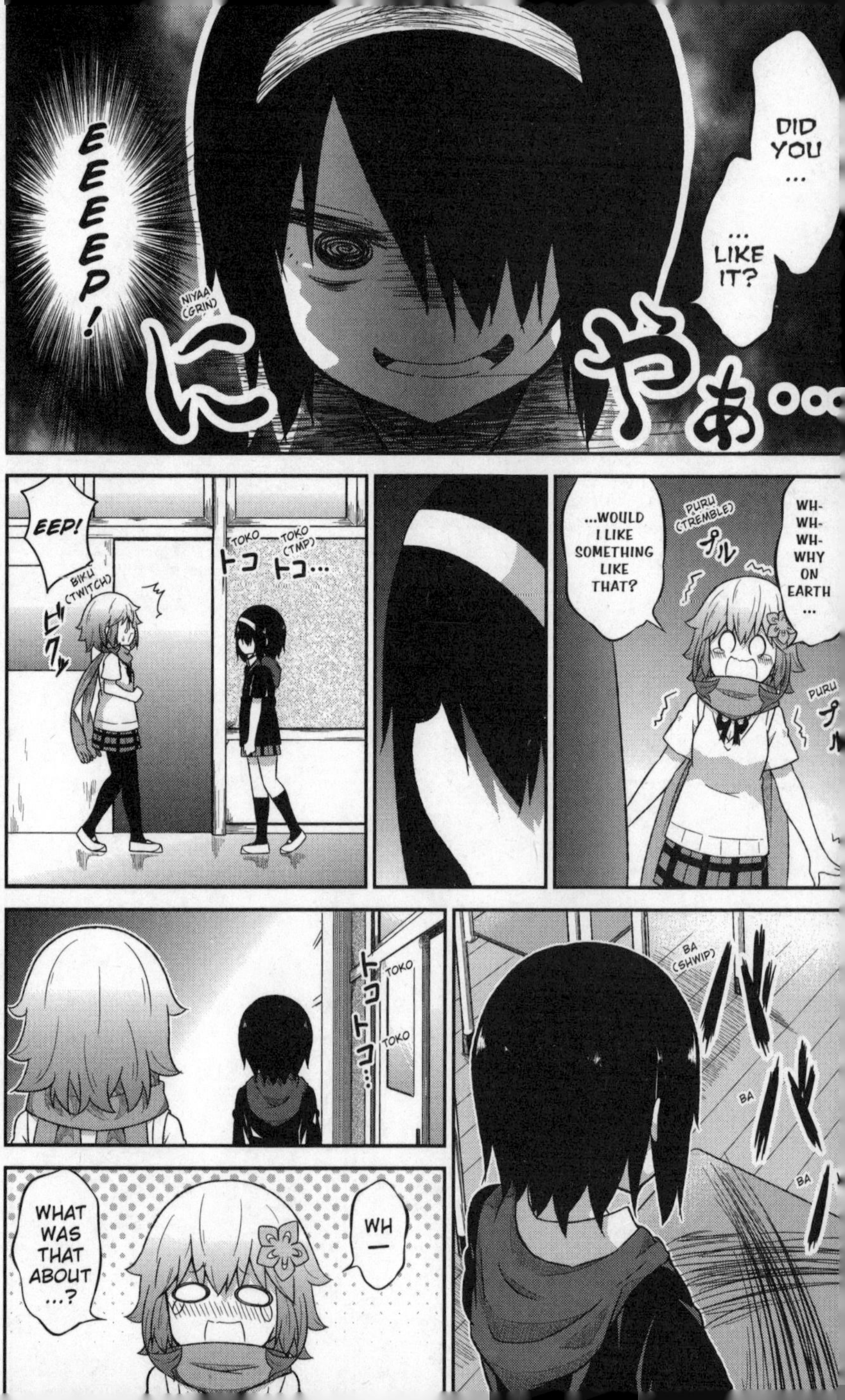
DID YOU ...
... LIKE IT?
NIYAA (GRIN)
にやぁ…
EEEEEP!
WH-WH-WH-WHY ON EARTH ...
PURU (TREMBLE)
プル
PURU
プル
...WOULD I LIKE SOMETHING LIKE THAT?
TOKO TOKO (TMP)
トコトコ…
EEP!
BIKU (TWITCH)
ビクッ
BA (SHWIP)
BA
BA
TOKO
TOKO
トコトコ…
WH—
WHAT WAS THAT ABOUT ...?

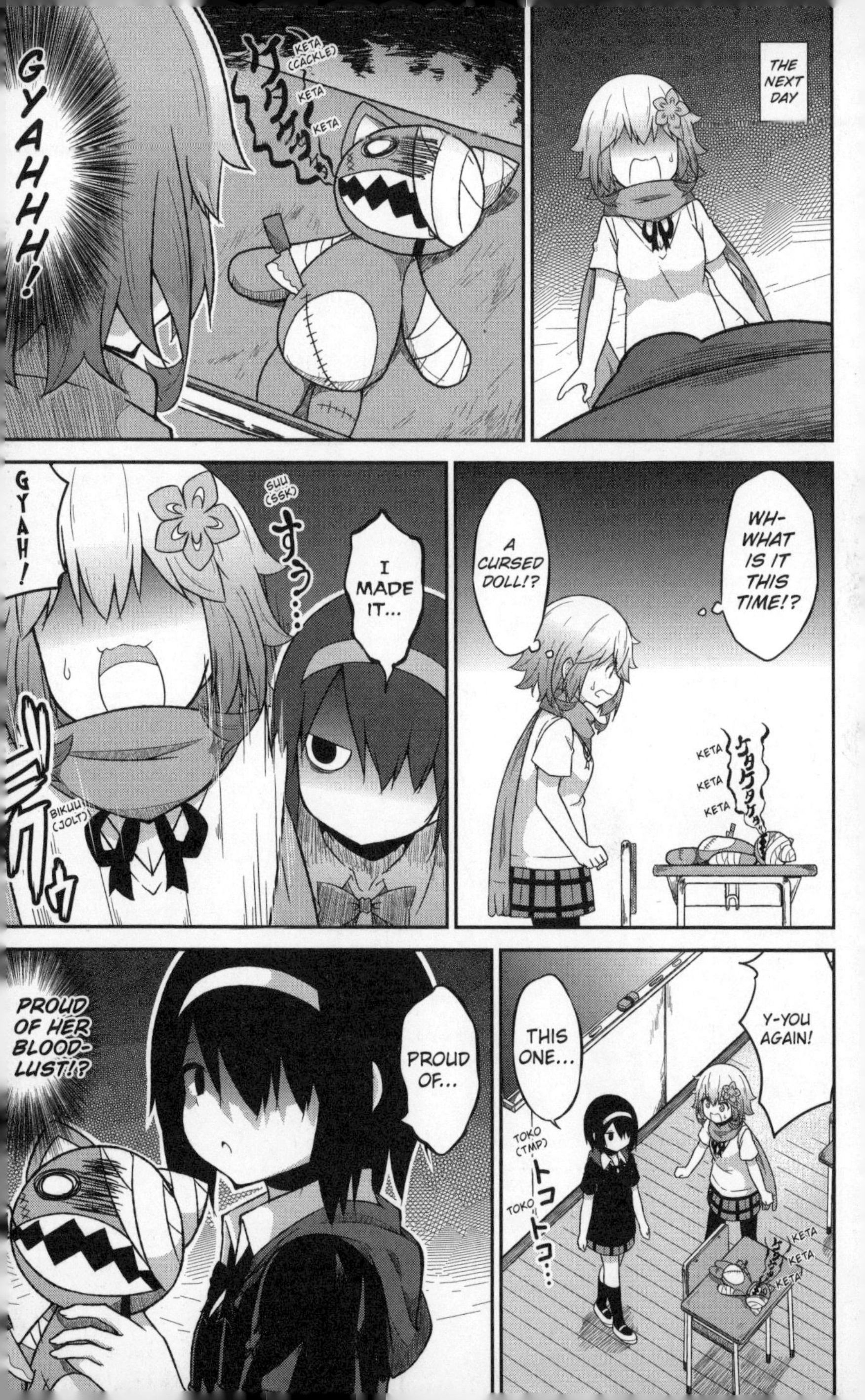
THE NEXT DAY
KETA (CACKLE)
KETA
KETA
GYAHHHH!
WH- WHAT IS IT THIS TIME!?
A CURSED DOLL!?
KETA
KETA
KETA
I MADE IT...
SUU (SSK)
GYAH!
BIKUU (JOLT)
Y-YOU AGAIN!
THIS ONE...
TOKO (TMP)
TOKO
KETA
KETA
KETA
PROUD OF...
PROUD OF HER BLOOD-LUST!?

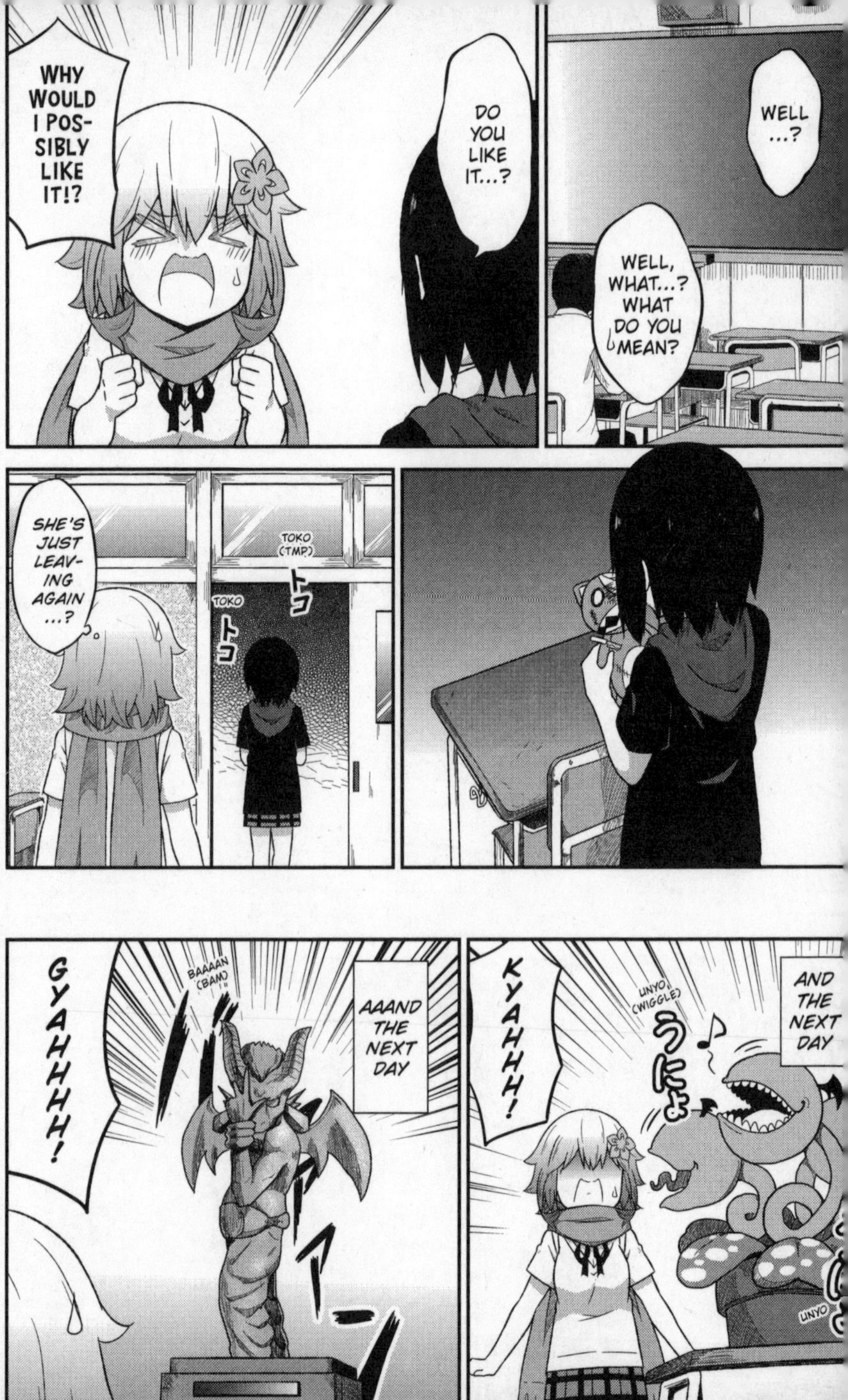
WELL ...?
WELL, WHAT...? WHAT DO YOU MEAN?
DO YOU LIKE IT...?
WHY WOULD I POS-SIBLY LIKE IT!?
TOKO (TMP)
トコ
TOKO
トコ
SHE'S JUST LEAV-ING AGAIN ...?
AND THE NEXT DAY
UNYO (WIGGLE)
うにょ
KYAHHH!
UNYO
AAAND THE NEXT DAY
BAAAAN (BAM)
GYAHHHHH!

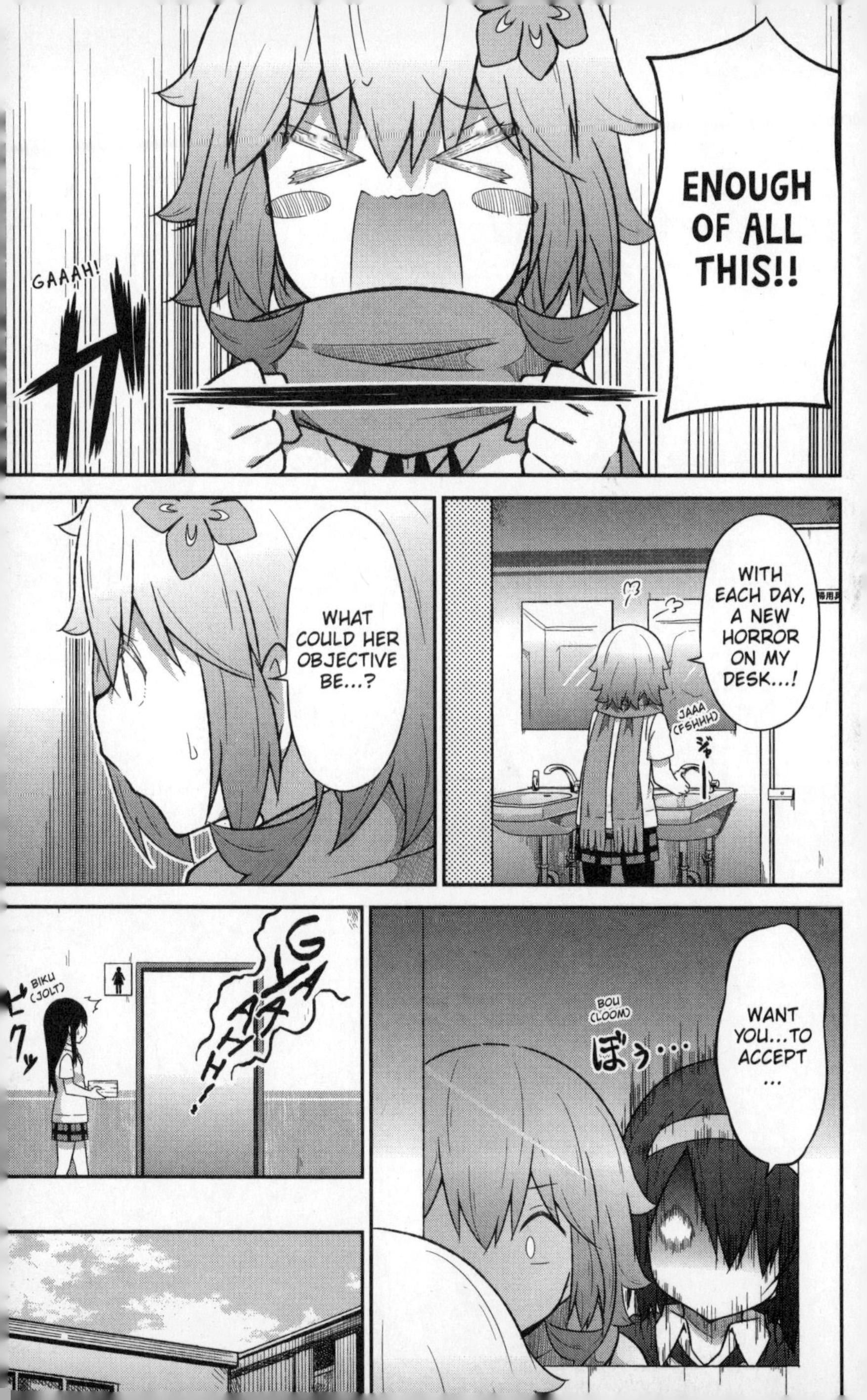
ENOUGH OF ALL THIS!!
GAAAH!
ガッ
WITH EACH DAY, A NEW HORROR ON MY DESK...!
JAAA (FSHHH)
ジャ
WHAT COULD HER OBJECTIVE BE...?
BOU (LOOM)
ぼぅ...
WANT YOU...TO ACCEPT ...
GYAAAH-!
BIKU (JOLT)
ビクッ

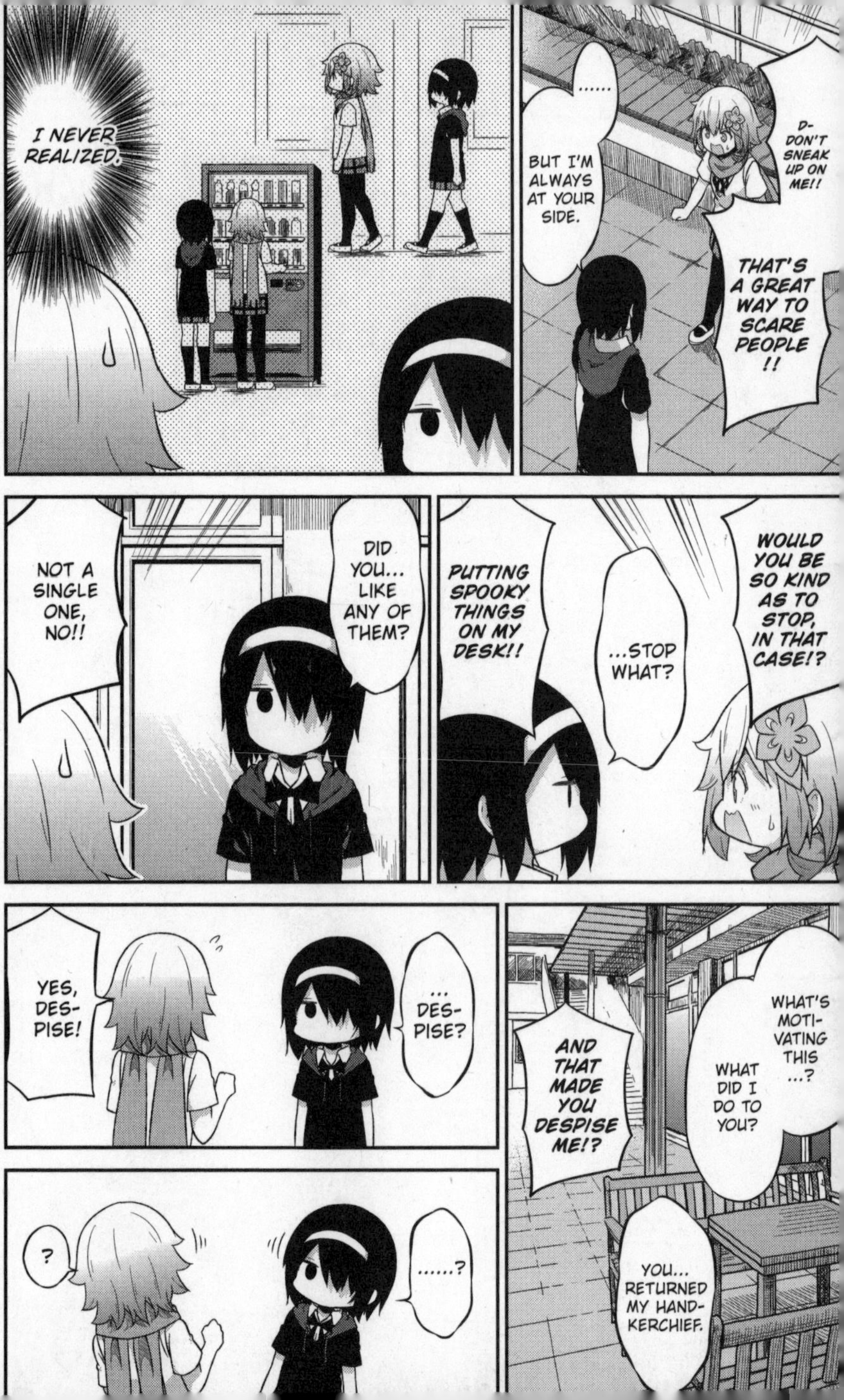
D-DON'T SNEAK UP ON ME!!
......
BUT I'M ALWAYS AT YOUR SIDE.
THAT'S A GREAT WAY TO SCARE PEOPLE!!
I NEVER REALIZED.
WOULD YOU BE SO KIND AS TO STOP, IN THAT CASE!?
...STOP WHAT?
PUTTING SPOOKY THINGS ON MY DESK!!
DID YOU... LIKE ANY OF THEM?
NOT A SINGLE ONE, NO!!
WHAT'S MOTI-VATING THIS ...?
WHAT DID I DO TO YOU?
YOU... RETURNED MY HAND-KERCHIEF.
AND THAT MADE YOU DESPISE ME!?
... DES-PISE?
YES, DES-PISE!
......?
?

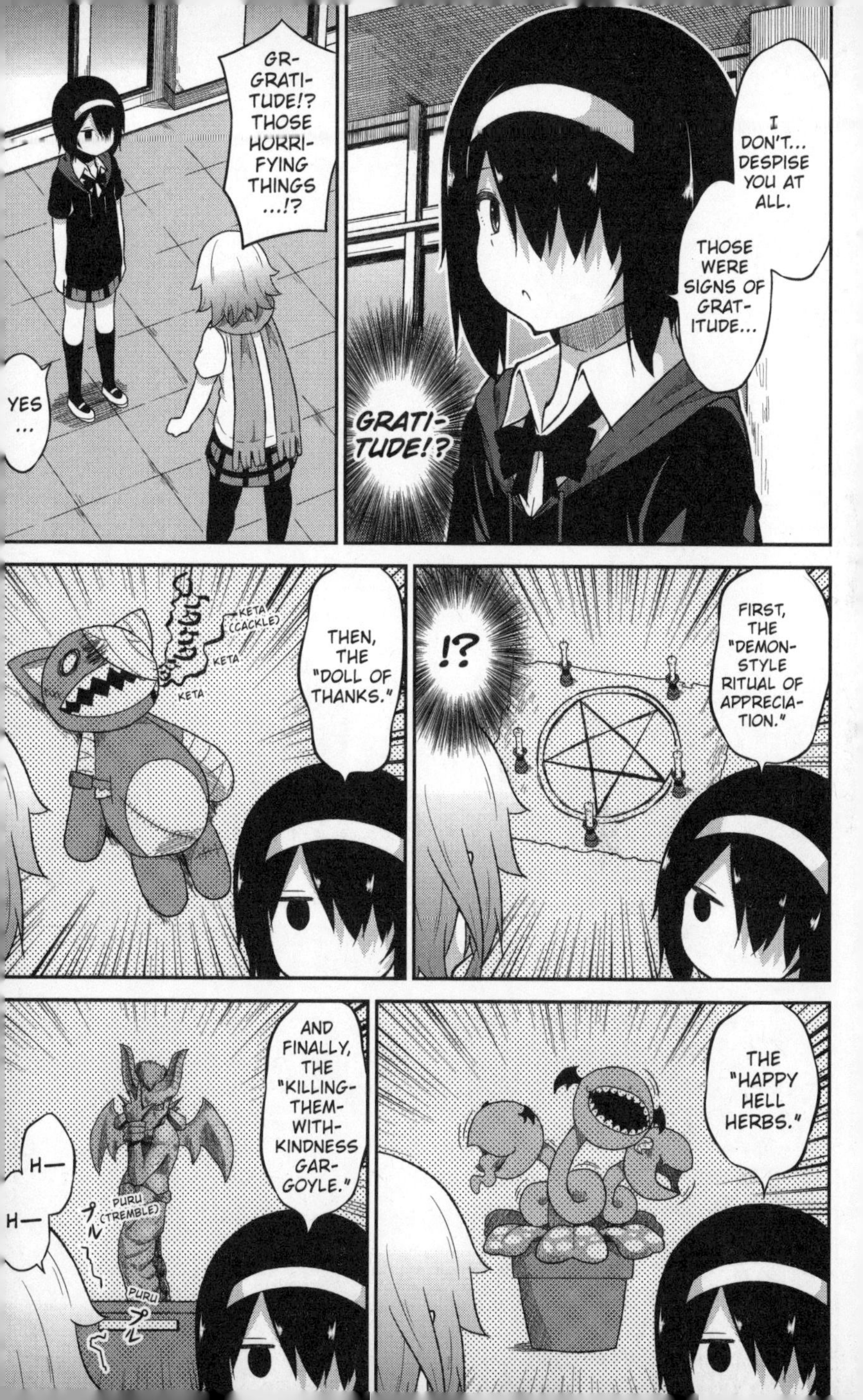
I DON'T... DESPISE YOU AT ALL.
THOSE WERE SIGNS OF GRATITUDE...
GRATITUDE!?
GR-GRATITUDE!? THOSE HORRIFYING THINGS...!?
YES...
FIRST, THE "DEMON-STYLE RITUAL OF APPRECIATION."
!?
THEN, THE "DOLL OF THANKS."
KETA (CACKLE)
KETA
KETA
THE "HAPPY HELL HERBS."
AND FINALLY, THE "KILLING-THEM-WITH-KINDNESS GARGOYLE."
H—
H—
PURU (TREMBLE)
PURU

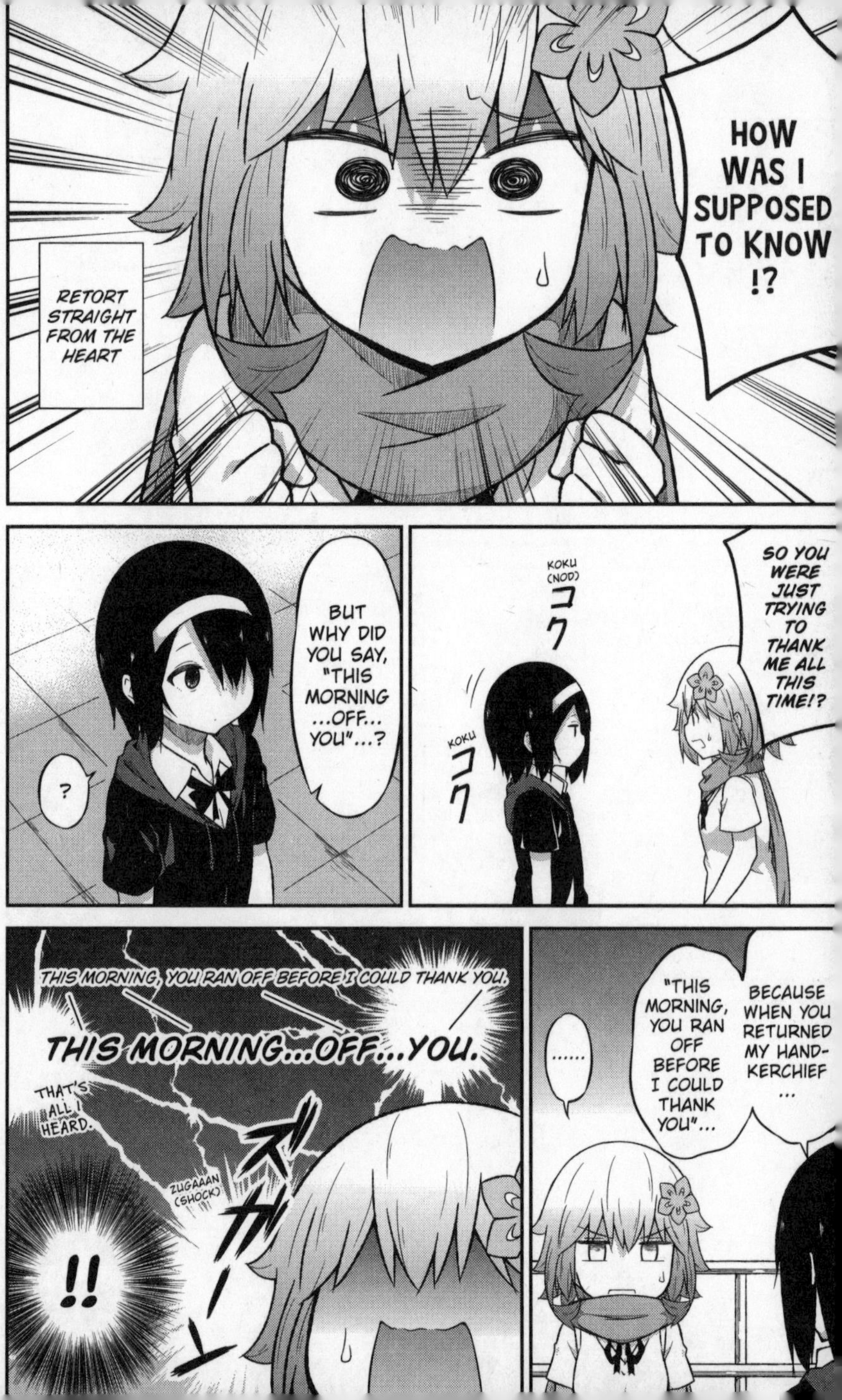
HOW WAS I SUPPOSED TO KNOW !?
RETORT STRAIGHT FROM THE HEART
SO YOU WERE JUST TRYING TO THANK ME ALL THIS TIME!?
KOKU (NOD)
KOKU
BUT WHY DID YOU SAY, "THIS MORNING ...OFF... YOU"...?
?
BECAUSE WHEN YOU RETURNED MY HAND-KERCHIEF ...
"THIS MORNING, YOU RAN OFF BEFORE I COULD THANK YOU"...
......
THIS MORNING, YOU RAN OFF BEFORE I COULD THANK YOU.
THIS MORNING...OFF...YOU.
THAT'S ALL I HEARD.
ZUGAAAN (SHOCK)
!!

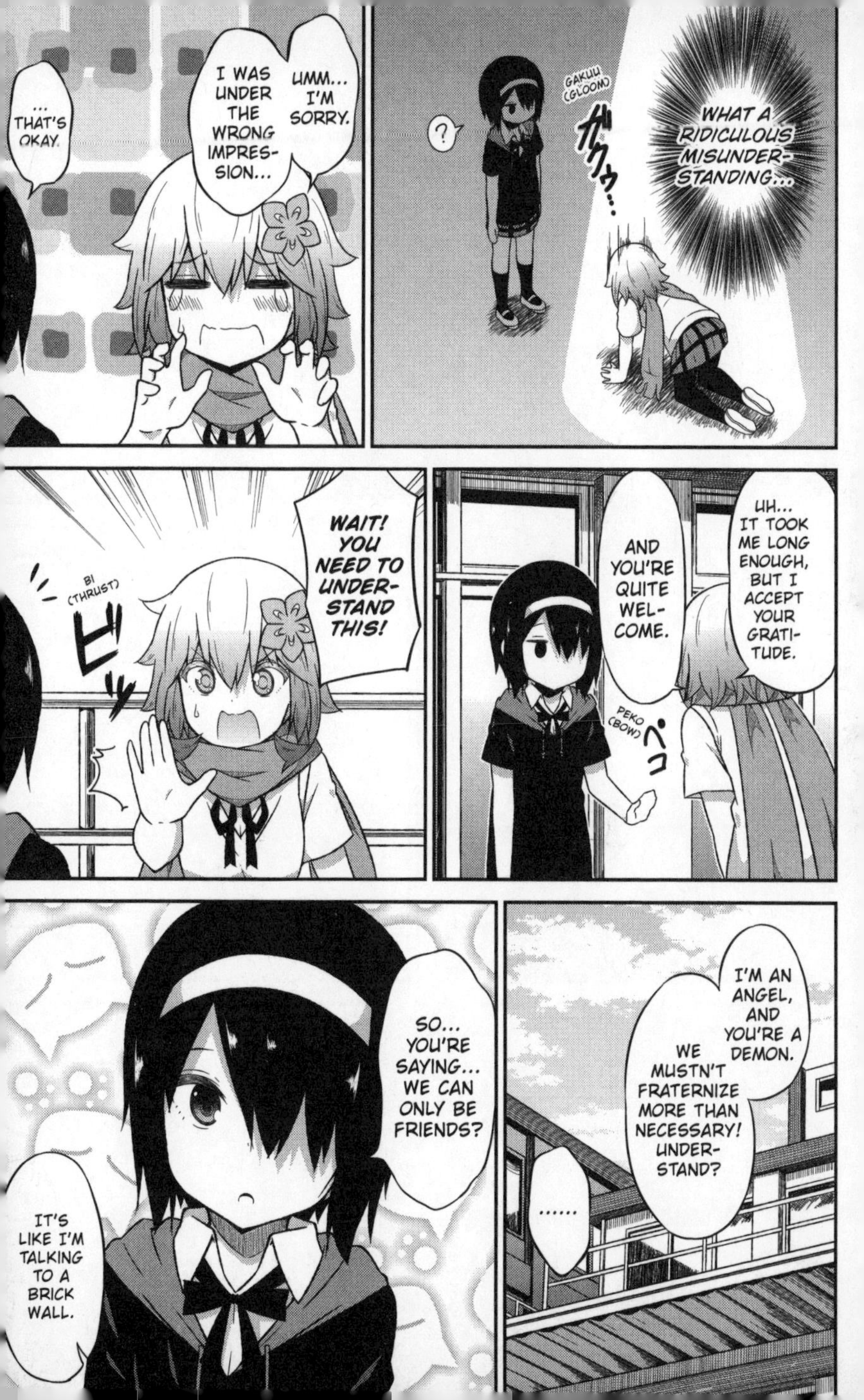
WHAT A RIDICULOUS MISUNDERSTANDING...
GAKUU (GLOOM)
ガクゥ…
?
UMM... I'M SORRY.
I WAS UNDER THE WRONG IMPRESSION...
...THAT'S OKAY.
UH... IT TOOK ME LONG ENOUGH, BUT I ACCEPT YOUR GRATITUDE.
AND YOU'RE QUITE WELCOME.
PEKO (BOW)
ペコ
WAIT! YOU NEED TO UNDERSTAND THIS!
BI (THRUST)
ビッ
I'M AN ANGEL, AND YOU'RE A DEMON.
WE MUSTN'T FRATERNIZE MORE THAN NECESSARY! UNDERSTAND?
......
SO... YOU'RE SAYING... WE CAN ONLY BE FRIENDS?
IT'S LIKE I'M TALKING TO A BRICK WALL.

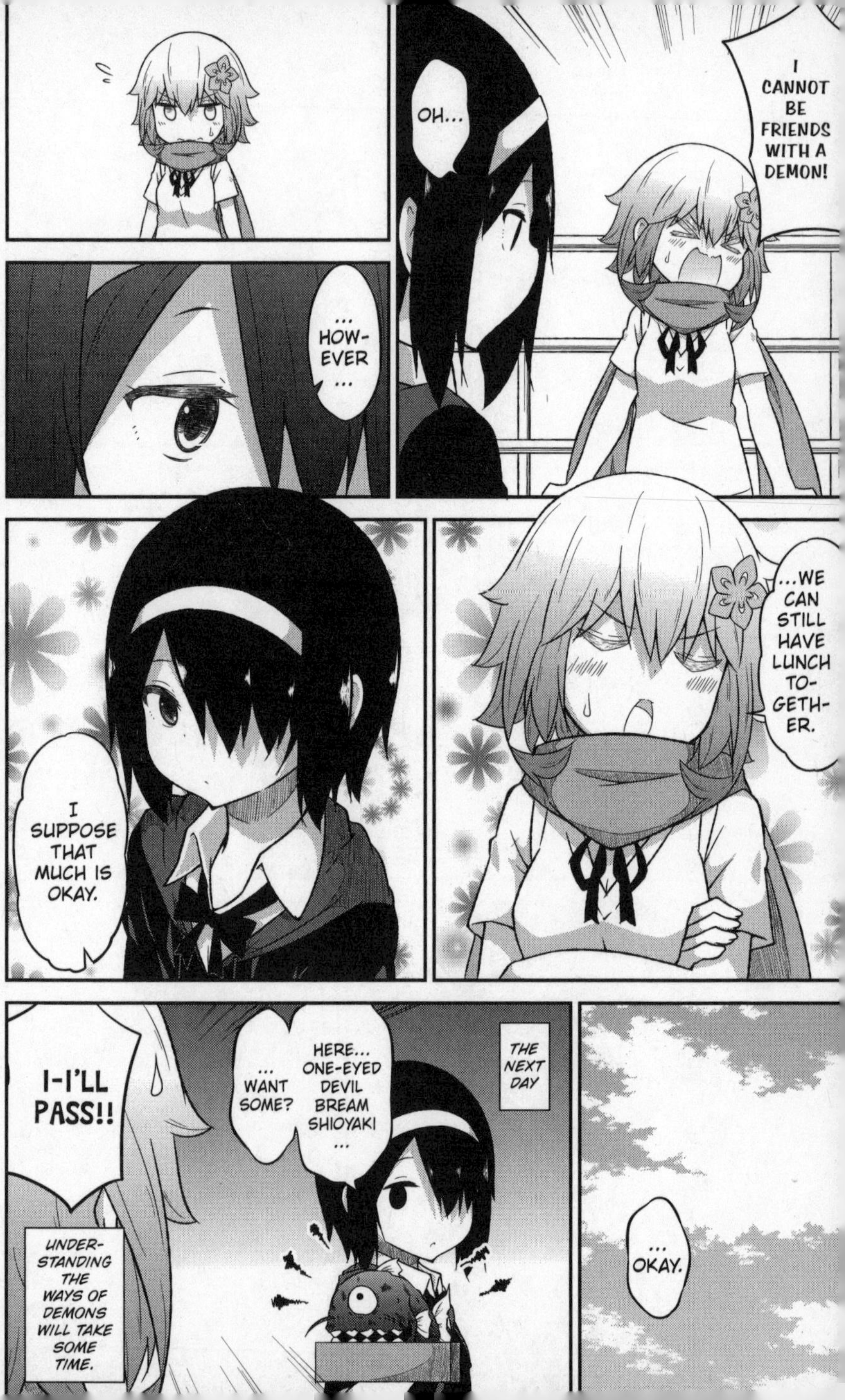
I CANNOT BE FRIENDS WITH A DEMON!
OH...
...HOWEVER...
...WE CAN STILL HAVE LUNCH TOGETHER.
I SUPPOSE THAT MUCH IS OKAY.
...OKAY.
THE NEXT DAY
HERE... ONE-EYED DEVIL BREAM SHIOYAKI...
...WANT SOME?
I-I'LL PASS!!
UNDERSTANDING THE WAYS OF DEMONS WILL TAKE SOME TIME.

YOU DO, THOUGH.

I AM A NEW CHARACTER...

...YET I HAVE NO NAME...

NEW

Gabriel Dropout

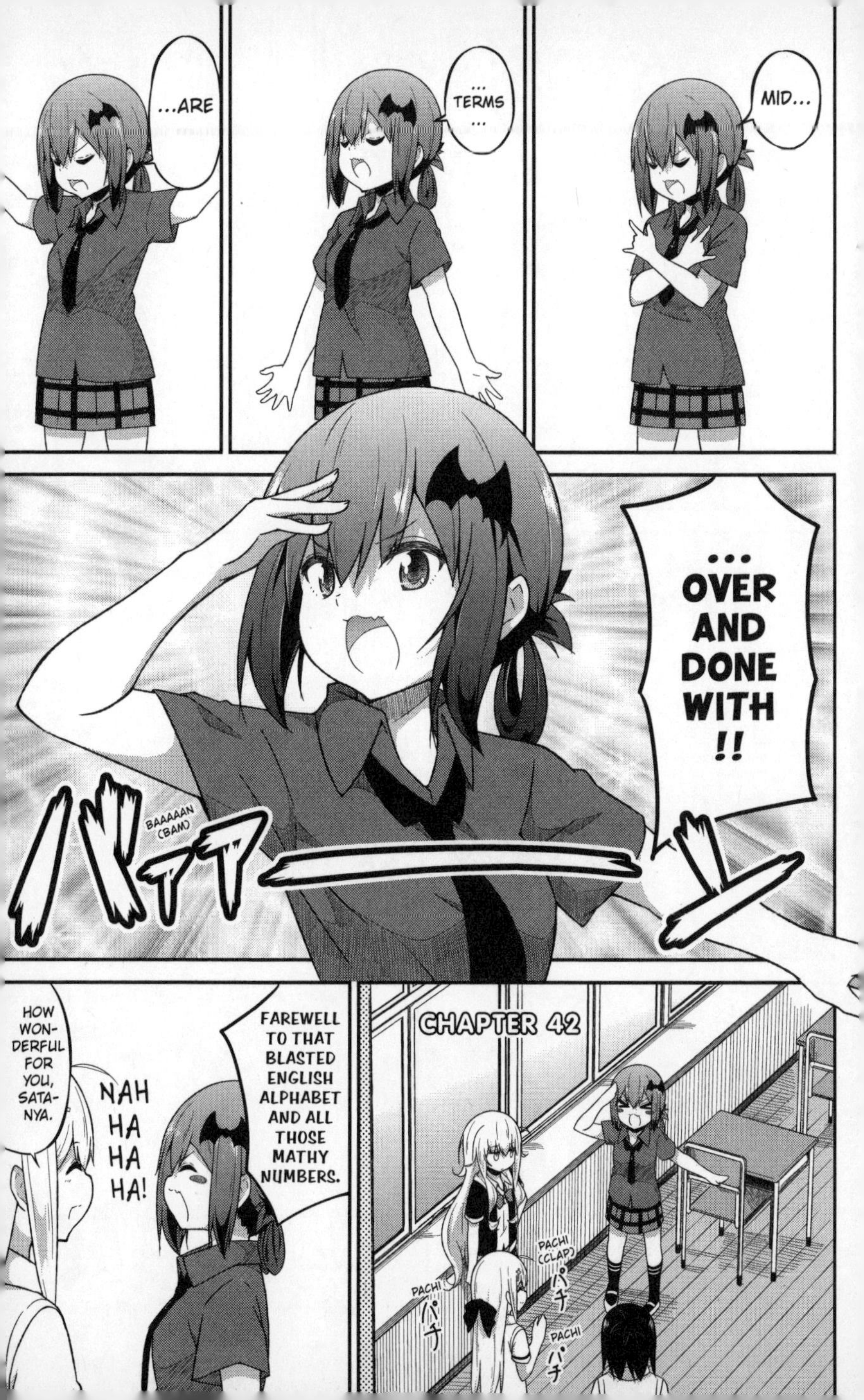
MID...
...TERMS...
...ARE
...OVER AND DONE WITH!!
BAAAAAN (BAM)
CHAPTER 42
PACHI (CLAP)
パチ
PACHI
パチ
PACHI
パチ
FAREWELL TO THAT BLASTED ENGLISH ALPHABET AND ALL THOSE MATHY NUMBERS.
NAH HA HA HA!
HOW WONDERFUL FOR YOU, SATANYA.

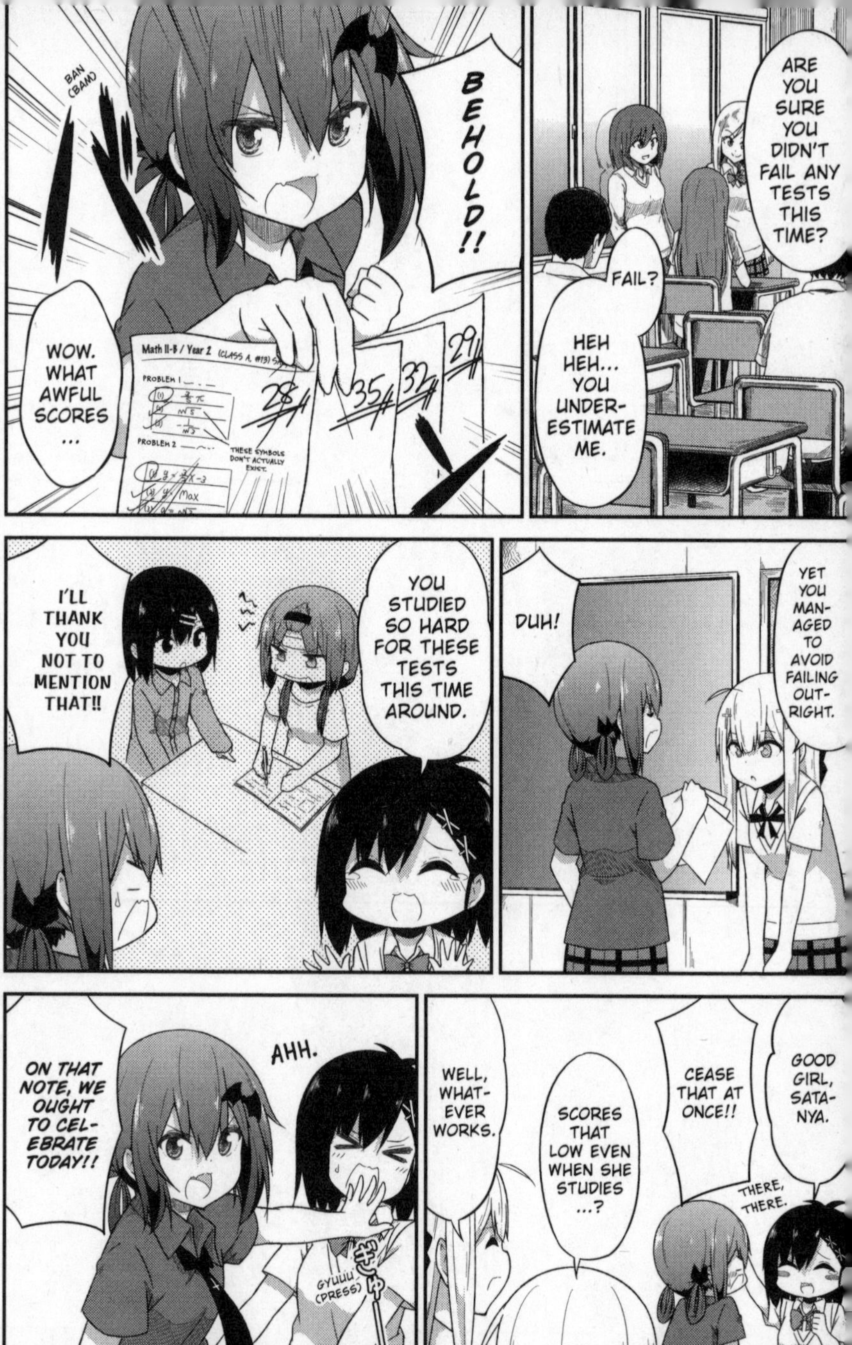

ARE YOU SURE YOU DIDN'T FAIL ANY TESTS THIS TIME?
FAIL?
HEH HEH... YOU UNDER-ESTIMATE ME.
BEHOLD!!
BAN (BAM)
WOW. WHAT AWFUL SCORES...
Math II-B / Year 2 (CLASS A, #13)
PROBLEM 1
PROBLEM 2
THESE SYMBOLS DON'T ACTUALLY EXIST.
28
35
32
29
YET YOU MAN-AGED TO AVOID FAILING OUT-RIGHT.
DUH!
YOU STUDIED SO HARD FOR THESE TESTS THIS TIME AROUND.
I'LL THANK YOU NOT TO MENTION THAT!!
GOOD GIRL, SATA-NYA.
THERE, THERE.
CEASE THAT AT ONCE!!
SCORES THAT LOW EVEN WHEN SHE STUDIES...?
WELL, WHAT-EVER WORKS.
ON THAT NOTE, WE OUGHT TO CEL-EBRATE TODAY!!
AHH.
ぎゅ
GYUUU (PRESS)

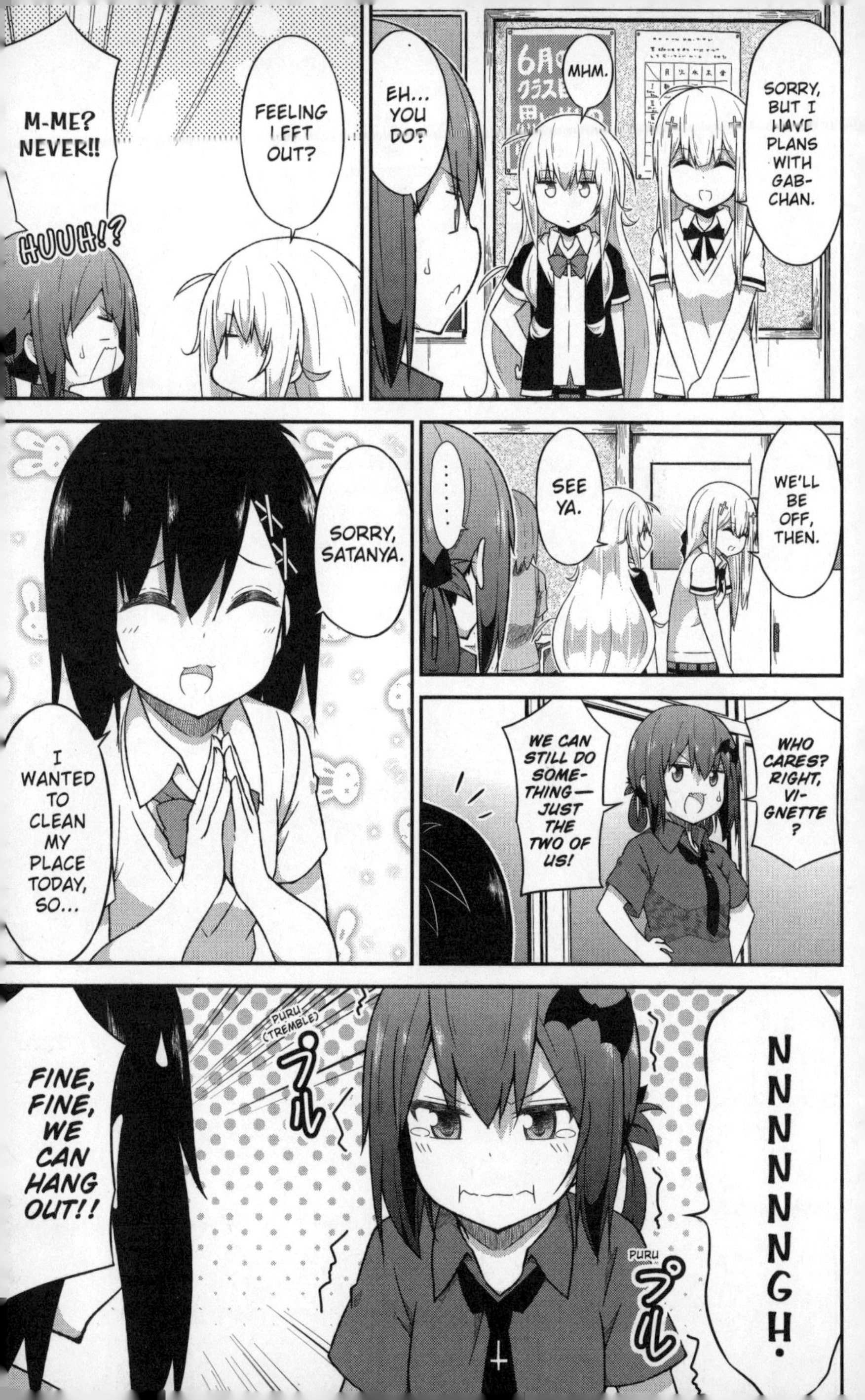
SORRY, BUT I HAVE PLANS WITH GAB-CHAN.
MHM.
EH... YOU DO?
FEELING LEFT OUT?
M-ME? NEVER!!
HUUH!?
WE'LL BE OFF, THEN.
SEE YA.
......
WHO CARES? RIGHT, VI-GNETTE?
WE CAN STILL DO SOME-THING—JUST THE TWO OF US!
SORRY, SATANYA.
I WANTED TO CLEAN MY PLACE TODAY, SO...
NNNNNNGH.
PURU (TREMBLE)
プル
PURU
プル
FINE, FINE, WE CAN HANG OUT!!

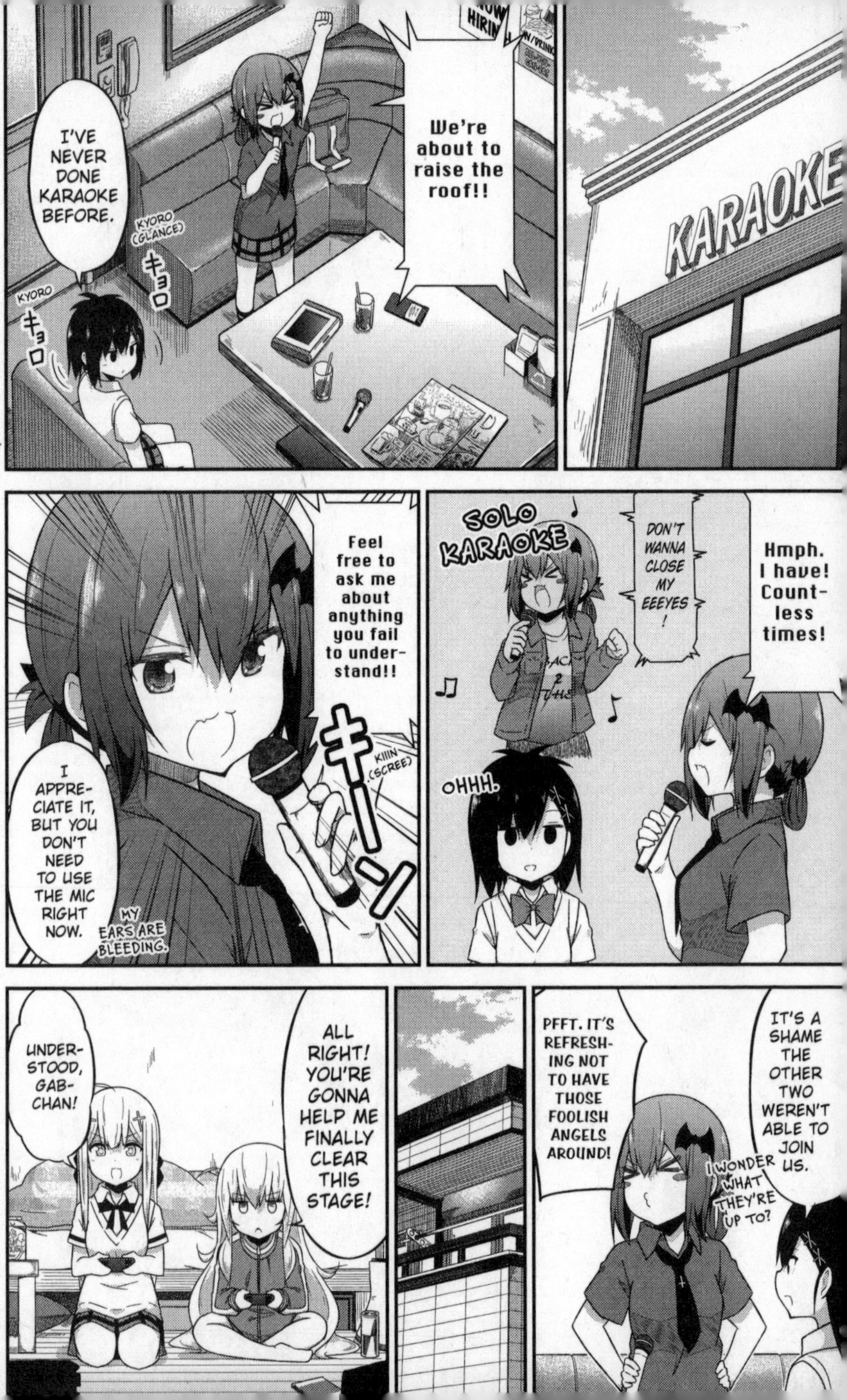
KARAOKE
We're about to raise the roof!!
I'VE NEVER DONE KARAOKE BEFORE.
KYORO (GLANCE)
キョロ
KYORO
キョロ
Hmph. I have! Countless times!
DON'T WANNA CLOSE MY EEEYES!
SOLO KARAOKE
OHHH.
Feel free to ask me about anything you fail to understand!!
キーン
KIIIN (SCREE)
I APPRECIATE IT, BUT YOU DON'T NEED TO USE THE MIC RIGHT NOW.
MY EARS ARE BLEEDING.
IT'S A SHAME THE OTHER TWO WEREN'T ABLE TO JOIN US.
PFFT. IT'S REFRESHING NOT TO HAVE THOSE FOOLISH ANGELS AROUND!
I WONDER WHAT THEY'RE UP TO?
ALL RIGHT! YOU'RE GONNA HELP ME FINALLY CLEAR THIS STAGE!
UNDERSTOOD, GAB-CHAN!

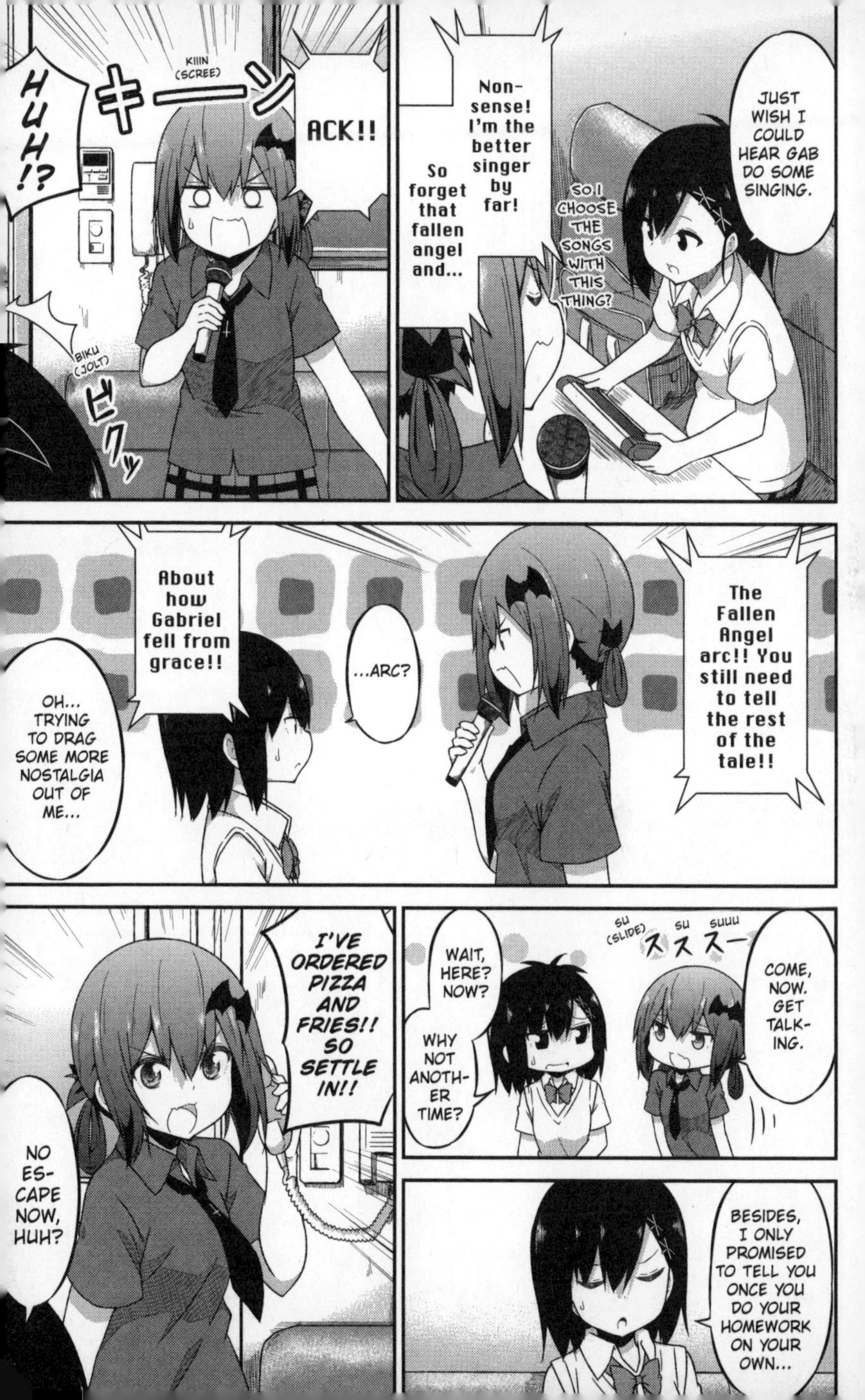
JUST WISH I COULD HEAR GAB DO SOME SINGING.
SO I CHOOSE THE SONGS WITH THIS THING?
Non-sense! I'm the better singer by far!
So forget that fallen angel and...
ACK!!
KIIIN (SCREE)
キーン
HUH!?
BIKU (JOLT)
ビクッ
The Fallen Angel arc!! You still need to tell the rest of the tale!!
...ARC?
About how Gabriel fell from grace!!
OH... TRYING TO DRAG SOME MORE NOSTALGIA OUT OF ME...
COME, NOW. GET TALK-ING.
SU (SLIDE) SU SUUU
スススー
WAIT, HERE? NOW?
WHY NOT ANOTH-ER TIME?
BESIDES, I ONLY PROMISED TO TELL YOU ONCE YOU DO YOUR HOMEWORK ON YOUR OWN...
I'VE ORDERED PIZZA AND FRIES!! SO SETTLE IN!!
NO ES-CAPE NOW, HUH?

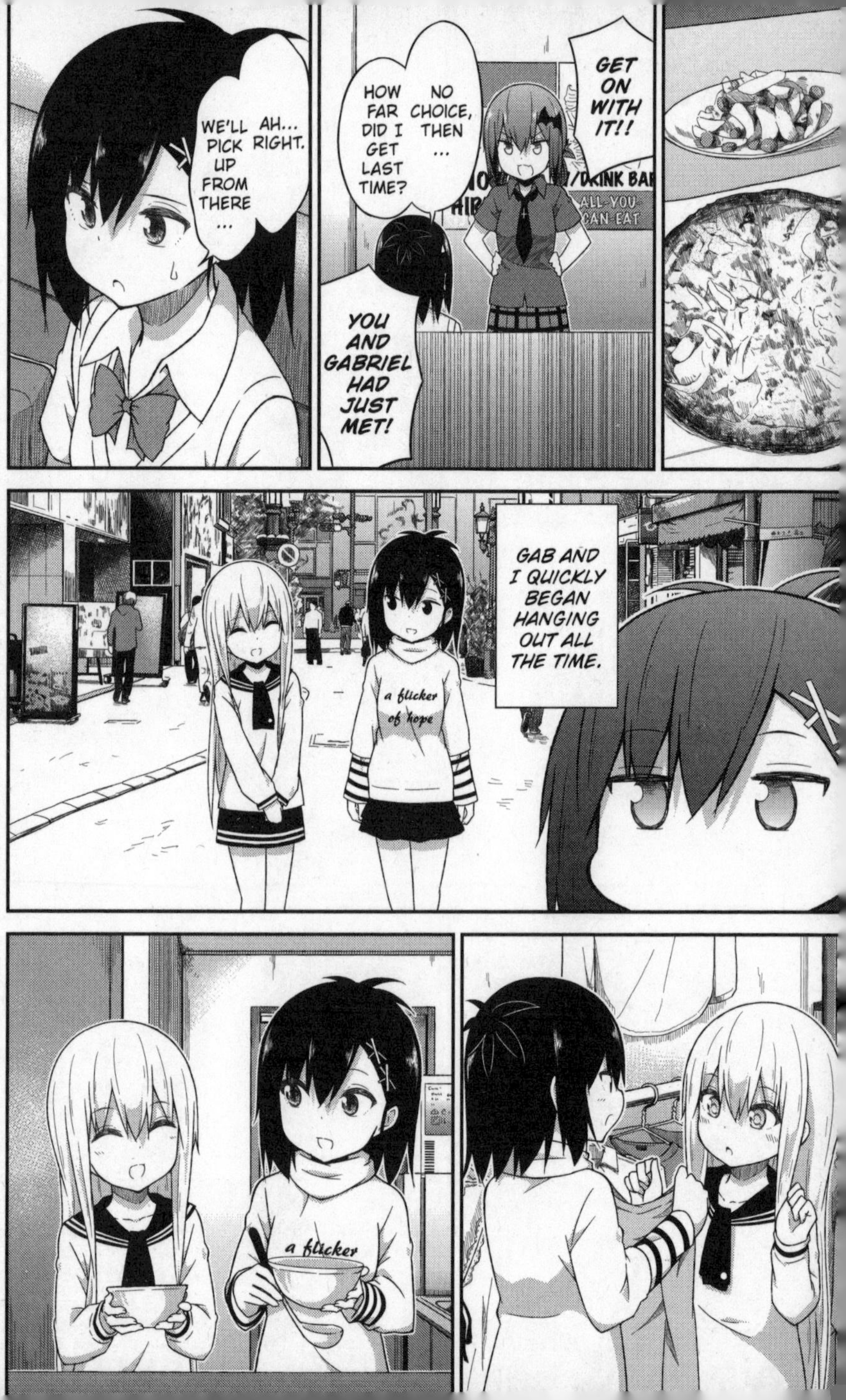
GET ON WITH IT!!
NO CHOICE, THEN...
HOW FAR DID I GET LAST TIME?
ALL-YOU-CAN-EAT
YOU AND GABRIEL HAD JUST MET!
AH... RIGHT.
WE'LL PICK UP FROM THERE...
GAB AND I QUICKLY BEGAN HANGING OUT ALL THE TIME.
a flicker of hope
a flicker

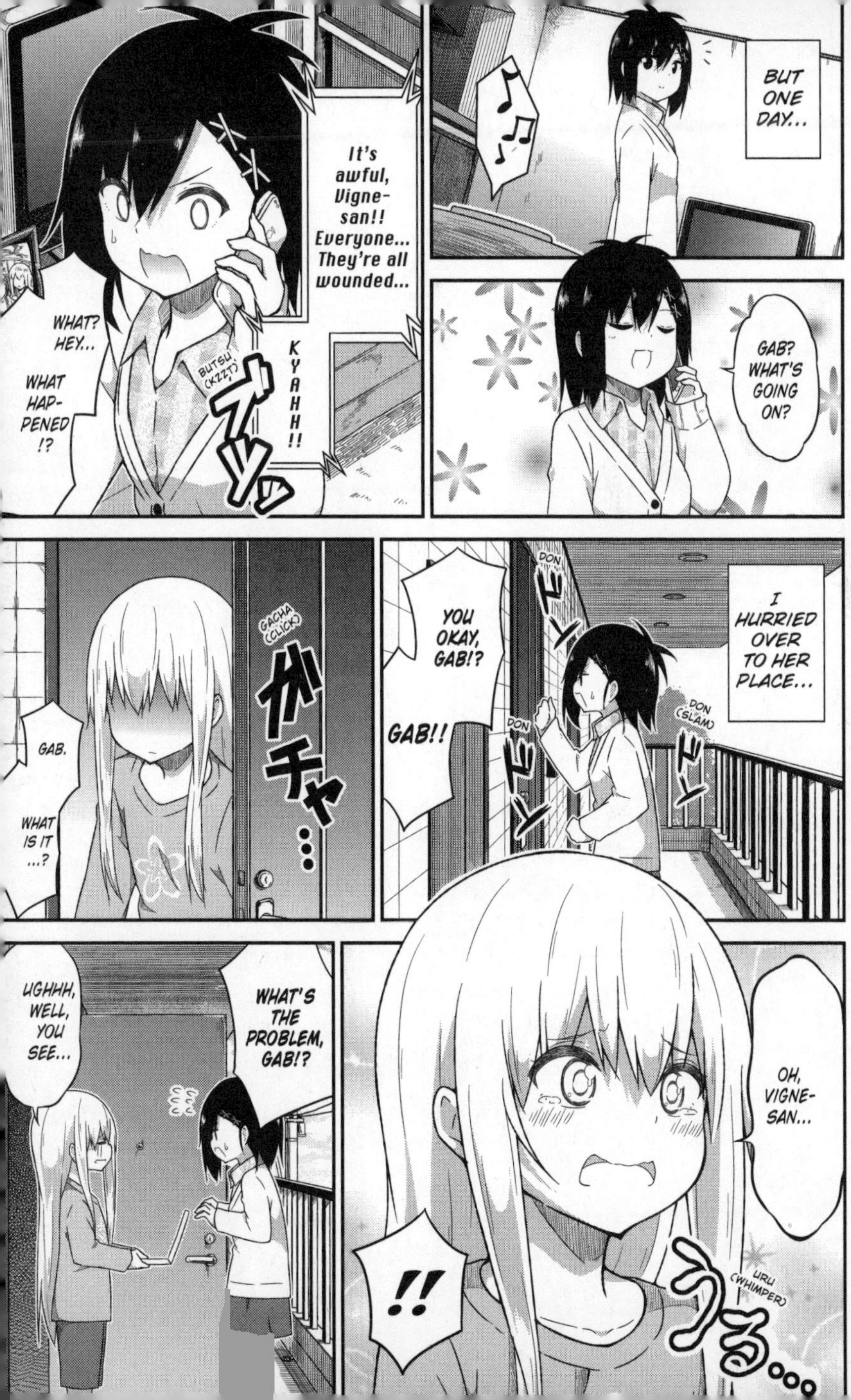
BUT ONE DAY...
GAB? WHAT'S GOING ON?
It's awful, Vigne-san!! Everyone... They're all wounded...
KYAHHH!!
BUTSU (KZZT)
WHAT? HEY...
WHAT HAPPENED!?
I HURRIED OVER TO HER PLACE...
DON (SLAM)
DON
DON
YOU OKAY, GAB!?
GAB!!
GACHA (CLICK)
GAB.
WHAT IS IT ...?
OH, VIGNE-SAN...
URU (WHIMPER)
!!
WHAT'S THE PROBLEM, GAB!?
UGHHH, WELL, YOU SEE...

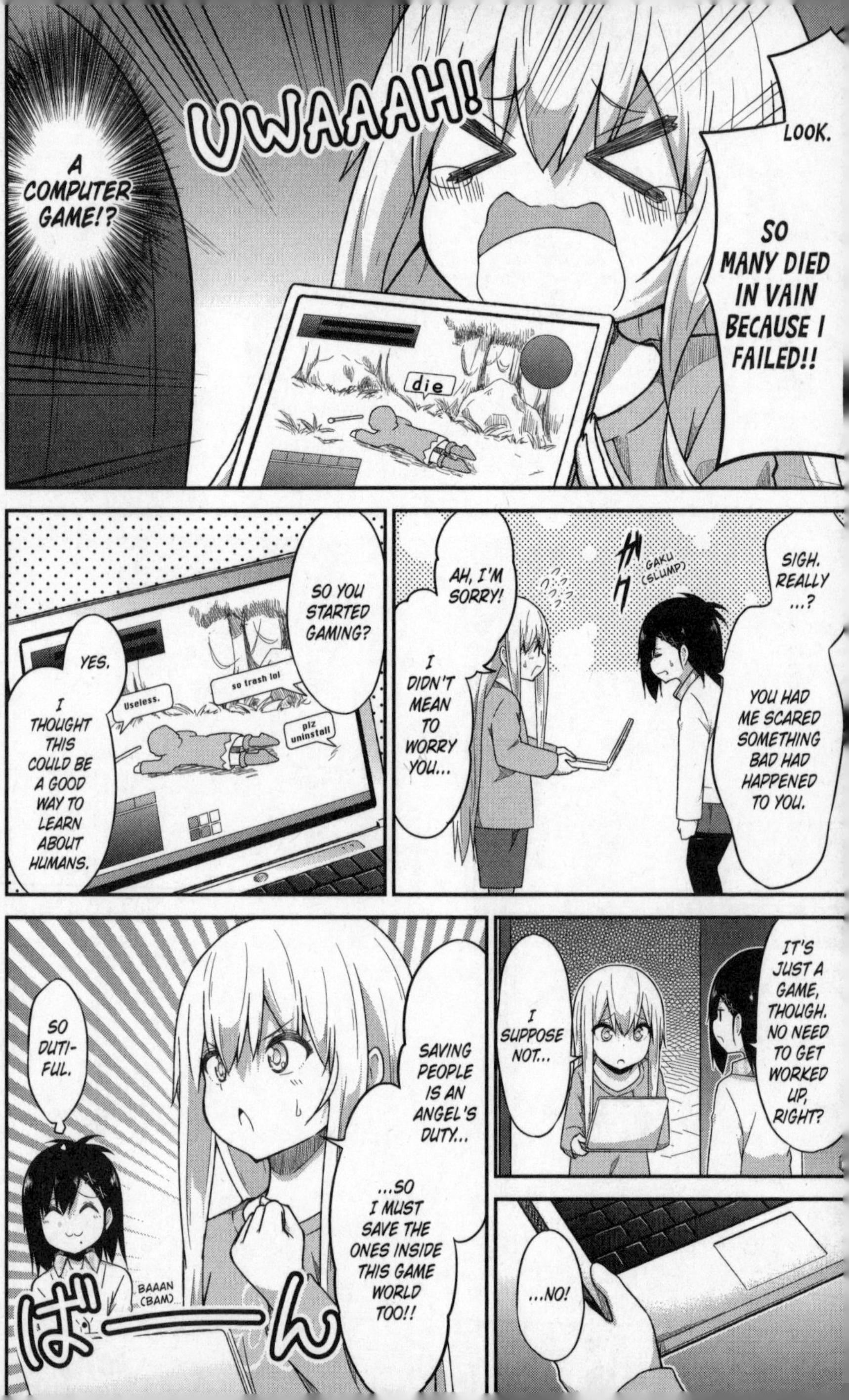
LOOK.
SO MANY DIED IN VAIN BECAUSE I FAILED!!
UWAAAAH!
A COMPUTER GAME!?
die
SIGH. REALLY ...?
GAKU (SLUMP)
YOU HAD ME SCARED SOMETHING BAD HAD HAPPENED TO YOU.
AH, I'M SORRY!
I DIDN'T MEAN TO WORRY YOU...
SO YOU STARTED GAMING?
so trash lol
Useless.
plz uninstall
YES.
I THOUGHT THIS COULD BE A GOOD WAY TO LEARN ABOUT HUMANS.
IT'S JUST A GAME, THOUGH. NO NEED TO GET WORKED UP, RIGHT?
I SUPPOSE NOT...
...NO!
SAVING PEOPLE IS AN ANGEL'S DUTY...
...SO I MUST SAVE THE ONES INSIDE THIS GAME WORLD TOO!!
SO DUTI-FUL.
BAAAN (BAM)
ばーん

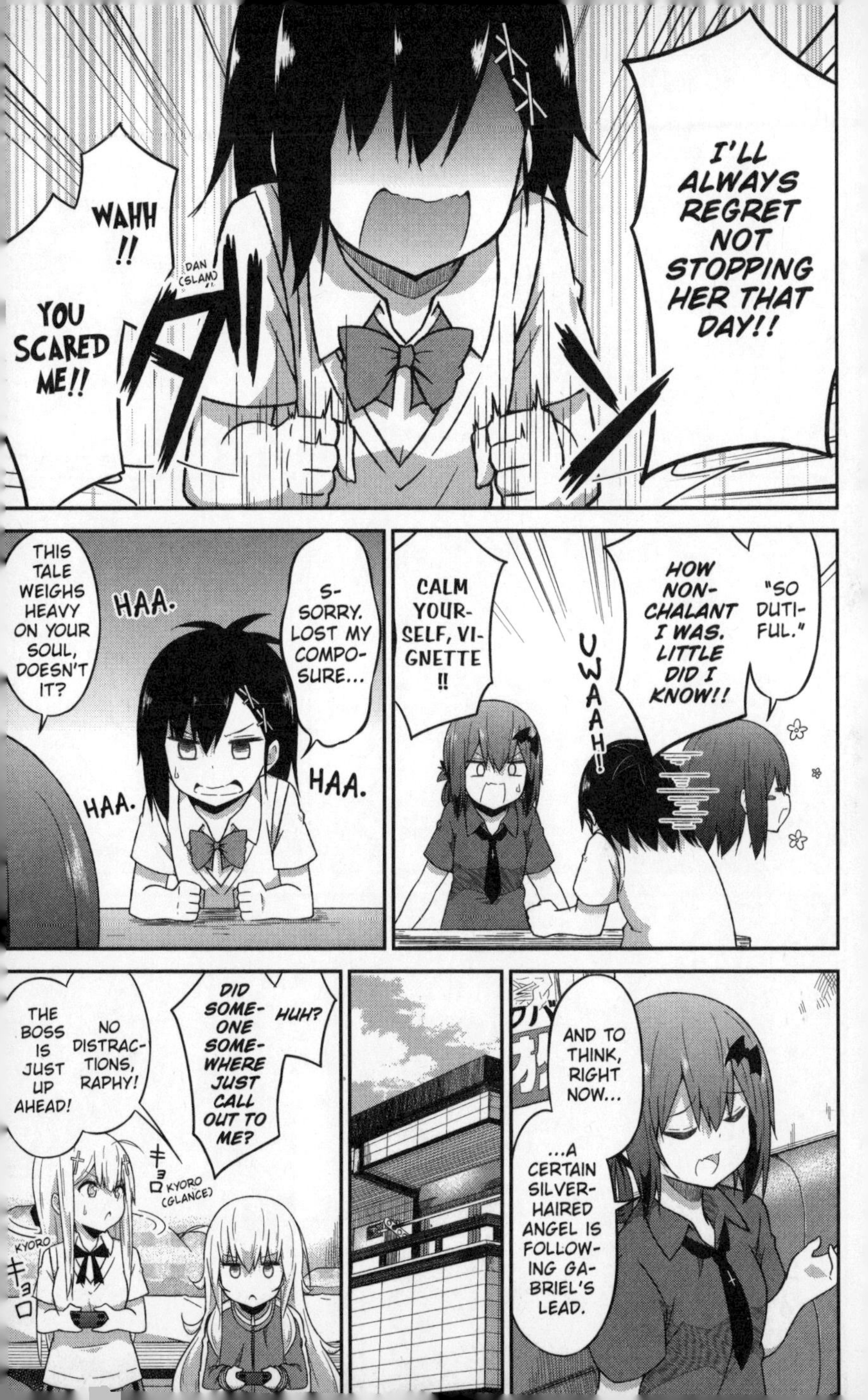
I'LL ALWAYS REGRET NOT STOPPING HER THAT DAY!!
WAHH!!
DAN (SLAM)
YOU SCARED ME!!
"SO DUTIFUL."
HOW NONCHALANT I WAS. LITTLE DID I KNOW!!
UWAAAH!
CALM YOURSELF, VIGNETTE!!
S-SORRY. LOST MY COMPOSURE...
HAA.
THIS TALE WEIGHS HEAVY ON YOUR SOUL, DOESN'T IT?
HAA.
HAA.
AND TO THINK, RIGHT NOW...
...A CERTAIN SILVER-HAIRED ANGEL IS FOLLOWING GABRIEL'S LEAD.
HUH?
DID SOMEONE SOMEWHERE JUST CALL OUT TO ME?
NO DISTRACTIONS, RAPHY!
THE BOSS IS JUST UP AHEAD!
キョロ KYORO (GLANCE)
KYORO キョロ

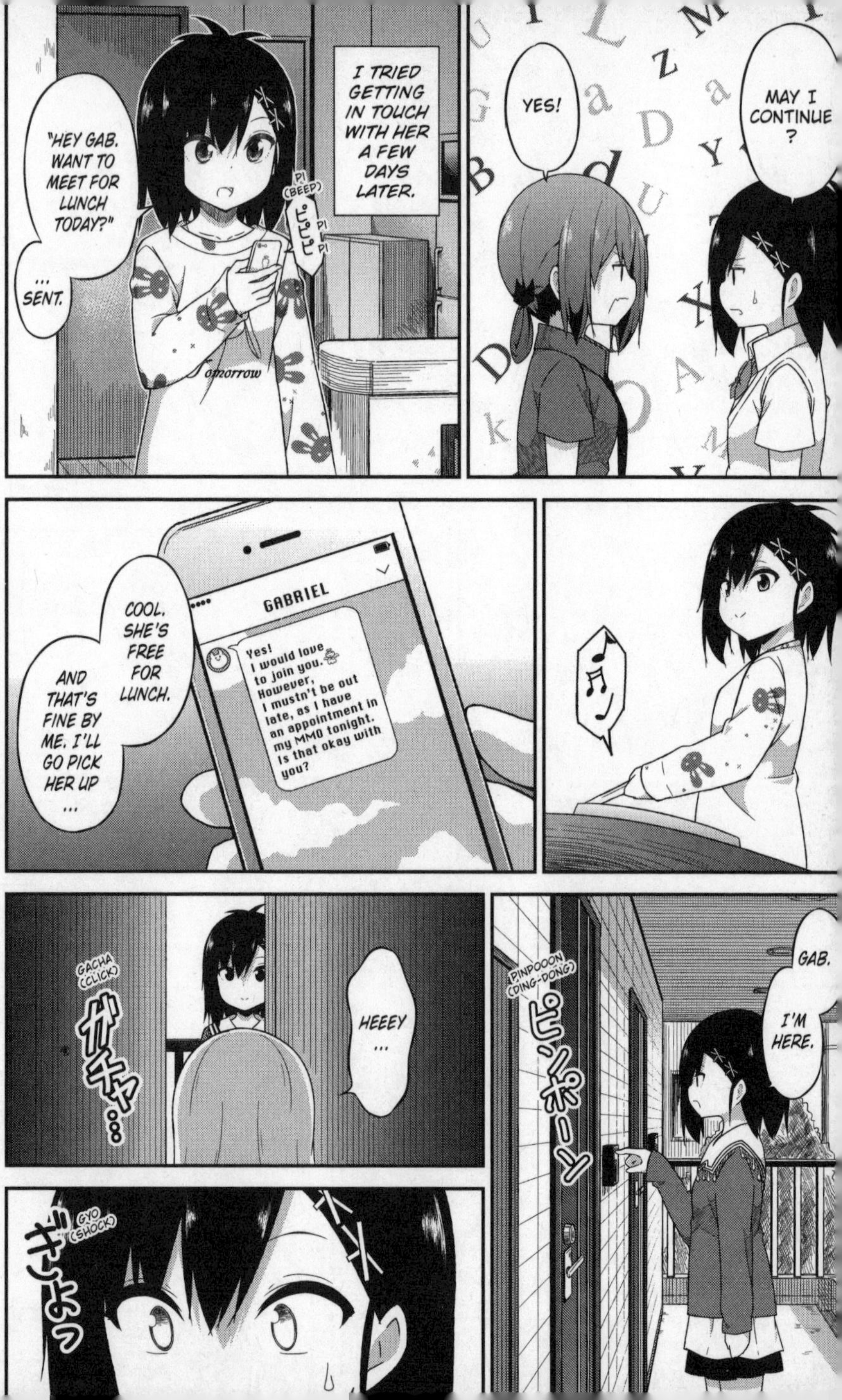
MAY I CONTINUE ?
YES!
I TRIED GETTING IN TOUCH WITH HER A FEW DAYS LATER.
PI PI PI (BEEP)
"HEY GAB. WANT TO MEET FOR LUNCH TODAY?"
... SENT.
Tomorrow
GABRIEL
Yes! I would love to join you. However, I mustn't be out late, as I have an appointment in my MMO tonight. Is that okay with you?
COOL. SHE'S FREE FOR LUNCH.
AND THAT'S FINE BY ME. I'LL GO PICK HER UP ...
GAB. I'M HERE.
PINPOOON (DING-DONG)
HEEEY ...
GACHA (CLICK)
GYO (SHOCK)

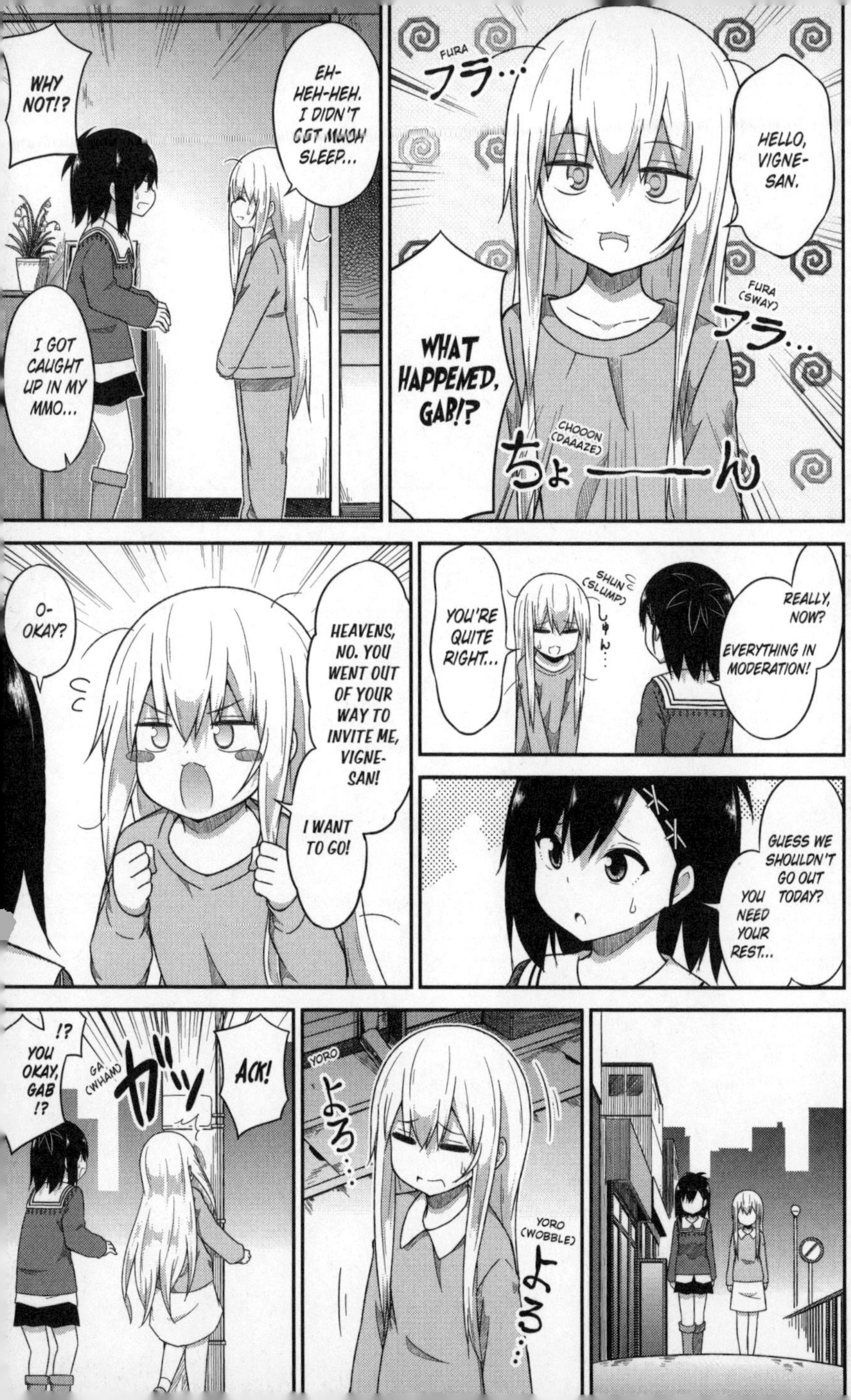
FURA
フラ…
HELLO, VIGNE-SAN.
FURA (SWAY)
フラ…
WHAT HAPPENED, GAB!?
CHOOON (DAAAZE)
ちょーーん
EH-HEH-HEH. I DIDN'T GET MUCH SLEEP...
WHY NOT!?
I GOT CAUGHT UP IN MY MMO...
REALLY, NOW?
EVERYTHING IN MODERATION!
SHUN (SLUMP)
しゅん…
YOU'RE QUITE RIGHT...
GUESS WE SHOULDN'T GO OUT TODAY? YOU NEED YOUR REST...
HEAVENS, NO. YOU WENT OUT OF YOUR WAY TO INVITE ME, VIGNE-SAN!
I WANT TO GO!
O-OKAY?
YORO
よろ…
YORO (WOBBLE)
よろ…
ACK!
GA (WHAM)
ガッ
!? YOU OKAY, GAB !?

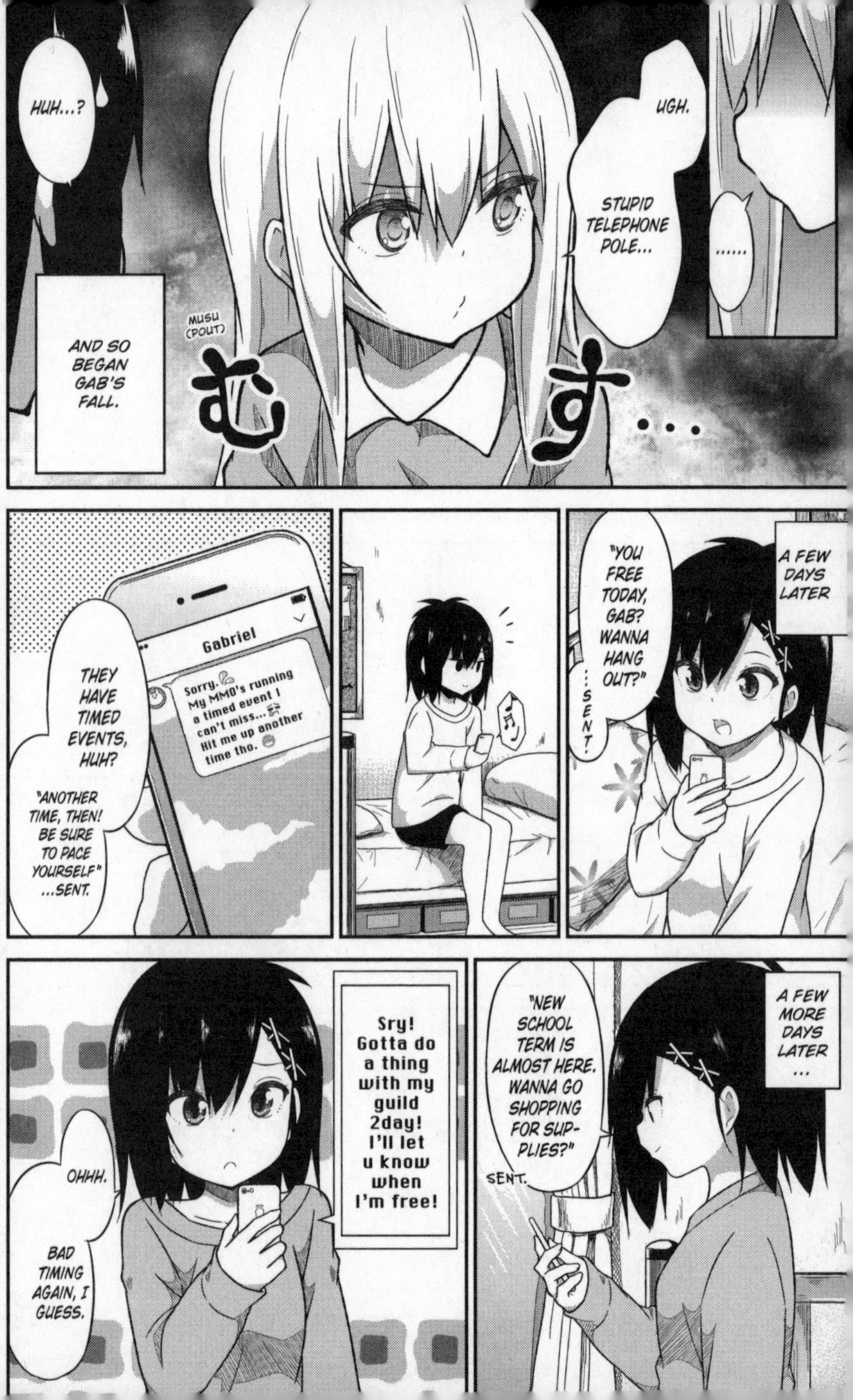
UGH.
STUPID TELEPHONE POLE...
......
HUH...?
MUSU (POUT)
むす...
AND SO BEGAN GAB'S FALL.
A FEW DAYS LATER
"YOU FREE TODAY, GAB? WANNA HANG OUT?"
...SENT.
Gabriel
Sorry. My MMO's running a timed event I can't miss... Hit me up another time tho.
THEY HAVE TIMED EVENTS, HUH?
"ANOTHER TIME, THEN! BE SURE TO PACE YOURSELF" ...SENT.
A FEW MORE DAYS LATER ...
"NEW SCHOOL TERM IS ALMOST HERE. WANNA GO SHOPPING FOR SUP-PLIES?"
SENT.
Sry! Gotta do a thing with my guild 2day! I'll let u know when I'm free!
OHHH.
BAD TIMING AGAIN, I GUESS.

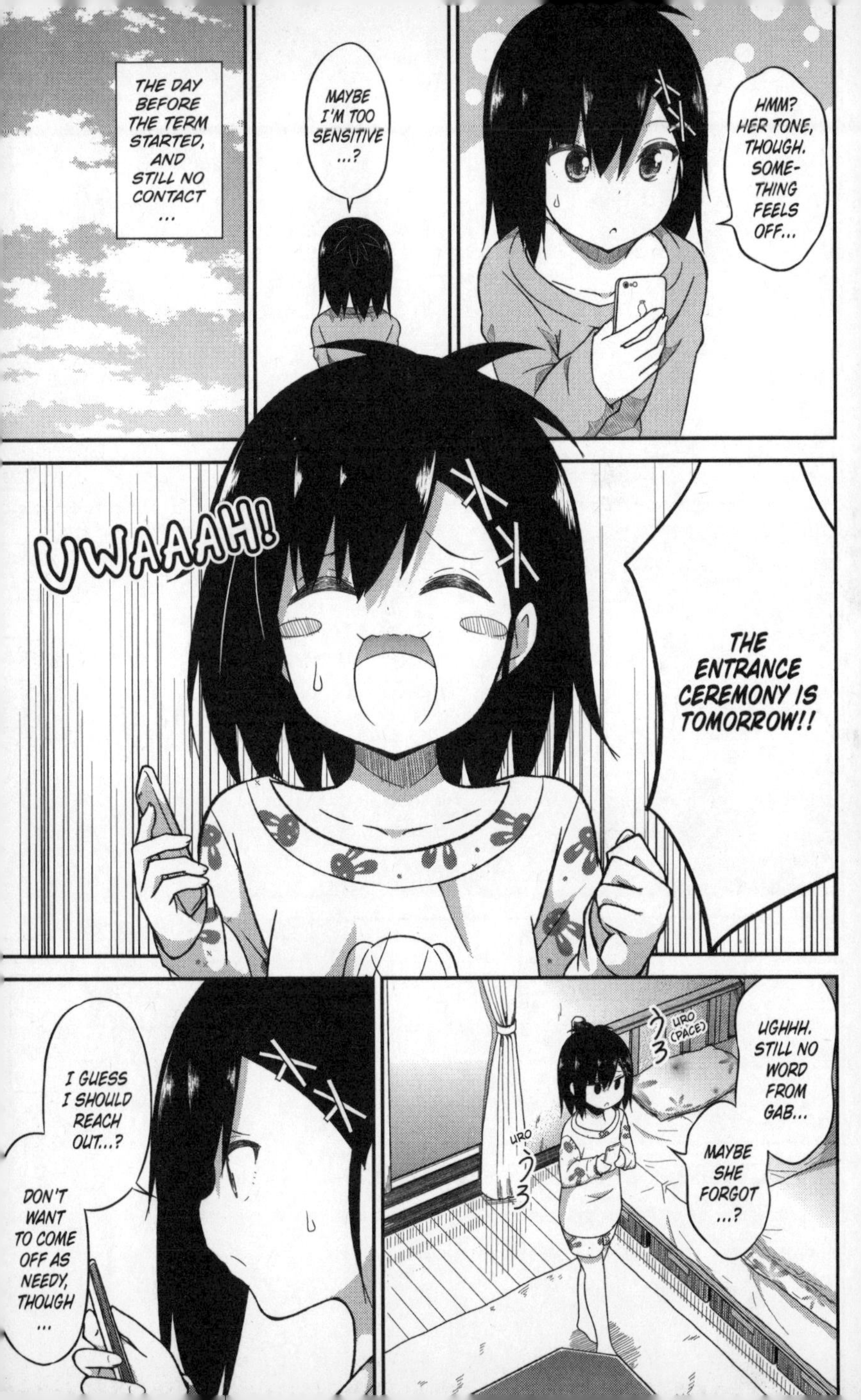

HMM? HER TONE, THOUGH. SOME-THING FEELS OFF...
MAYBE I'M TOO SENSITIVE...?
THE DAY BEFORE THE TERM STARTED, AND STILL NO CONTACT...
THE ENTRANCE CEREMONY IS TOMORROW!!
UWAAAAH!
UGHHH. STILL NO WORD FROM GAB...
URO (PACE)
URO
MAYBE SHE FORGOT...?
I GUESS I SHOULD REACH OUT...?
DON'T WANT TO COME OFF AS NEEDY, THOUGH...

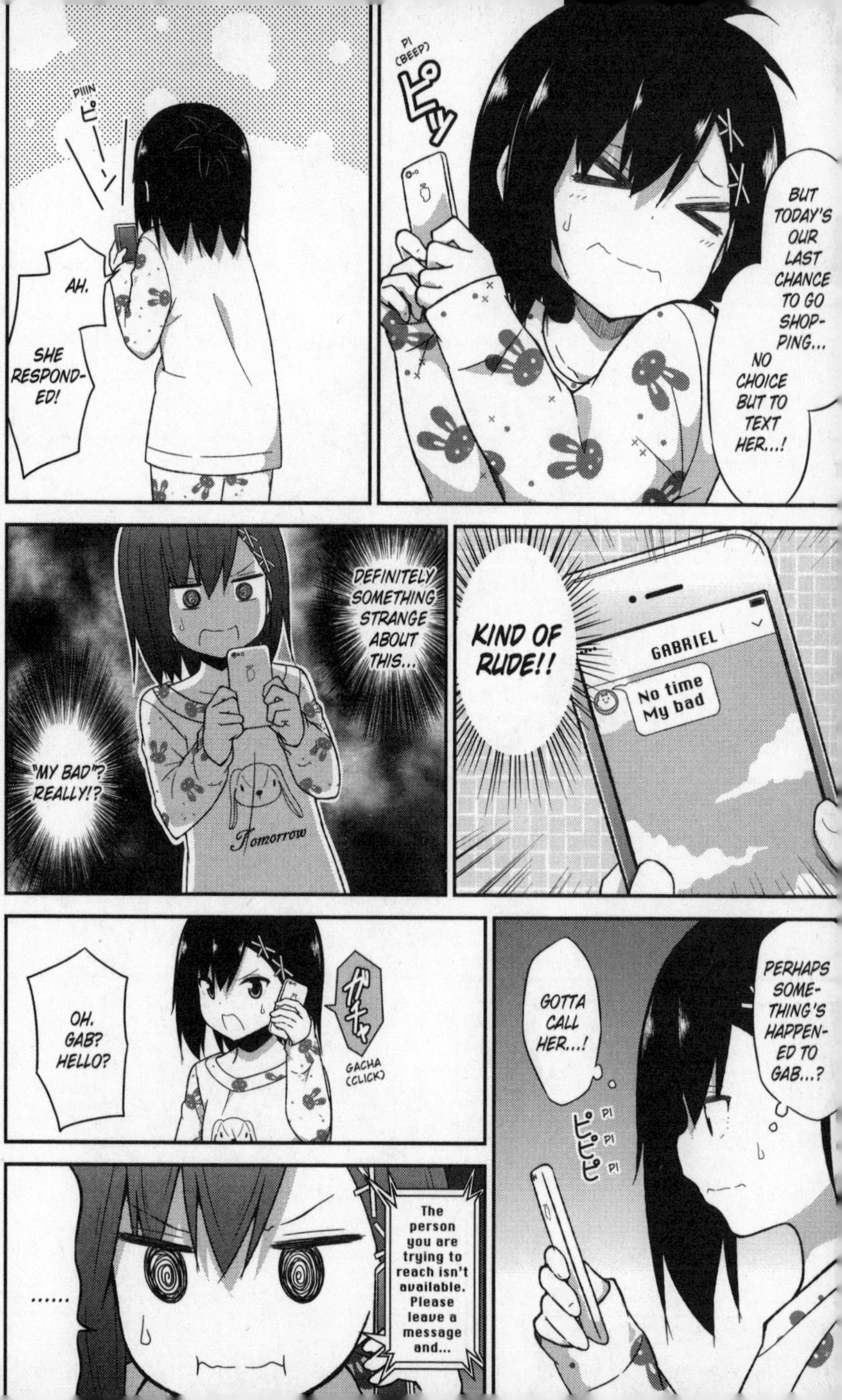
PI (BEEP)
ピッ
BUT TODAY'S OUR LAST CHANCE TO GO SHOPPING...
NO CHOICE BUT TO TEXT HER...!
PIIIN
ピーン
AH.
SHE RESPONDED!
KIND OF RUDE!!
GABRIEL
No time
My bad
DEFINITELY SOMETHING STRANGE ABOUT THIS...
"MY BAD"? REALLY!?
Tomorrow
PERHAPS SOMETHING'S HAPPENED TO GAB...?
GOTTA CALL HER...!
ピピピ
PI PI PI
ガチャ
GACHA (CLICK)
OH. GAB? HELLO?
The person you are trying to reach isn't available. Please leave a message and...
......

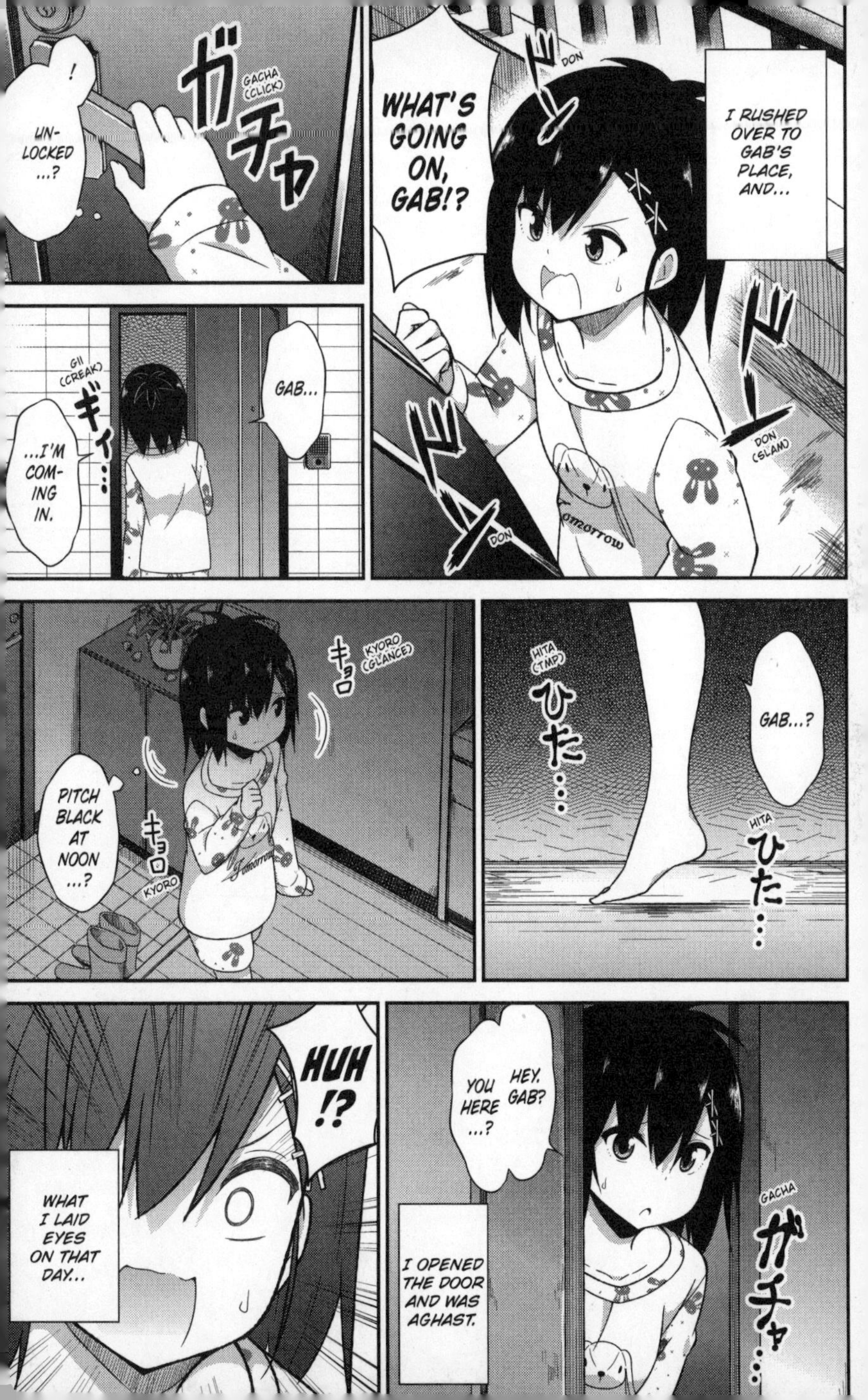
I RUSHED OVER TO GAB'S PLACE, AND...
DON
WHAT'S GOING ON, GAB!?
DON (SLAM)
DON
GACHA (CLICK)
!
UN-LOCKED ...?
GII (CREAK)
GAB...
...I'M COM-ING IN.
GAB...?
HITA (TMP)
HITA
KYORO (GLANCE)
KYORO
PITCH BLACK AT NOON ...?
HEY. GAB?
YOU HERE ...?
GACHA
I OPENED THE DOOR AND WAS AGHAST.
HUH !?
WHAT I LAID EYES ON THAT DAY...

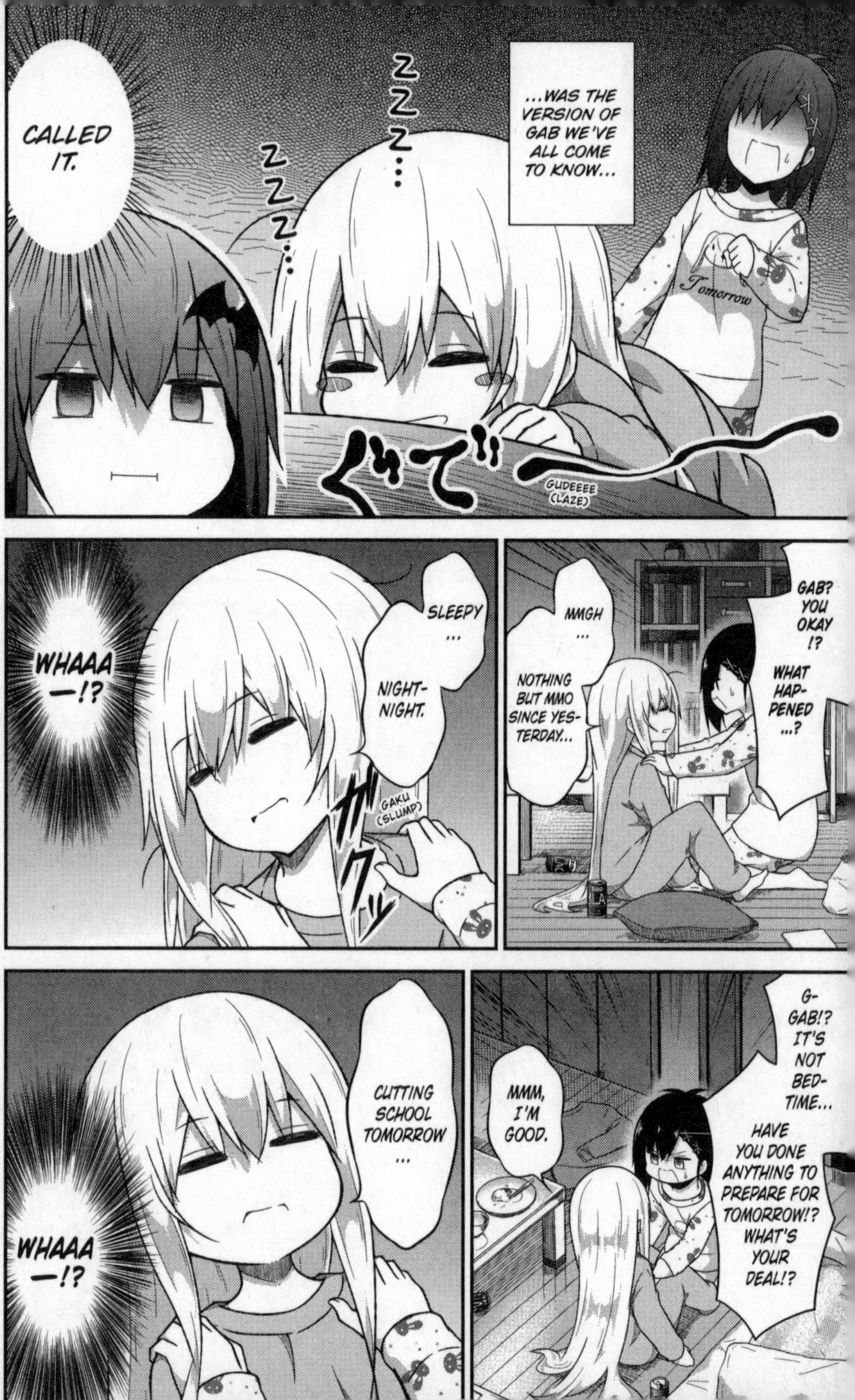
...WAS THE VERSION OF GAB WE'VE ALL COME TO KNOW...
Tomorrow
Z Z Z...
Z Z Z...
CALLED IT.
GUDEEEE (LAZE)
GAB? YOU OKAY!? WHAT HAP-PENED...?
MMGH... NOTHING BUT MMO SINCE YES-TERDAY...
SLEEPY... NIGHT-NIGHT.
GAKU (SLUMP)
WHAAA—!?
G-GAB!? IT'S NOT BED-TIME... HAVE YOU DONE ANYTHING TO PREPARE FOR TOMORROW!? WHAT'S YOUR DEAL!?
MMM, I'M GOOD.
CUTTING SCHOOL TOMORROW...
WHAAA—!?

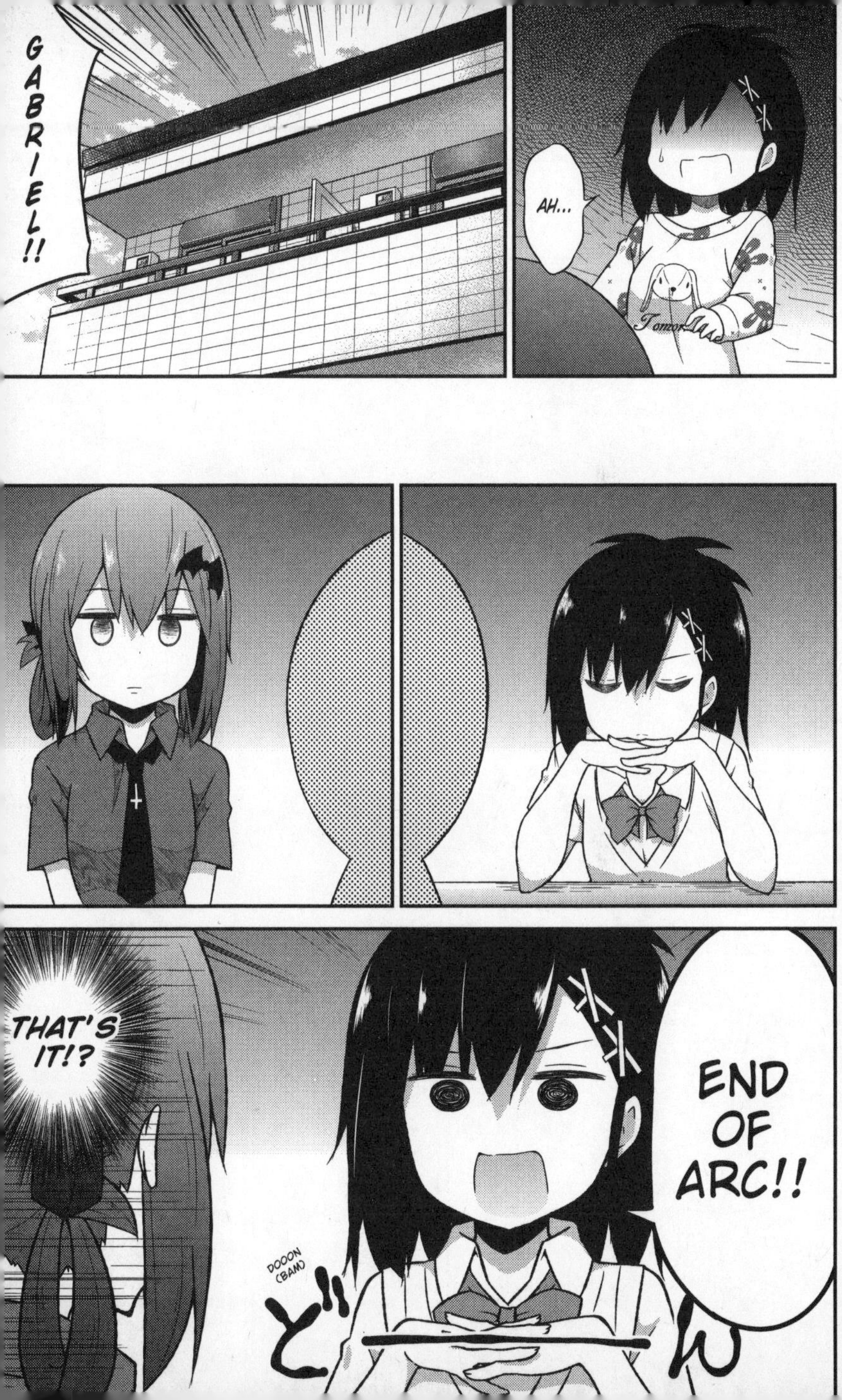
AH...
GABRIEL!!
END OF ARC!!
DOOON (BAM)
THAT'S IT!?

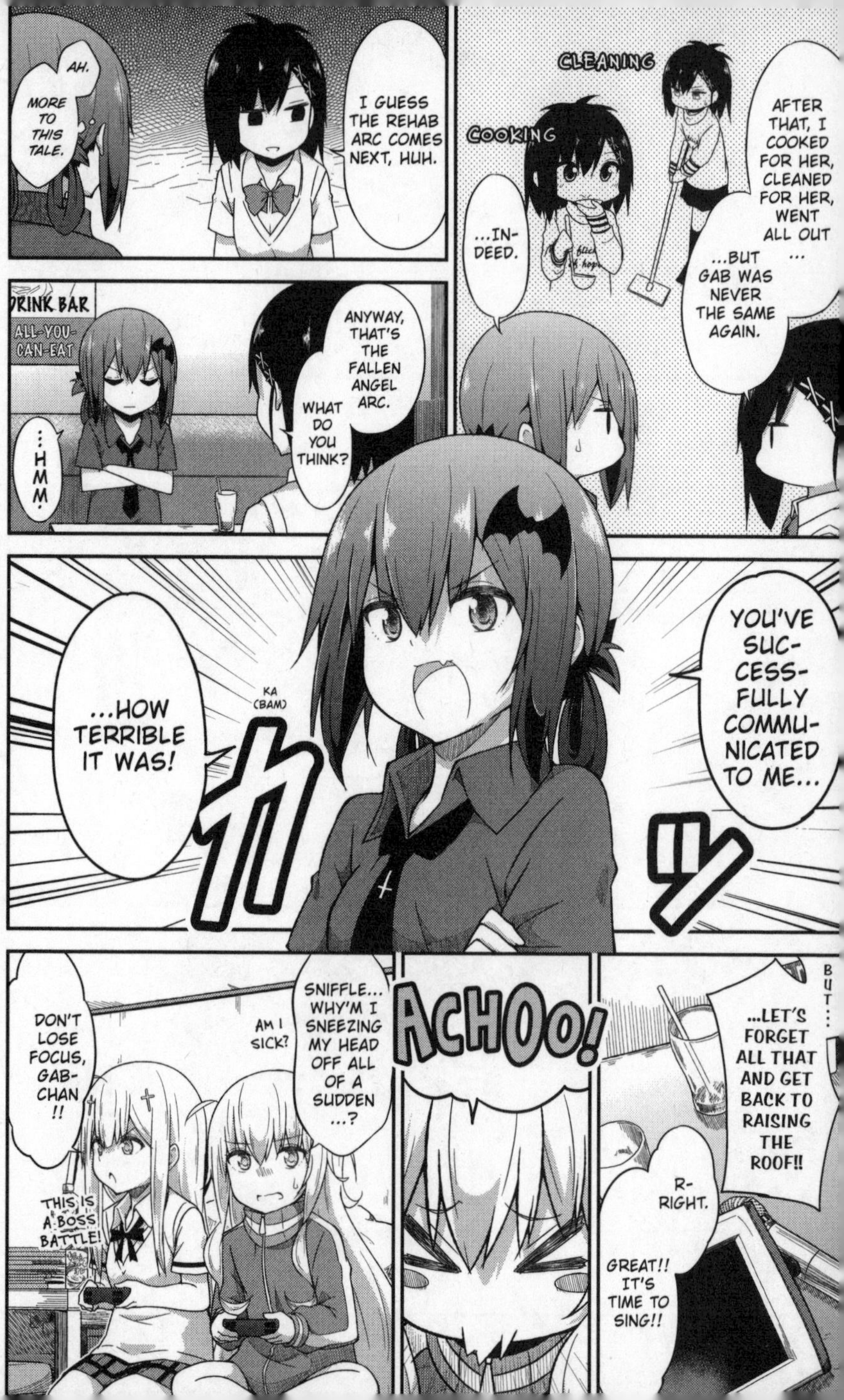
AFTER THAT, I COOKED FOR HER, CLEANED FOR HER, WENT ALL OUT ...
CLEANING
COOKING
...IN-DEED.
...BUT GAB WAS NEVER THE SAME AGAIN.
I GUESS THE REHAB ARC COMES NEXT, HUH.
AH. MORE TO THIS TALE.
ANYWAY, THAT'S THE FALLEN ANGEL ARC.
WHAT DO YOU THINK?
DRINK BAR
ALL-YOU-CAN-EAT
...HMM.
YOU'VE SUCCESSFULLY COMMUNICATED TO ME...
KA (BAM)
...HOW TERRIBLE IT WAS!
BUT...
...LET'S FORGET ALL THAT AND GET BACK TO RAISING THE ROOF!!
R-RIGHT.
GREAT!! IT'S TIME TO SING!!
ACHOO!
SNIFFLE... WHY'M I SNEEZING MY HEAD OFF ALL OF A SUDDEN ...?
AM I SICK?
DON'T LOSE FOCUS, GAB-CHAN!!
THIS IS A BOSS BATTLE!

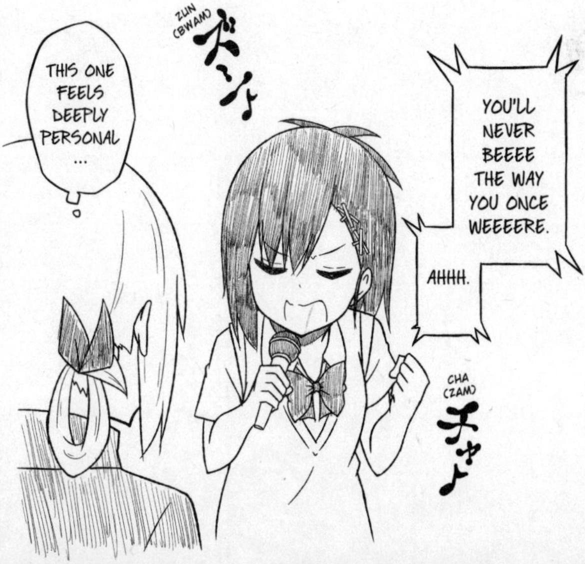
YOU'LL NEVER BEEEE THE WAY YOU ONCE WEEEERE.
AHHH.
CHA (ZAM)
ZUN (BWAM)
THIS ONE FEELS DEEPLY PERSONAL ...

Gabriel Dropout

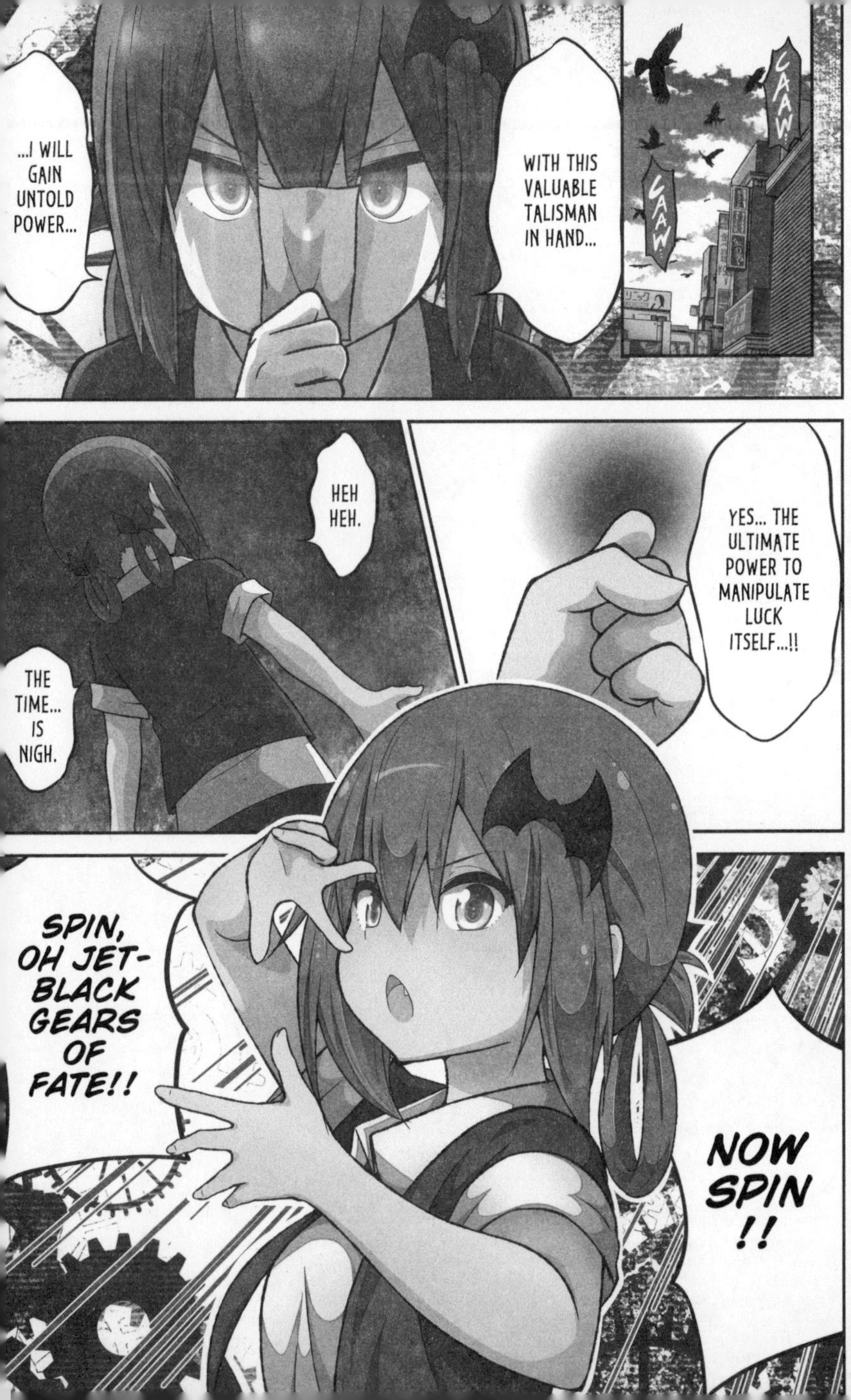
CAAW!
CAAW!
WITH THIS VALUABLE TALISMAN IN HAND...
...I WILL GAIN UNTOLD POWER...
YES... THE ULTIMATE POWER TO MANIPULATE LUCK ITSELF...!!
HEH HEH.
THE TIME... IS NIGH.
SPIN, OH JET-BLACK GEARS OF FATE!!
NOW SPIN!!

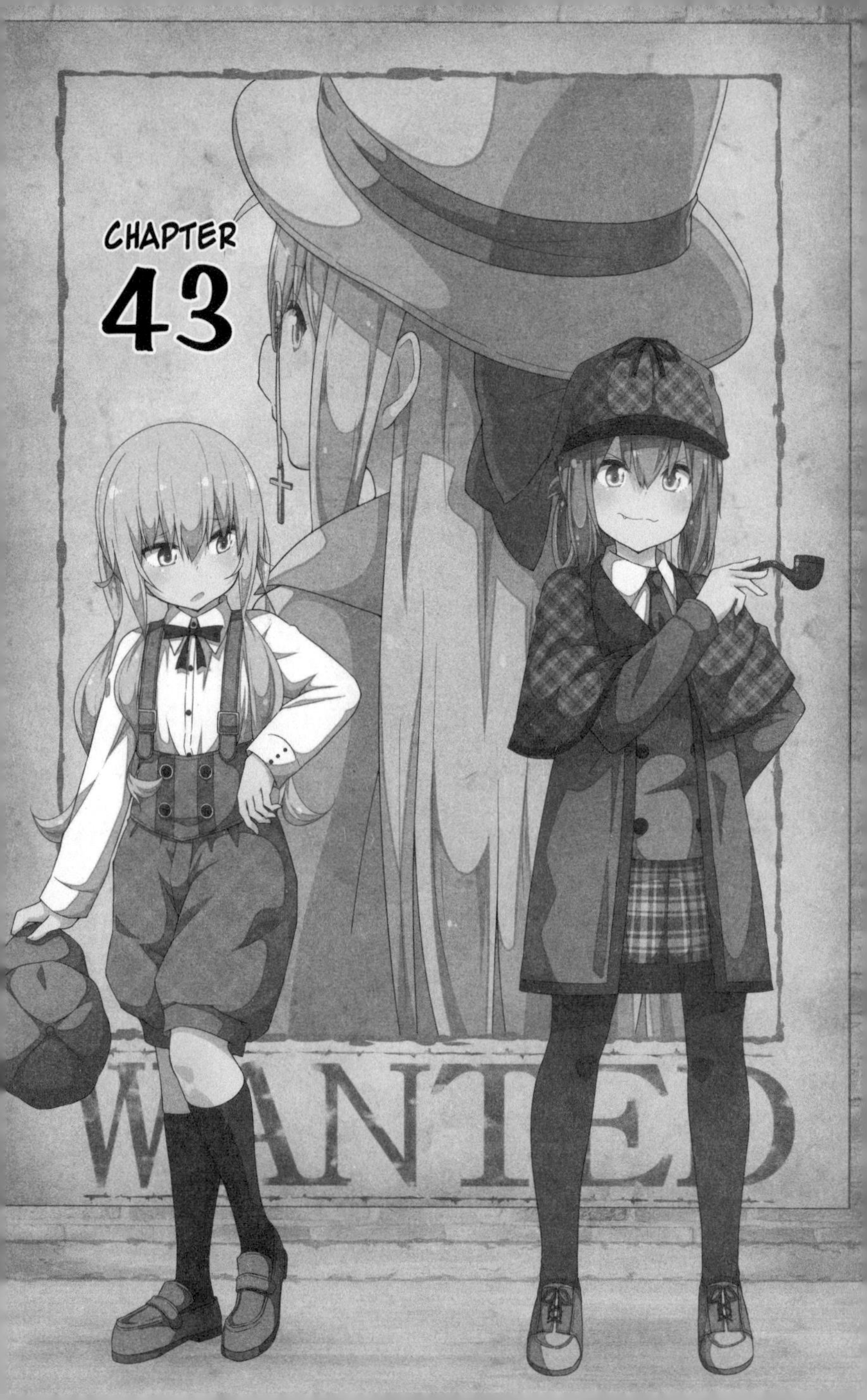
CHAPTER
43
WANTED

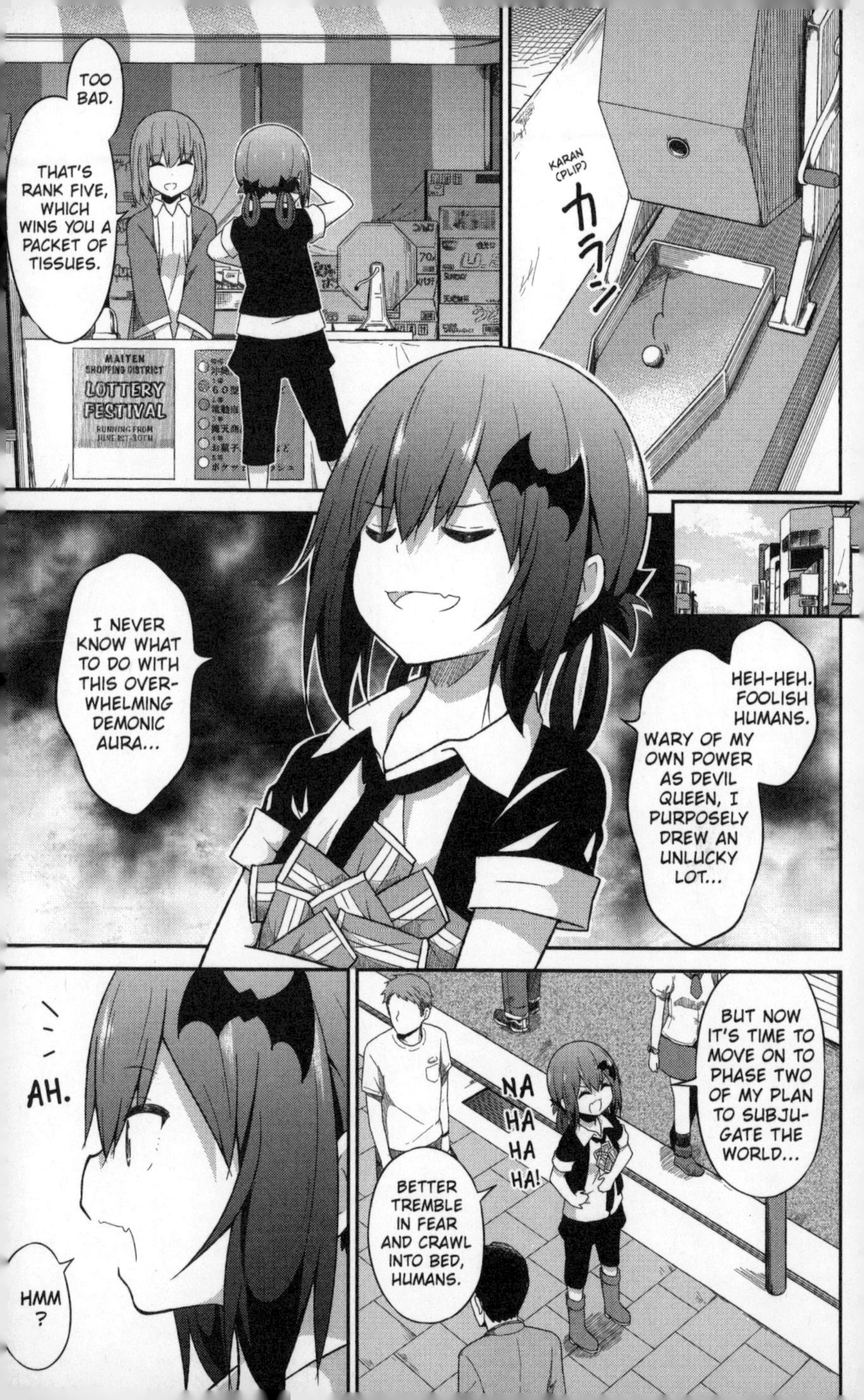
KARAN (PLIP)
カラン
TOO BAD.
THAT'S RANK FIVE, WHICH WINS YOU A PACKET OF TISSUES.
MAITEN SHOPPING DISTRICT
LOTTERY FESTIVAL
RUNNING FROM JUNE 1ST-30TH
HEH-HEH. FOOLISH HUMANS. WARY OF MY OWN POWER AS DEVIL QUEEN, I PURPOSELY DREW AN UNLUCKY LOT...
I NEVER KNOW WHAT TO DO WITH THIS OVER-WHELMING DEMONIC AURA...
BUT NOW IT'S TIME TO MOVE ON TO PHASE TWO OF MY PLAN TO SUBJU-GATE THE WORLD...
NA HA HA HA!
BETTER TREMBLE IN FEAR AND CRAWL INTO BED, HUMANS.
AH.
HMM?

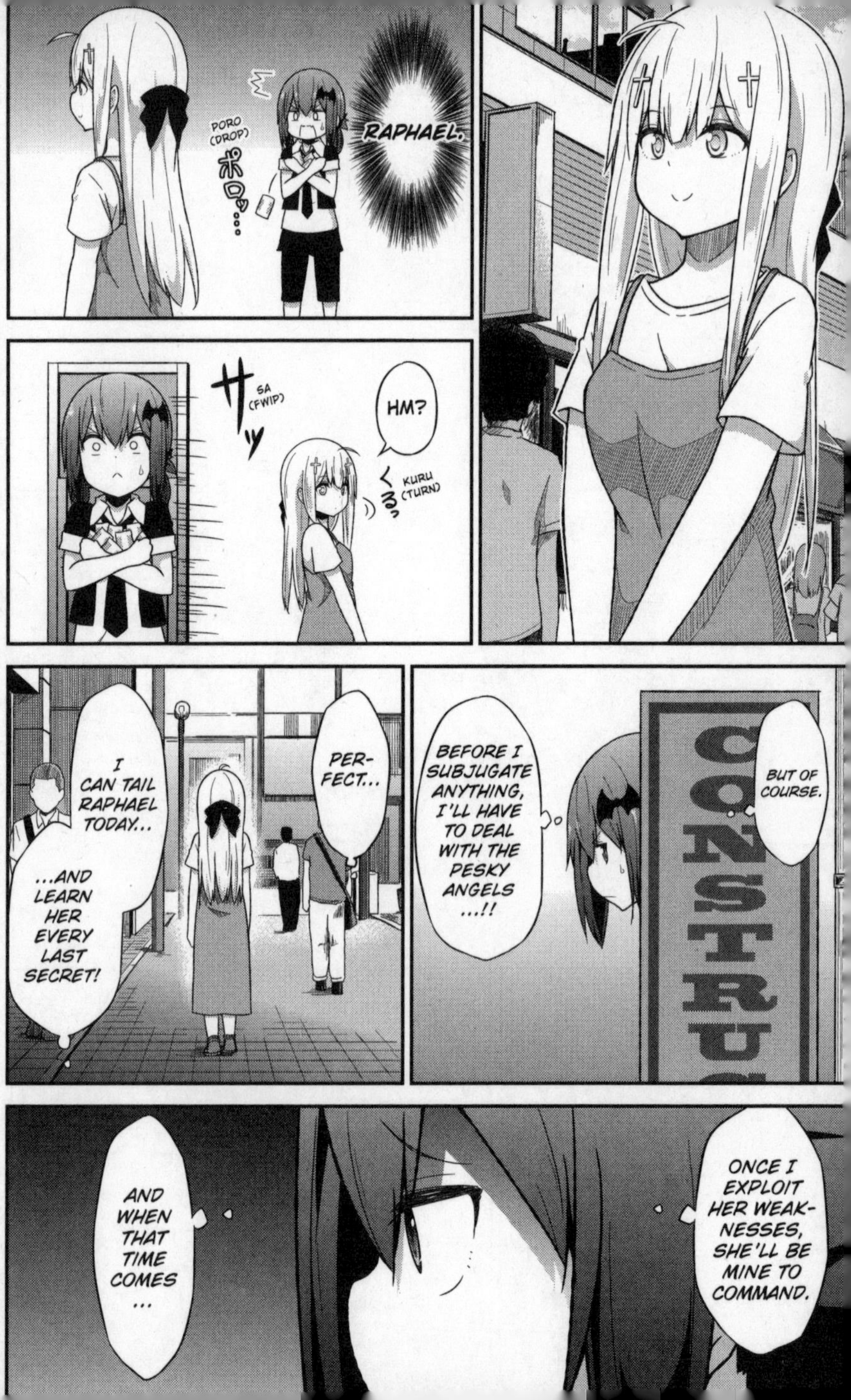
RAPHAEL.
PORO (DROP)
ポロッ…
HM?
KURU (TURN)
くるっ
SA (FWIP)
サッ
BUT OF COURSE.
BEFORE I SUBJUGATE ANYTHING, I'LL HAVE TO DEAL WITH THE PESKY ANGELS …!!
PER-FECT…
I CAN TAIL RAPHAEL TODAY…
…AND LEARN HER EVERY LAST SECRET!
ONCE I EXPLOIT HER WEAK-NESSES, SHE'LL BE MINE TO COMMAND.
AND WHEN THAT TIME COMES …

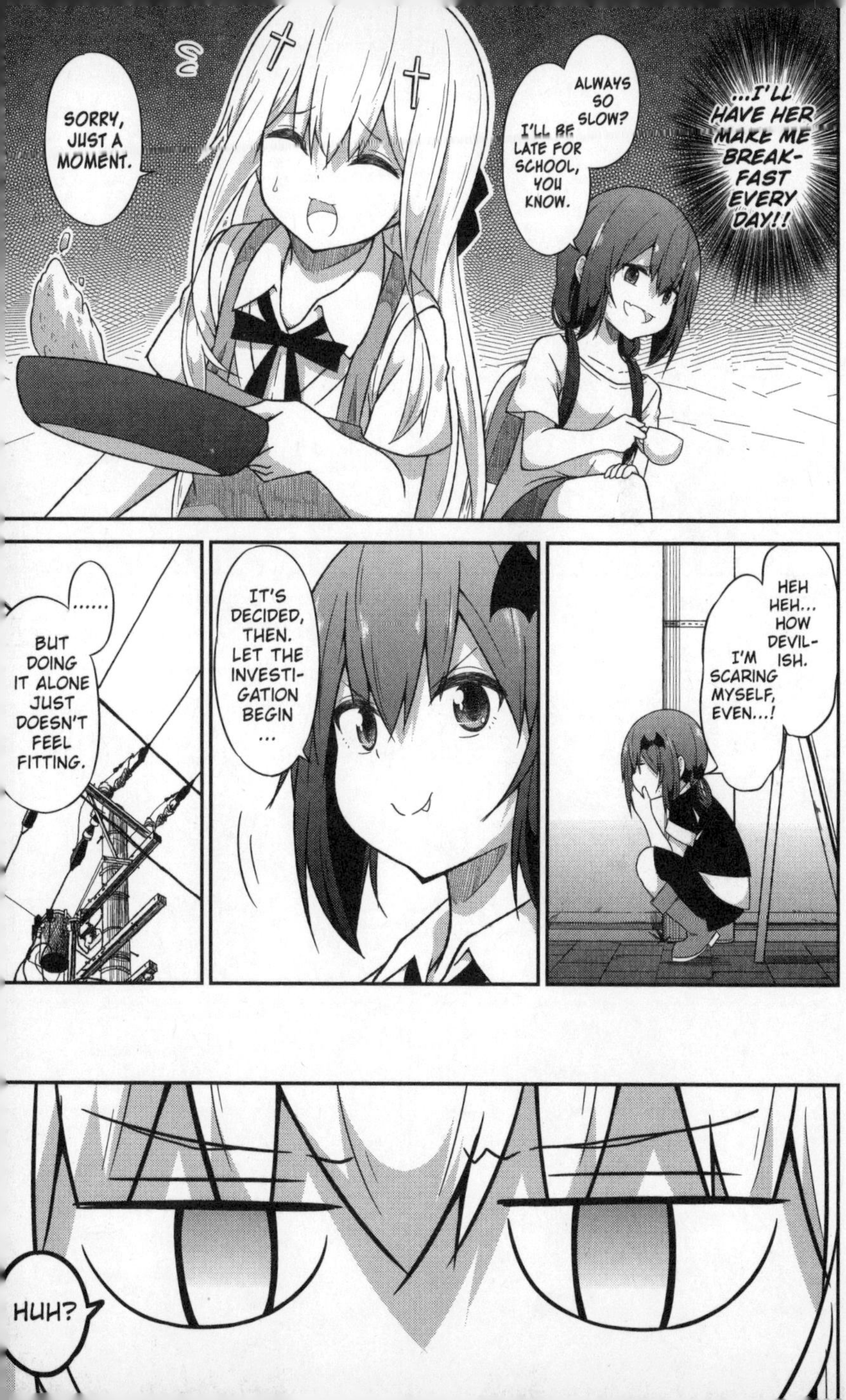

...I'LL HAVE HER MAKE ME BREAKFAST EVERY DAY!!
ALWAYS SO SLOW? I'LL BE LATE FOR SCHOOL, YOU KNOW.
SORRY, JUST A MOMENT.
HEH HEH... HOW DEVILISH. I'M SCARING MYSELF, EVEN...!
IT'S DECIDED, THEN. LET THE INVESTIGATION BEGIN...
......
BUT DOING IT ALONE JUST DOESN'T FEEL FITTING.
HUH?

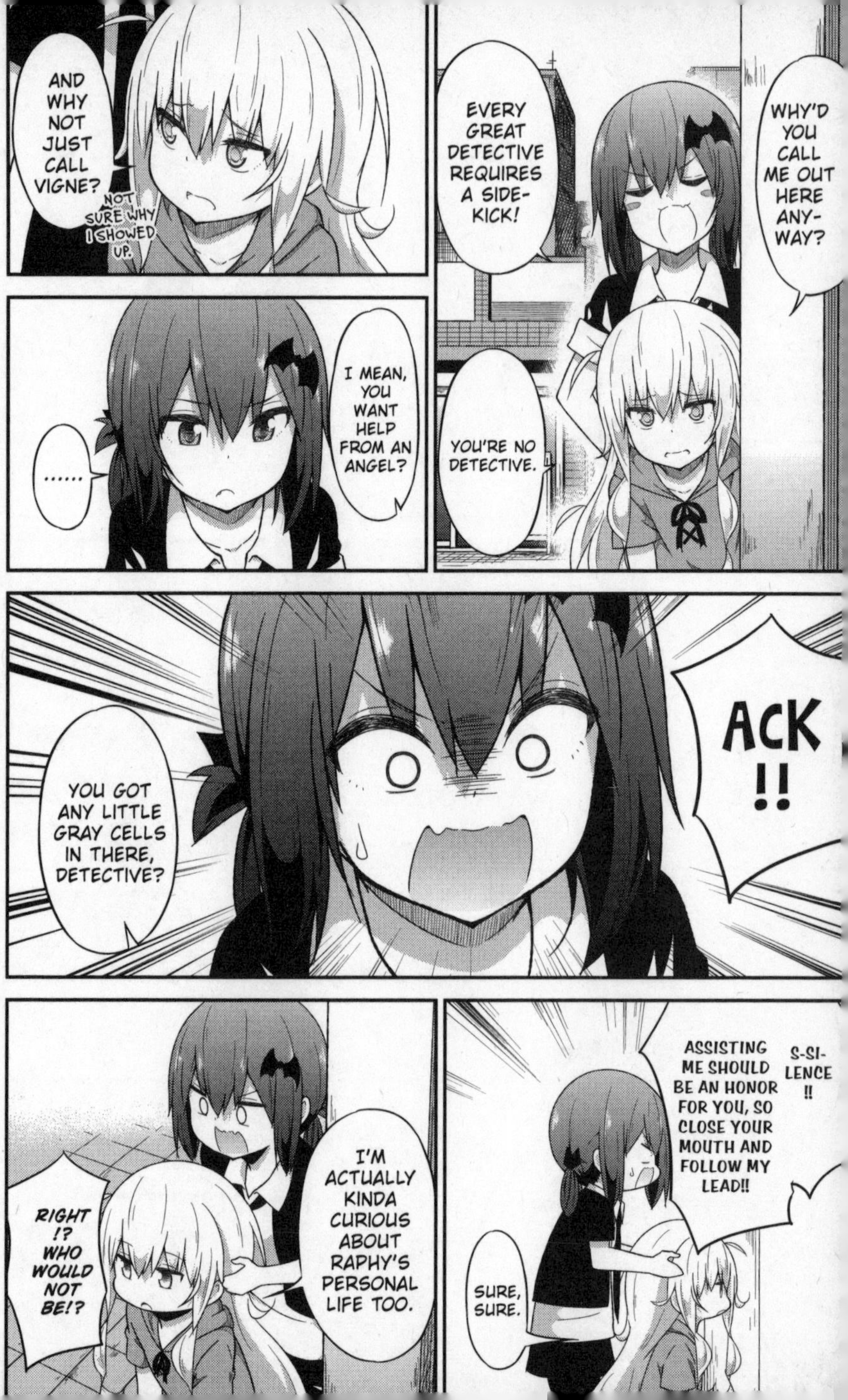
WHY'D YOU CALL ME OUT HERE ANY-WAY?
EVERY GREAT DETECTIVE REQUIRES A SIDE-KICK!
YOU'RE NO DETECTIVE.
AND WHY NOT JUST CALL VIGNE?
NOT SURE WHY I SHOWED UP.
I MEAN, YOU WANT HELP FROM AN ANGEL?
......
ACK!!
YOU GOT ANY LITTLE GRAY CELLS IN THERE, DETECTIVE?
S-SI-LENCE!!
ASSISTING ME SHOULD BE AN HONOR FOR YOU, SO CLOSE YOUR MOUTH AND FOLLOW MY LEAD!!
SURE, SURE.
I'M ACTUALLY KINDA CURIOUS ABOUT RAPHY'S PERSONAL LIFE TOO.
RIGHT!? WHO WOULD NOT BE!?

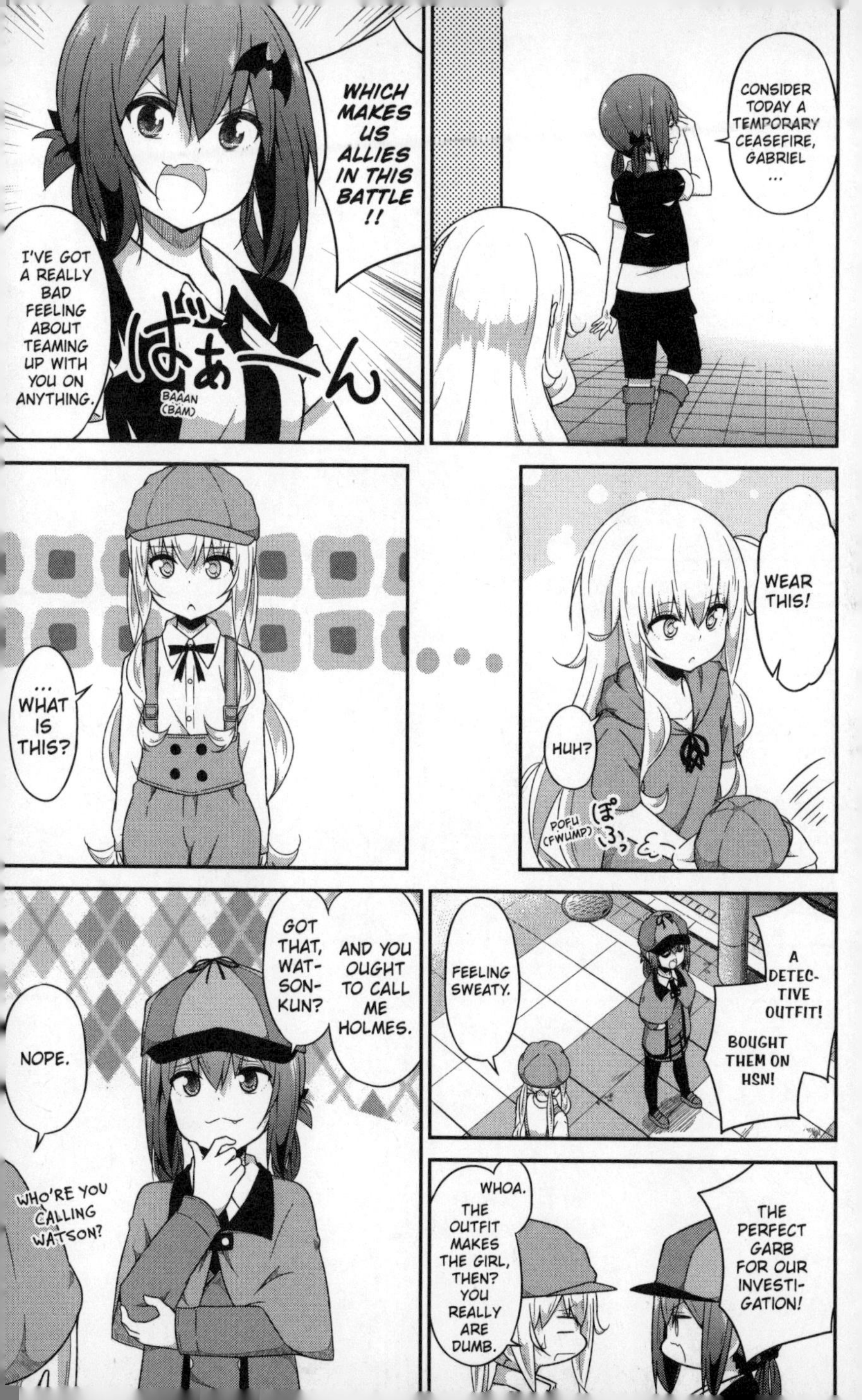
CONSIDER TODAY A TEMPORARY CEASEFIRE, GABRIEL...
WHICH MAKES US ALLIES IN THIS BATTLE!!
ばぁーん
BAAAN (BAM)
I'VE GOT A REALLY BAD FEELING ABOUT TEAMING UP WITH YOU ON ANYTHING.
WEAR THIS!
HUH?
ぽふっ
POFU (FWUMP)
...WHAT IS THIS?
A DETECTIVE OUTFIT!
BOUGHT THEM ON HSN!
FEELING SWEATY.
THE PERFECT GARB FOR OUR INVESTIGATION!
WHOA. THE OUTFIT MAKES THE GIRL, THEN? YOU REALLY ARE DUMB.
AND YOU OUGHT TO CALL ME HOLMES.
GOT THAT, WATSON-KUN?
NOPE.
WHO'RE YOU CALLING WATSON?

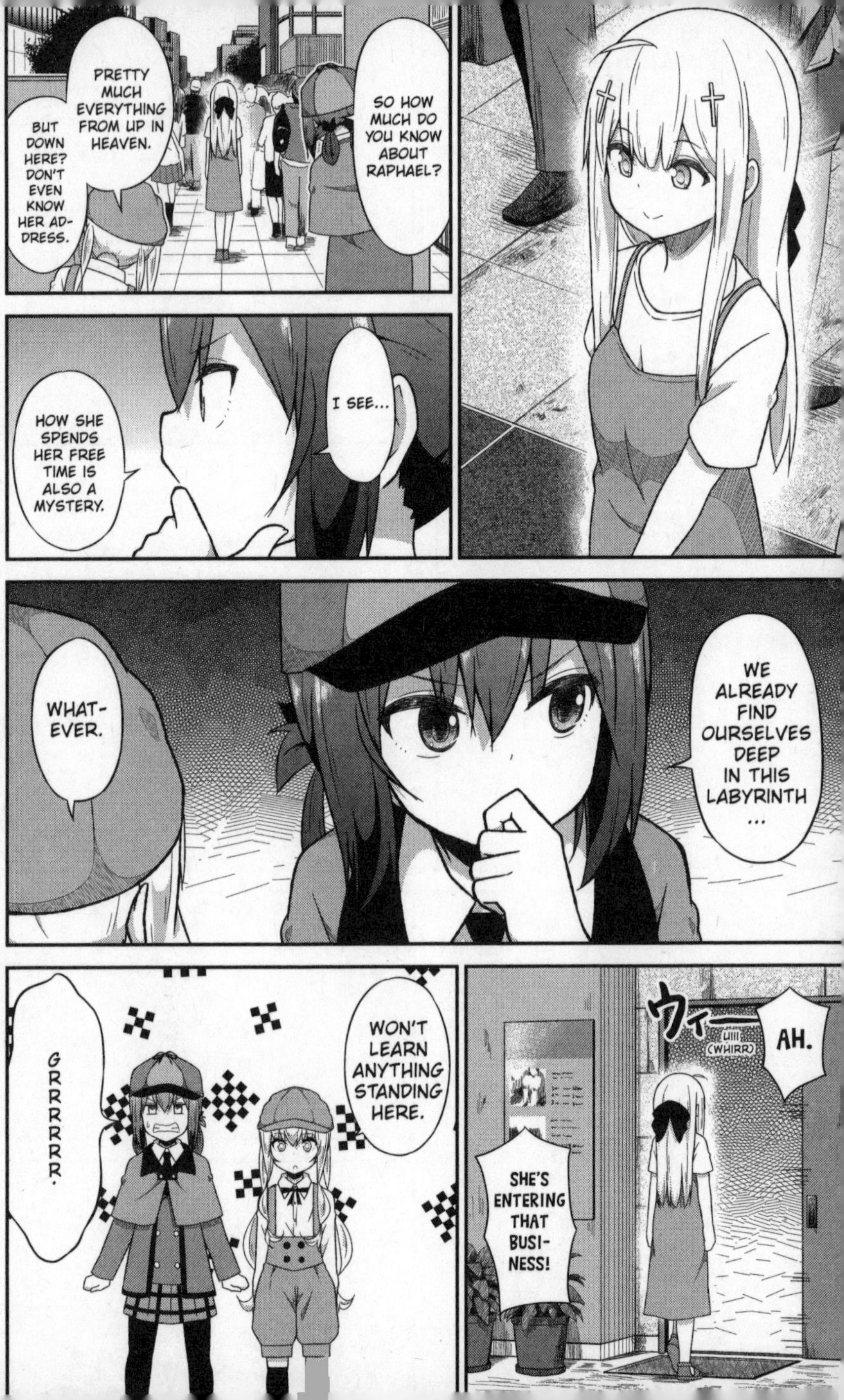
SO HOW MUCH DO YOU KNOW ABOUT RAPHAEL?
PRETTY MUCH EVERYTHING FROM UP IN HEAVEN.
BUT DOWN HERE? DON'T EVEN KNOW HER AD-DRESS.
I SEE...
HOW SHE SPENDS HER FREE TIME IS ALSO A MYSTERY.
WE ALREADY FIND OURSELVES DEEP IN THIS LABYRINTH ...
WHAT-EVER.
ウィー
UIII (WHIRR)
AH.
SHE'S ENTERING THAT BUSI-NESS!
WON'T LEARN ANYTHING STANDING HERE.
GRRRRRR.

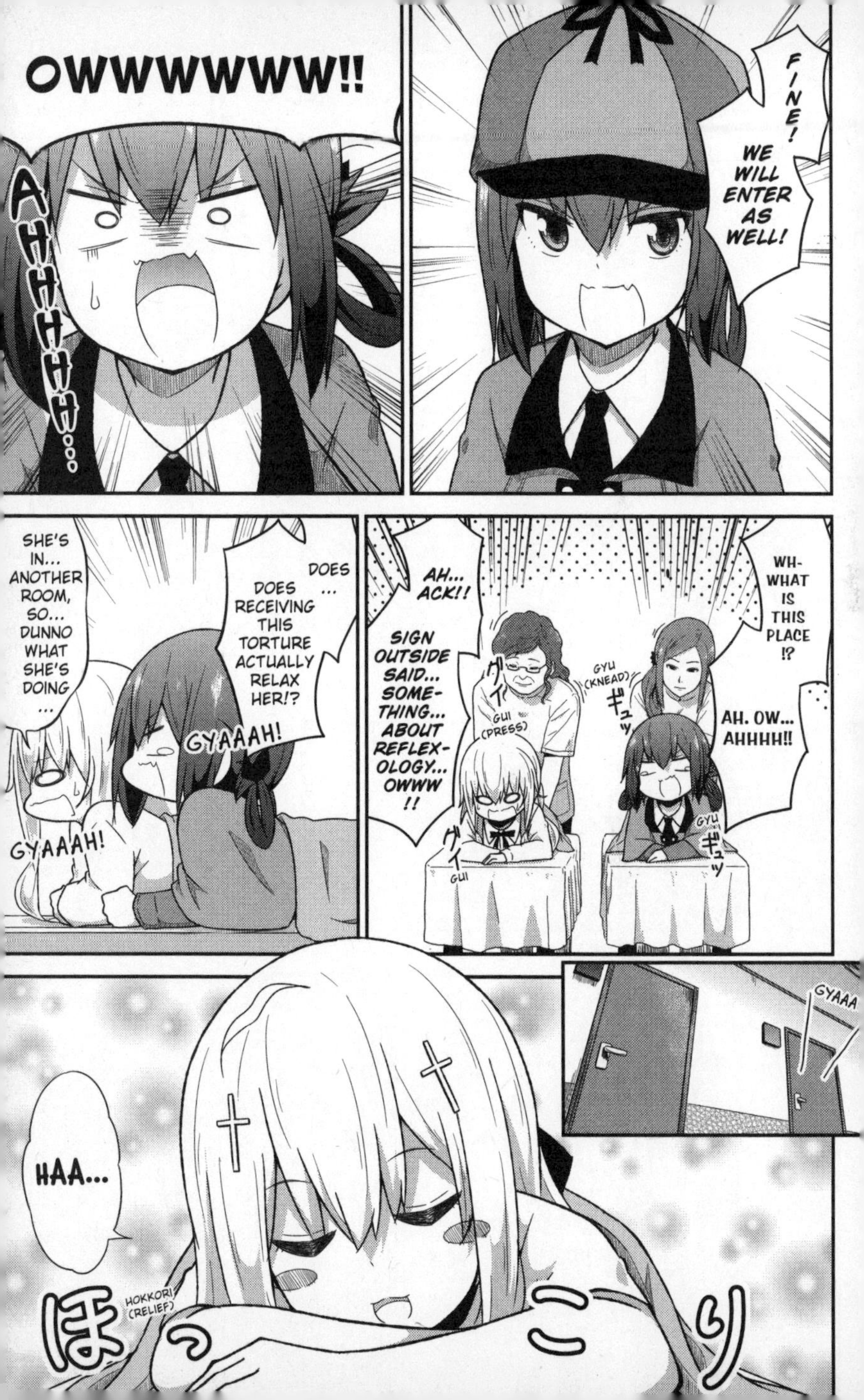
FINE! WE WILL ENTER AS WELL!
OWWWWWWW!!
AHHHHHHHooo
WH-WHAT IS THIS PLACE!?
AH. OW... AHHHHH!!
GYU (KNEAD)
AH... ACK!!
SIGN OUTSIDE SAID... SOMETHING... ABOUT REFLEXOLOGY... OWWW!!
GUI (PRESS)
GYU
GUI
DOES...
DOES RECEIVING THIS TORTURE ACTUALLY RELAX HER!?
SHE'S IN... ANOTHER ROOM, SO... DUNNO WHAT SHE'S DOING...
GYAAAH!
GYAAAH!
GYAAA
HAA...
HOKKORI (RELIEF)

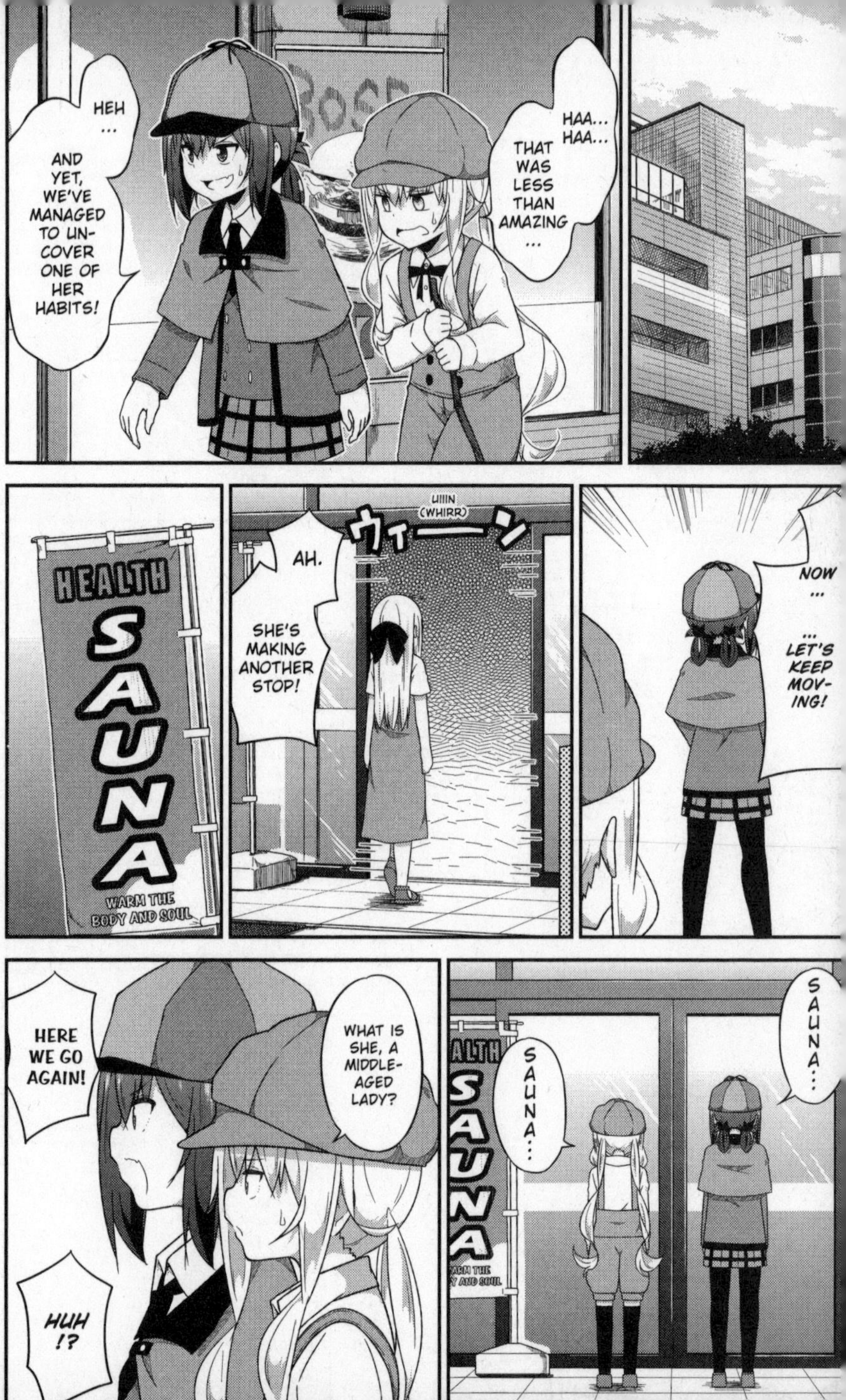
HAA... HAA...
THAT WAS LESS THAN AMAZING...
HEH...
AND YET, WE'VE MANAGED TO UN-COVER ONE OF HER HABITS!
NOW...
...LET'S KEEP MOVING!
UIIIN (WHIRR)
ウィーーン
AH.
SHE'S MAKING ANOTHER STOP!
HEALTH
SAUNA
WARM THE BODY AND SOUL
SAUNA...
SAUNA...
WHAT IS SHE, A MIDDLE-AGED LADY?
HERE WE GO AGAIN!
HUH!?

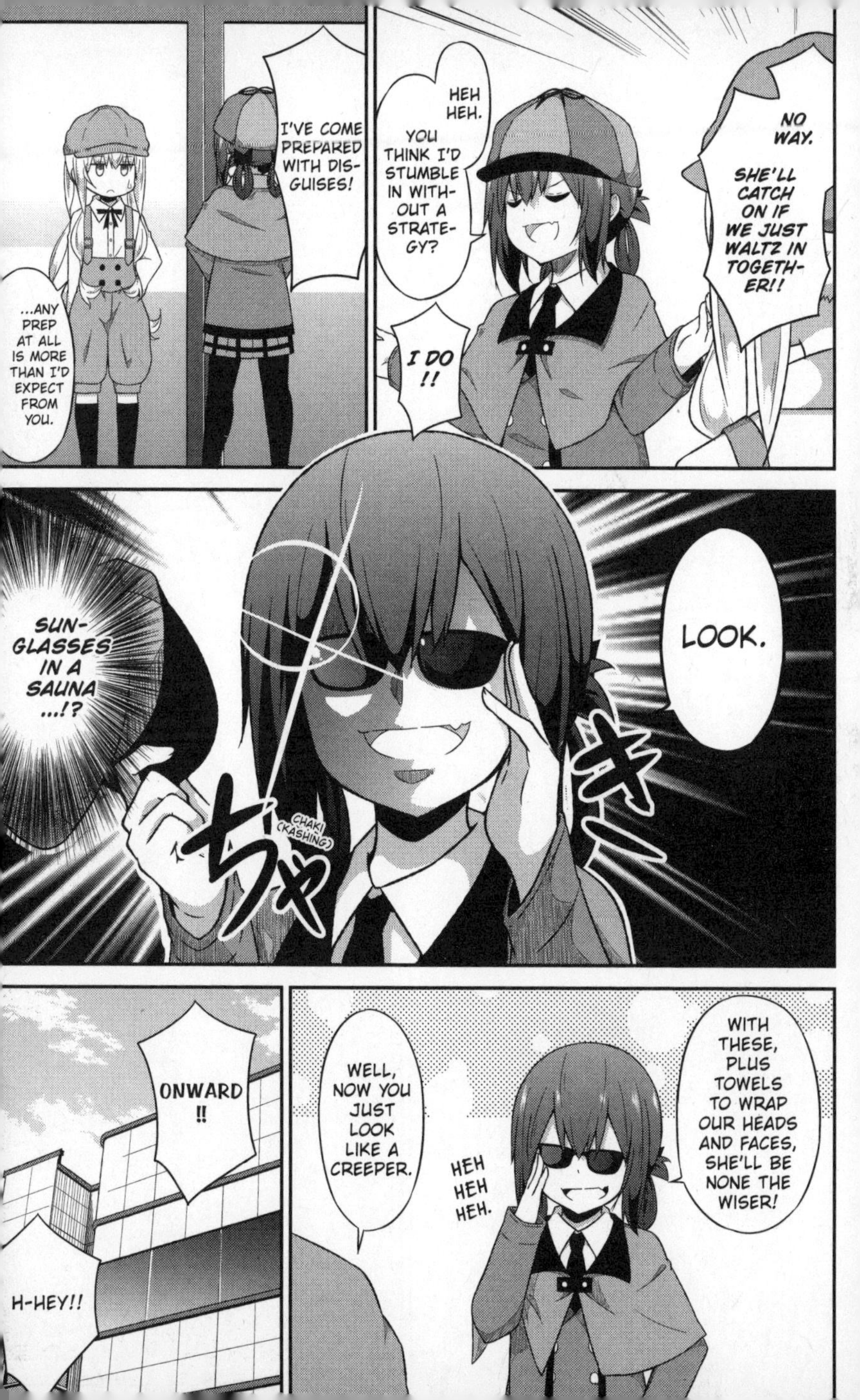
NO WAY.
SHE'LL CATCH ON IF WE JUST WALTZ IN TOGETHER!!
HEH HEH.
YOU THINK I'D STUMBLE IN WITHOUT A STRATEGY?
I DO!!
I'VE COME PREPARED WITH DISGUISES!
...ANY PREP AT ALL IS MORE THAN I'D EXPECT FROM YOU.
LOOK.
SUNGLASSES IN A SAUNA...!?
ちゃ
CHAKI (KASHING)
WITH THESE, PLUS TOWELS TO WRAP OUR HEADS AND FACES, SHE'LL BE NONE THE WISER!
HEH HEH HEH.
WELL, NOW YOU JUST LOOK LIKE A CREEPER.
ONWARD!!
H-HEY!!

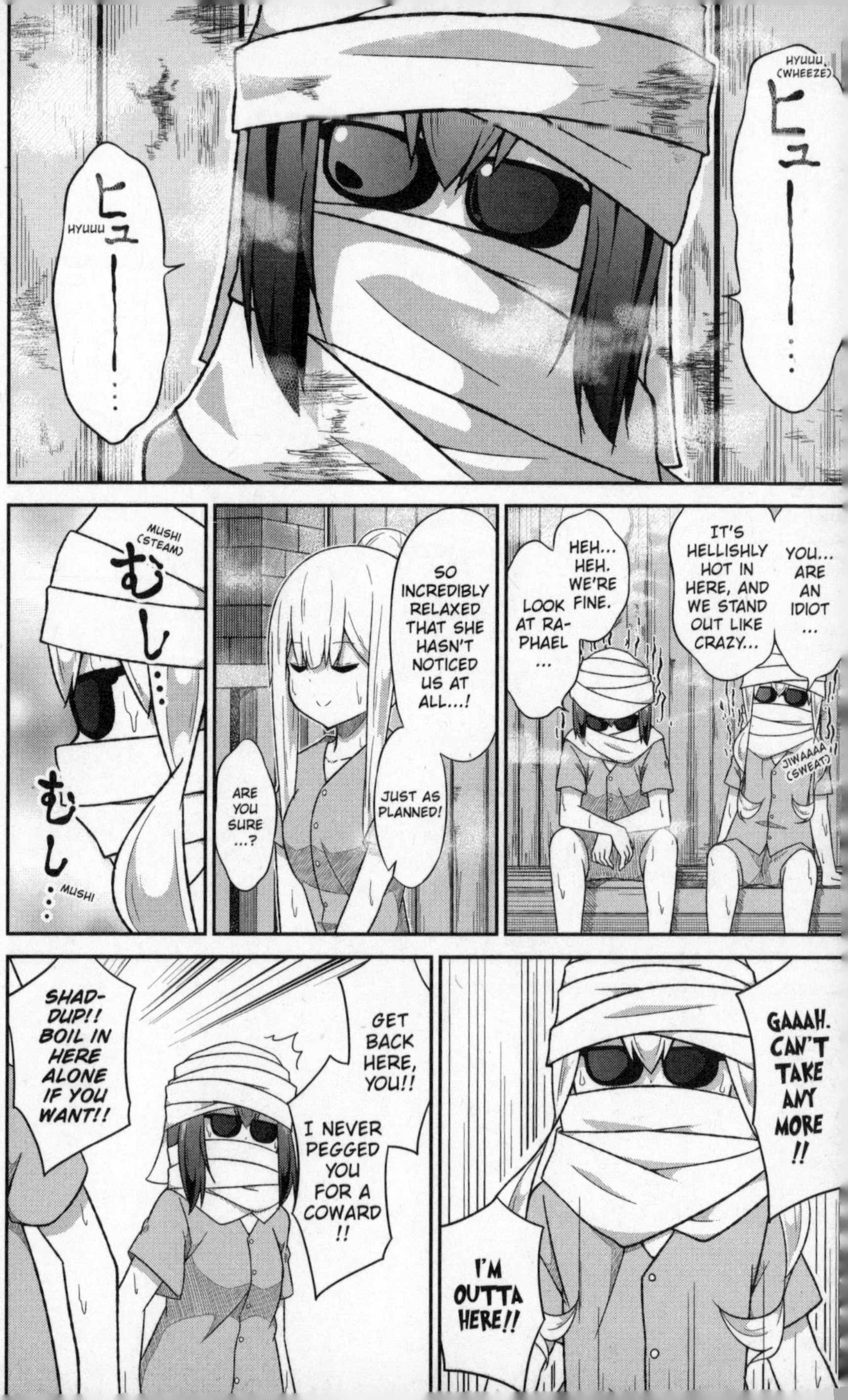
HYUUU (WHEEZE)
ヒュー…
ヒュー…
HYUUU
YOU... ARE AN IDIOT...
IT'S HELLISHLY HOT IN HERE, AND WE STAND OUT LIKE CRAZY...
HEH... HEH. WE'RE FINE.
LOOK AT RA-PHAEL...
JIWAAAA (SWEAT)
SO INCREDIBLY RELAXED THAT SHE HASN'T NOTICED US AT ALL...!
JUST AS PLANNED!
ARE YOU SURE...?
MUSHI (STEAM)
むし…
むし…
MUSHI
GAAAH. CAN'T TAKE ANY MORE!!
I'M OUTTA HERE!!
GET BACK HERE, YOU!!
I NEVER PEGGED YOU FOR A COWARD!!
SHAD-DUP!! BOIL IN HERE ALONE IF YOU WANT!!

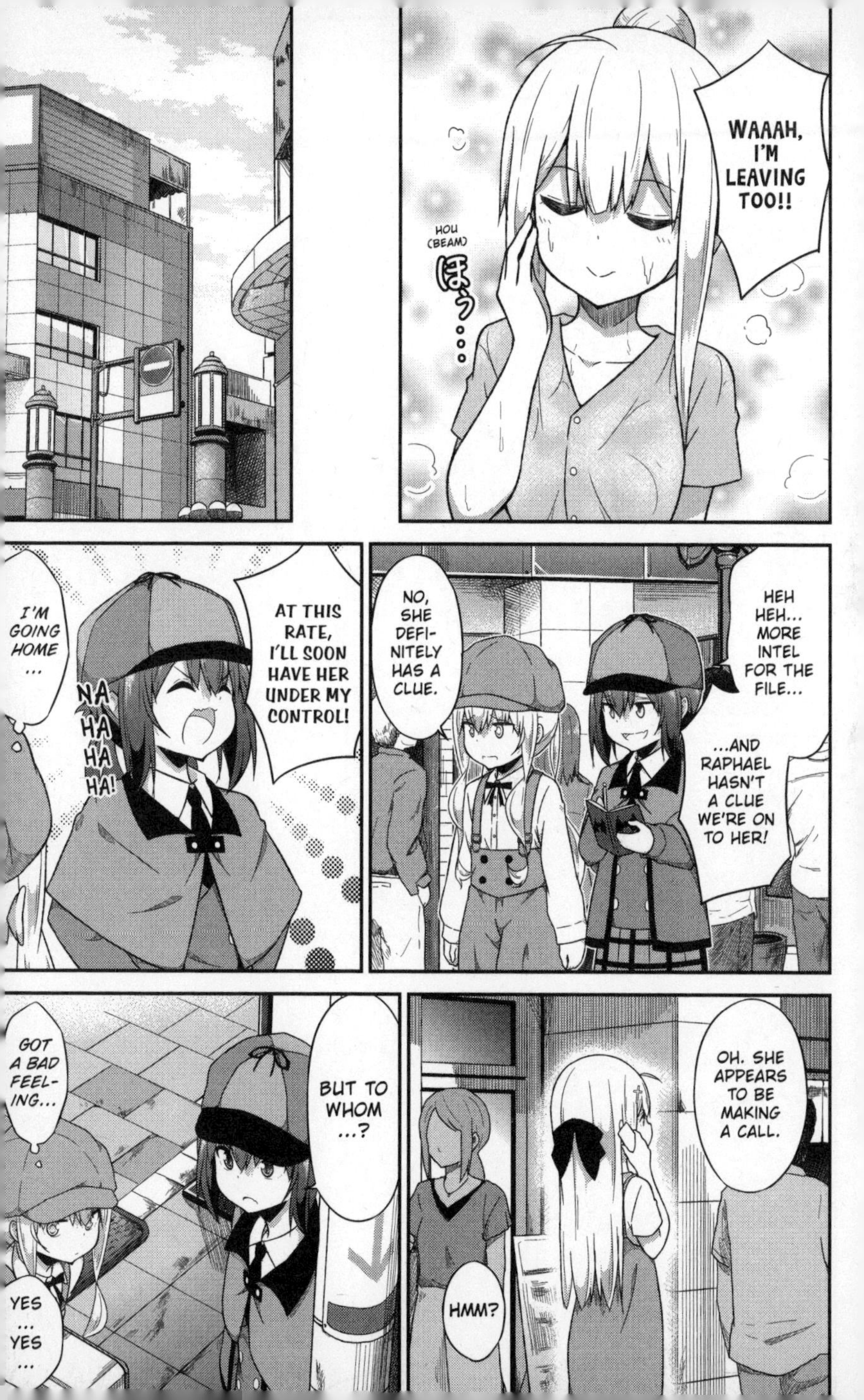
WAAAH, I'M LEAVING TOO!!
HOU (BEAM)
ほう・・・
HEH HEH... MORE INTEL FOR THE FILE...
...AND RAPHAEL HASN'T A CLUE WE'RE ON TO HER!
NO, SHE DEFINITELY HAS A CLUE.
AT THIS RATE, I'LL SOON HAVE HER UNDER MY CONTROL!
NA HA HA HA HA!
I'M GOING HOME...
OH. SHE APPEARS TO BE MAKING A CALL.
HMM?
BUT TO WHOM...?
GOT A BAD FEELING...
YES... YES...

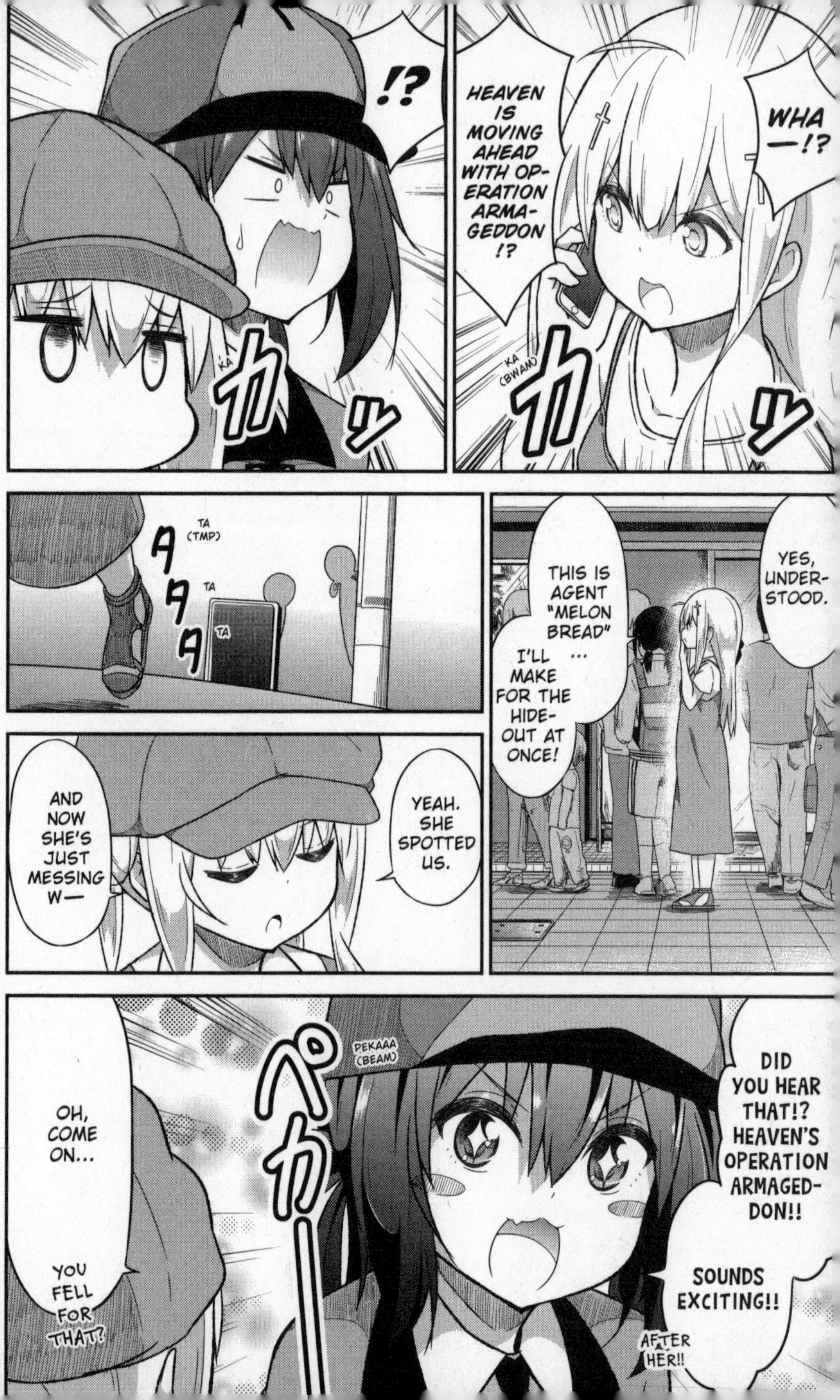
WHA—!?
HEAVEN IS MOVING AHEAD WITH OPERATION ARMAGEDDON!?
KA (BWAM)
カッ
!?
KA
カッ
YES, UNDERSTOOD.
THIS IS AGENT "MELON BREAD"...
I'LL MAKE FOR THE HIDEOUT AT ONCE!
TA (TMP)
TA
TA
タタタ
YEAH. SHE SPOTTED US.
AND NOW SHE'S JUST MESSING W—
DID YOU HEAR THAT!? HEAVEN'S OPERATION ARMAGEDDON!!
SOUNDS EXCITING!!
AFTER HER!!
PEKAAA (BEAM)
ぺかー
OH, COME ON...
YOU FELL FOR THAT?

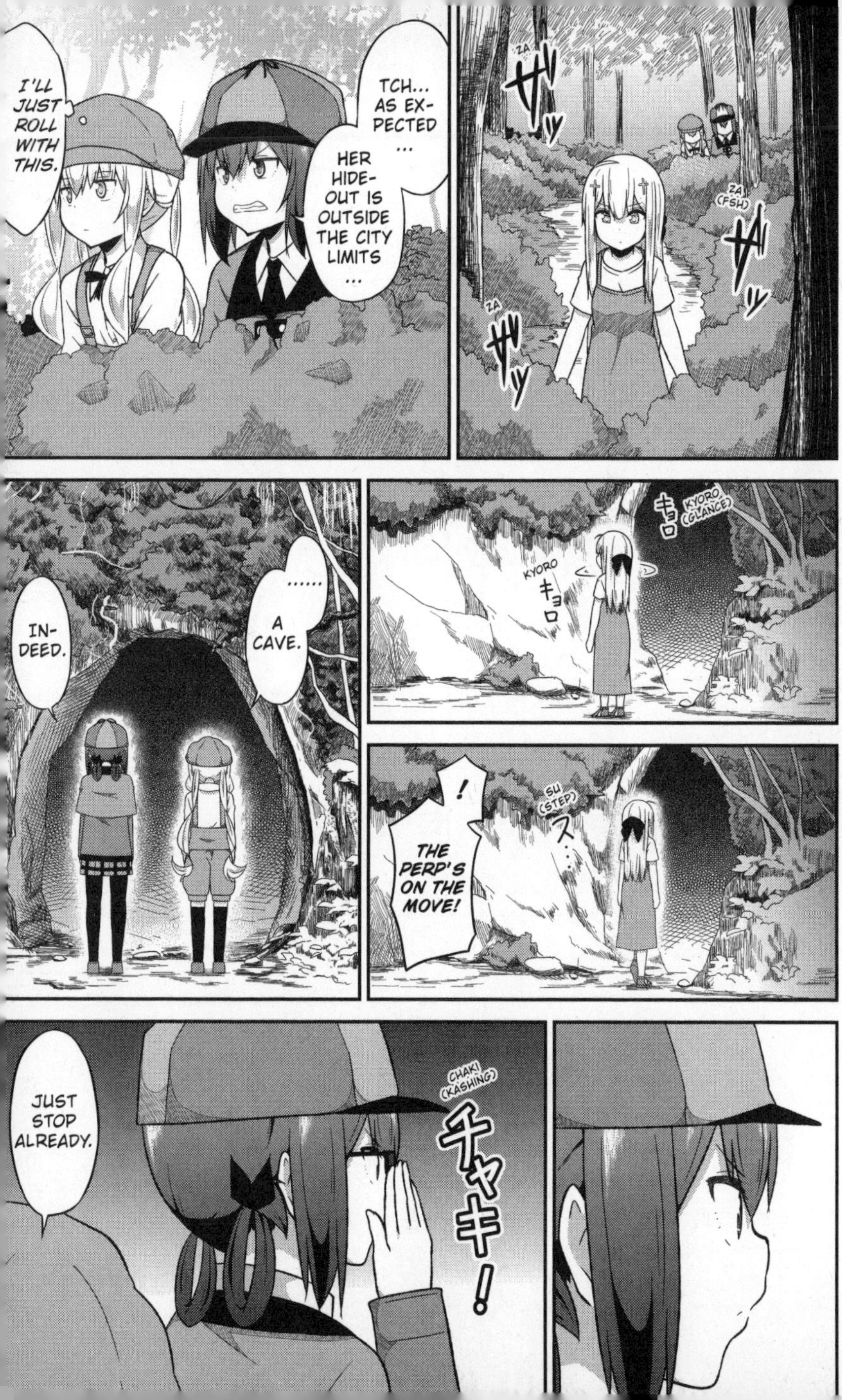
ZA ザッ
ZA (FSH) ザッ
ZA ザッ
TCH... AS EXPECTED ...
HER HIDEOUT IS OUTSIDE THE CITY LIMITS ...
I'LL JUST ROLL WITH THIS.
KYORO (GLANCE) キョロ
KYORO キョロ
SU (STEP) ス…
!
THE PERP'S ON THE MOVE!
......
A CAVE.
INDEED.
CHAKI (KASHING) チャキ!
JUST STOP ALREADY.

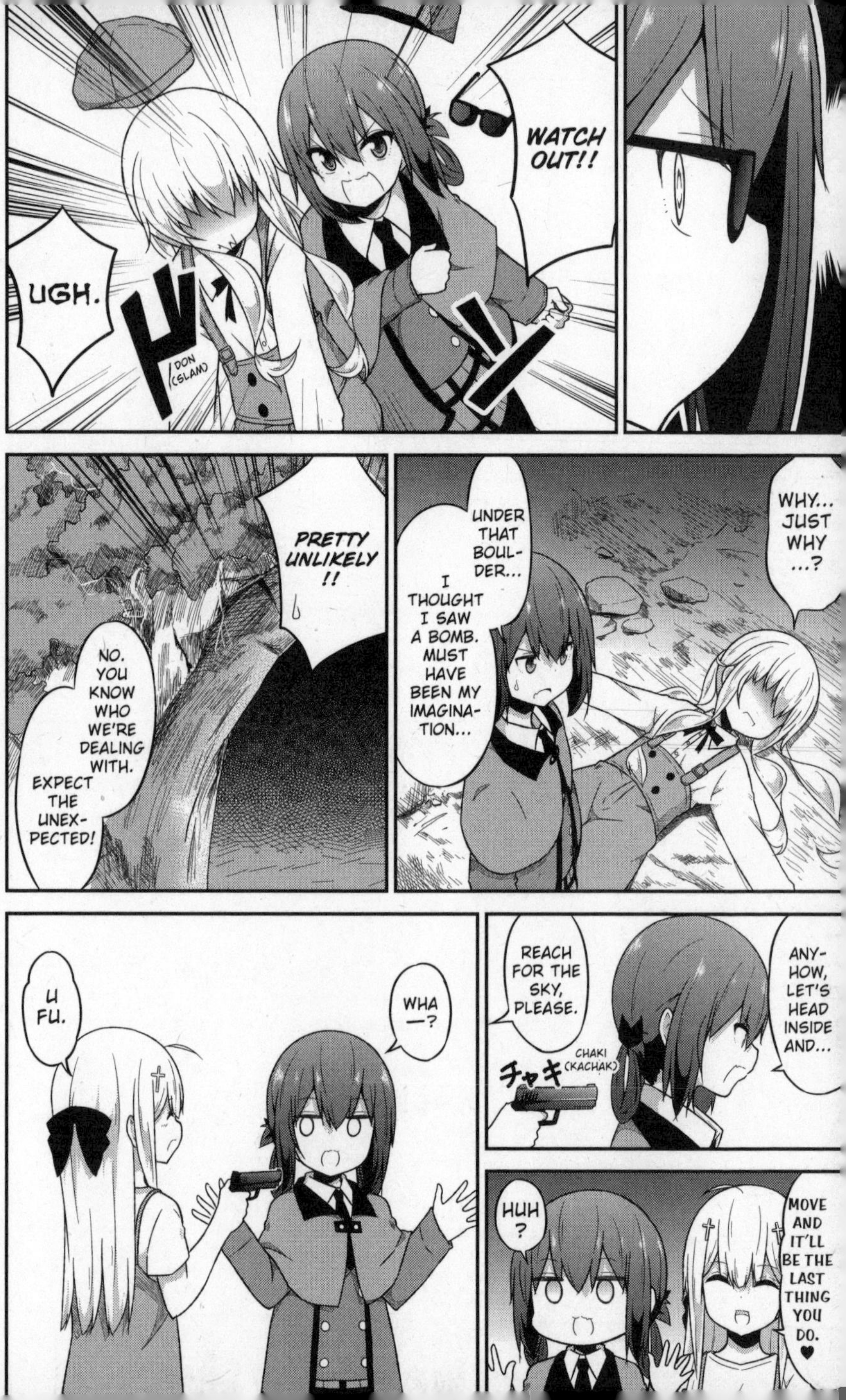
WATCH OUT!!
UGH.
DON (SLAM)
WHY... JUST WHY...?
UNDER THAT BOULDER...
I THOUGHT I SAW A BOMB. MUST HAVE BEEN MY IMAGINATION...
PRETTY UNLIKELY!!
NO. YOU KNOW WHO WE'RE DEALING WITH. EXPECT THE UNEXPECTED!
ANYHOW, LET'S HEAD INSIDE AND...
REACH FOR THE SKY, PLEASE.
チャキ
CHAKI (KACHAK)
MOVE AND IT'LL BE THE LAST THING YOU DO. ♥
HUH?
WHA—?
U FU.

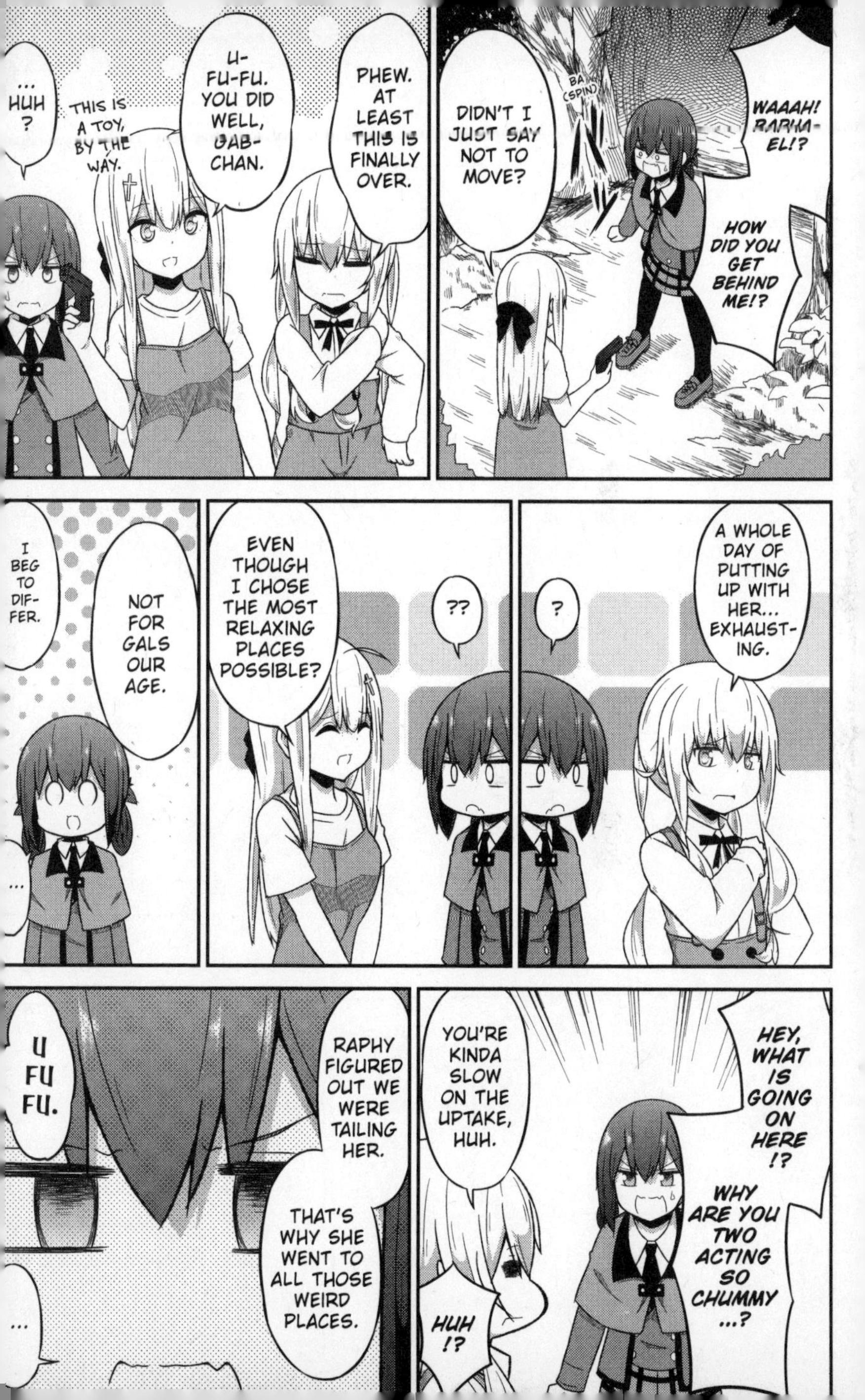
WAAAH! RAPHAEL!?
HOW DID YOU GET BEHIND ME!?
BA (SPIN)
DIDN'T I JUST SAY NOT TO MOVE?
PHEW. AT LEAST THIS IS FINALLY OVER.
U-FU-FU. YOU DID WELL, GAB-CHAN.
THIS IS A TOY, BY THE WAY.
... HUH?
A WHOLE DAY OF PUTTING UP WITH HER... EXHAUSTING.
?
??
EVEN THOUGH I CHOSE THE MOST RELAXING PLACES POSSIBLE?
NOT FOR GALS OUR AGE.
I BEG TO DIFFER.
...
HEY, WHAT IS GOING ON HERE!?
WHY ARE YOU TWO ACTING SO CHUMMY...?
YOU'RE KINDA SLOW ON THE UPTAKE, HUH.
HUH!?
RAPHY FIGURED OUT WE WERE TAILING HER.
THAT'S WHY SHE WENT TO ALL THOSE WEIRD PLACES.
U FU FU.
...

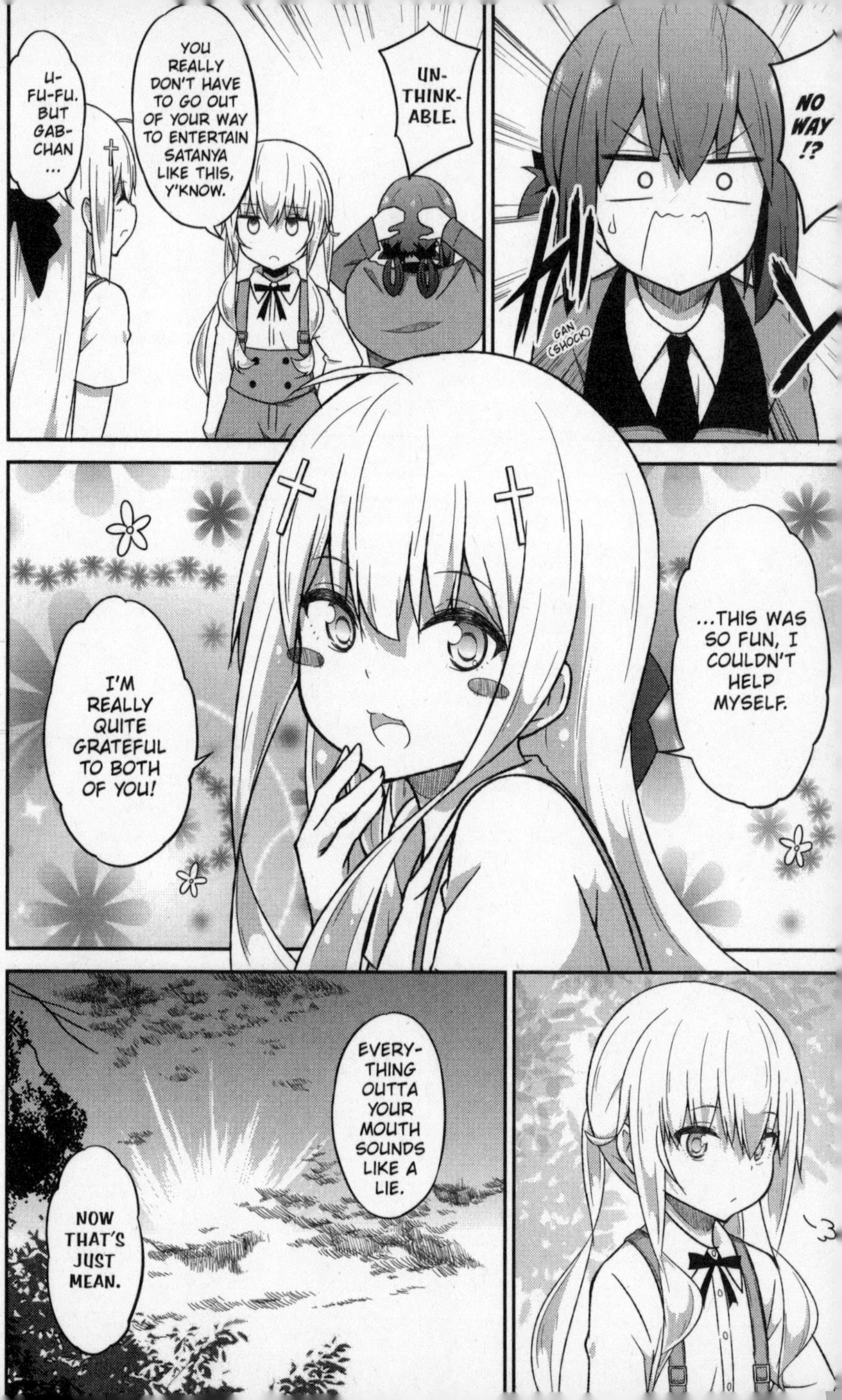
U-FU-FU. BUT GAB-CHAN...
YOU REALLY DON'T HAVE TO GO OUT OF YOUR WAY TO ENTERTAIN SATANYA LIKE THIS, Y'KNOW.
UN-THINK-ABLE.
NO WAY!?
GAN (SHOCK)
...THIS WAS SO FUN, I COULDN'T HELP MYSELF.
I'M REALLY QUITE GRATEFUL TO BOTH OF YOU!
EVERY-THING OUTTA YOUR MOUTH SOUNDS LIKE A LIE.
NOW THAT'S JUST MEAN.

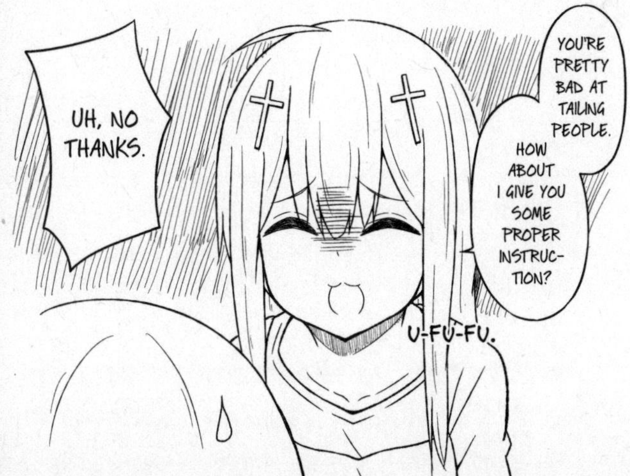
YOU'RE PRETTY BAD AT TAILING PEOPLE.
HOW ABOUT I GIVE YOU SOME PROPER INSTRUCTION?
U-FU-FU.
UH, NO THANKS.

Gabriel Dropout

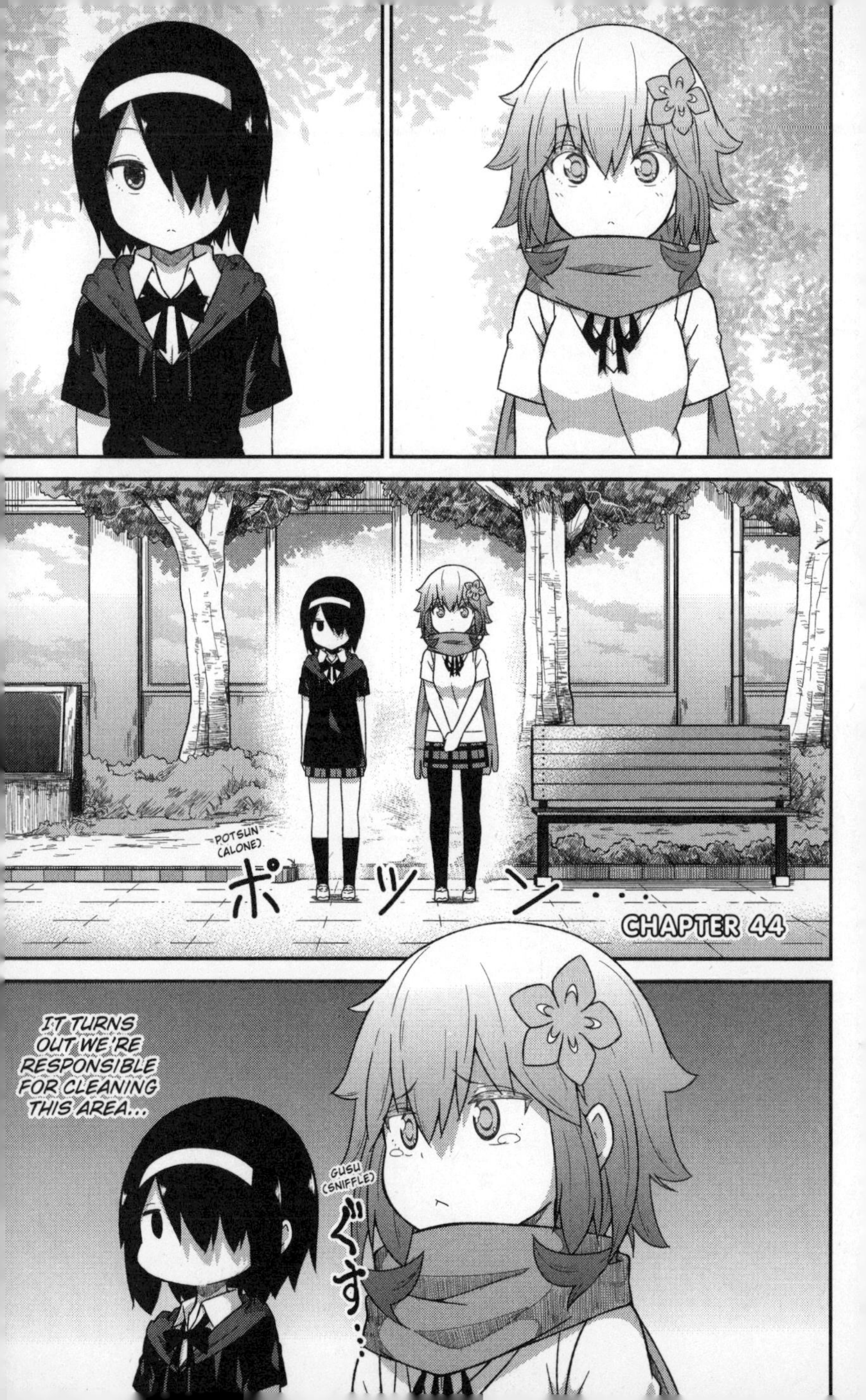
POTSUN (ALONE)
ポッン…
CHAPTER 44
IT TURNS OUT WE'RE RESPONSIBLE FOR CLEANING THIS AREA...
GUSU (SNIFFLE)
ぐす…

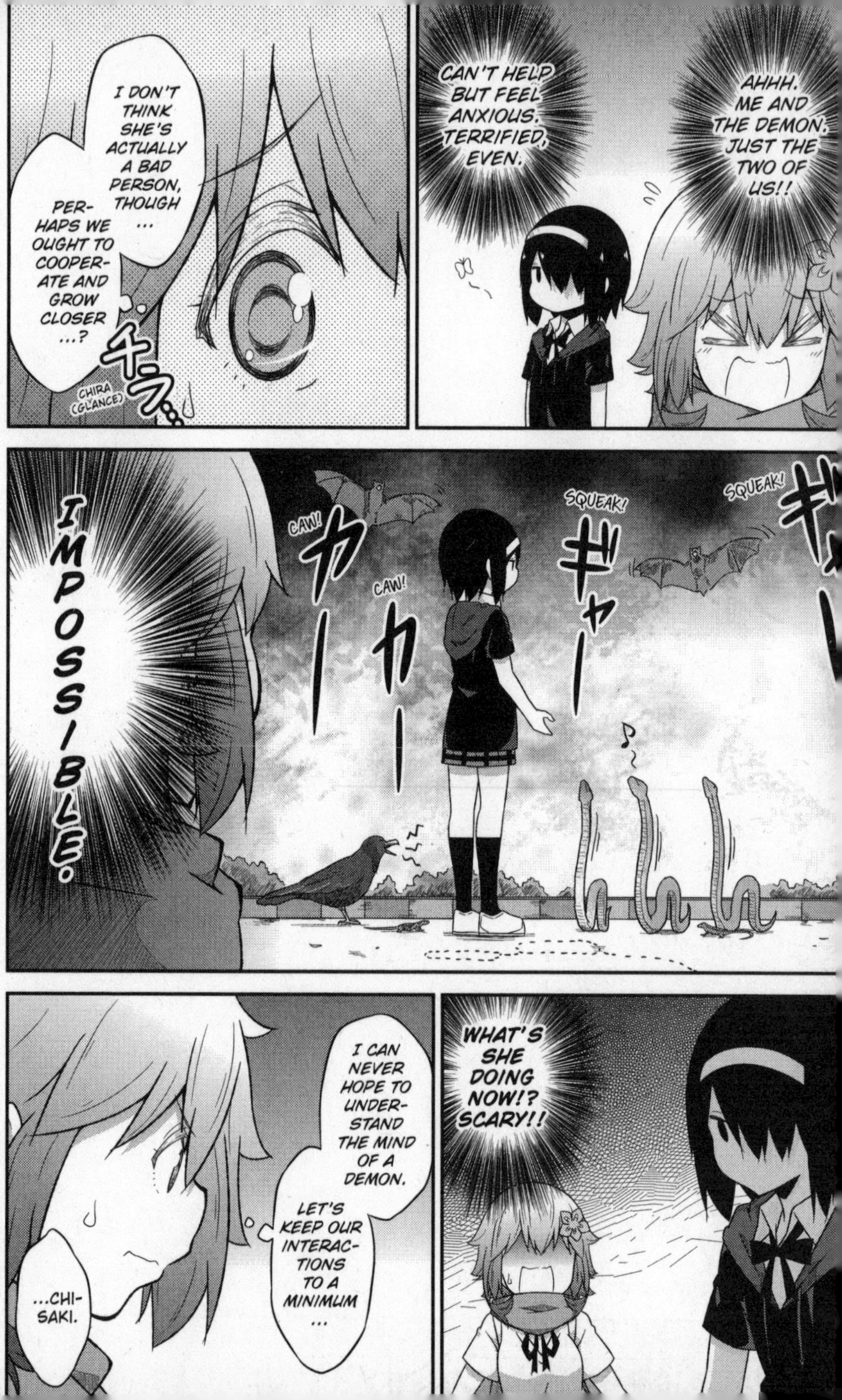
AHHH. ME AND THE DEMON. JUST THE TWO OF US!!
CAN'T HELP BUT FEEL ANXIOUS. TERRIFIED, EVEN.
I DON'T THINK SHE'S ACTUALLY A BAD PERSON, THOUGH...
PERHAPS WE OUGHT TO COOPERATE AND GROW CLOSER...?
CHIRA (GLANCE)
SQUEAK!
SQUEAK!
CAW!
CAW!
IMPOSSIBLE.
WHAT'S SHE DOING NOW!? SCARY!!
I CAN NEVER HOPE TO UNDERSTAND THE MIND OF A DEMON.
LET'S KEEP OUR INTERACTIONS TO A MINIMUM...
...CHISAKI.

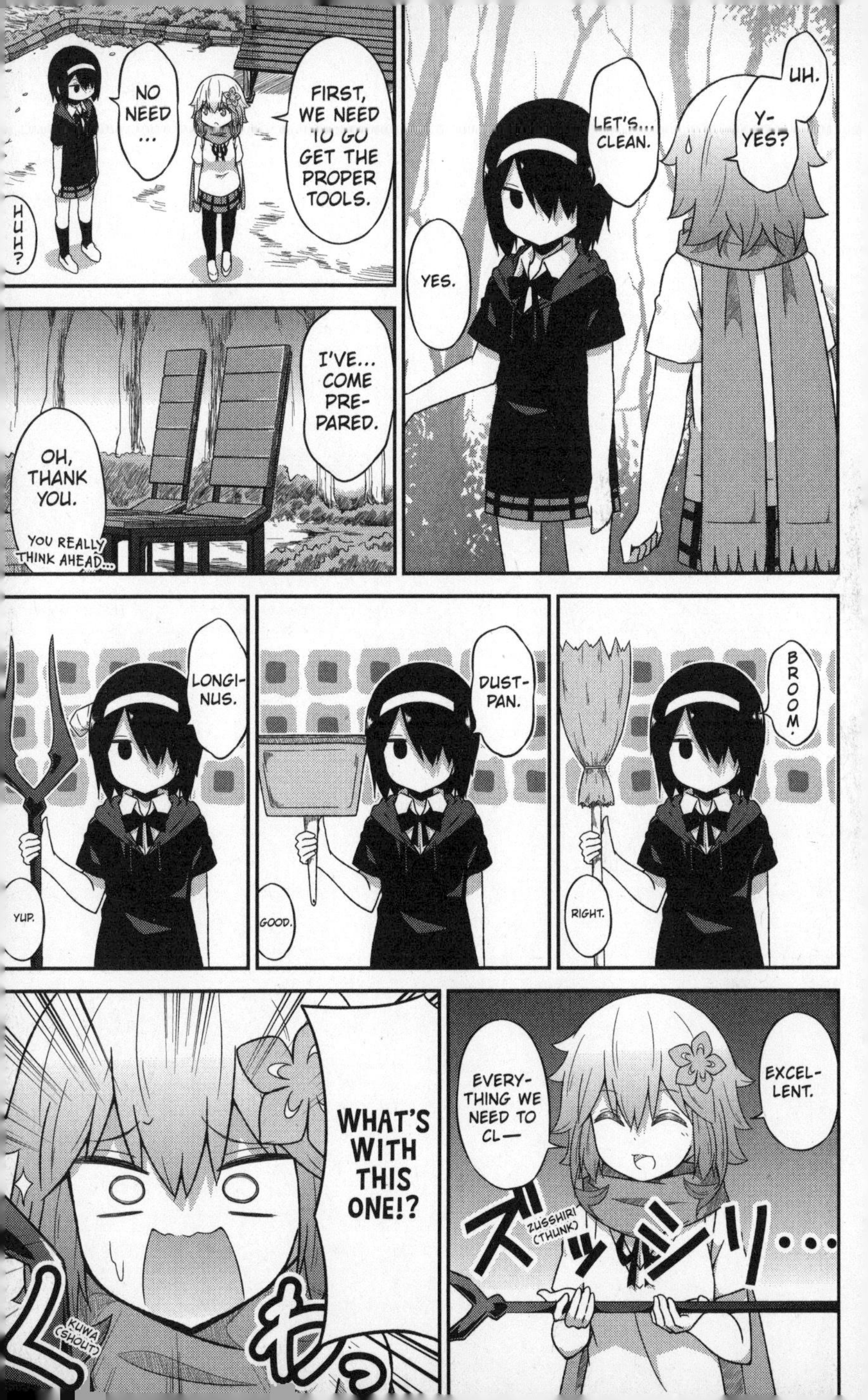
UH. Y-YES?
LET'S... CLEAN.
YES.
FIRST, WE NEED TO GO GET THE PROPER TOOLS.
NO NEED...
HUH?
I'VE... COME PREPARED.
OH, THANK YOU.
YOU REALLY THINK AHEAD...
BROOM.
RIGHT.
DUSTPAN.
GOOD.
LONGINUS.
YUP.
EXCELLENT.
EVERYTHING WE NEED TO CL—
ZUSSHIRI (THUNK)
WHAT'S WITH THIS ONE!?
KUWA (SHOUT)

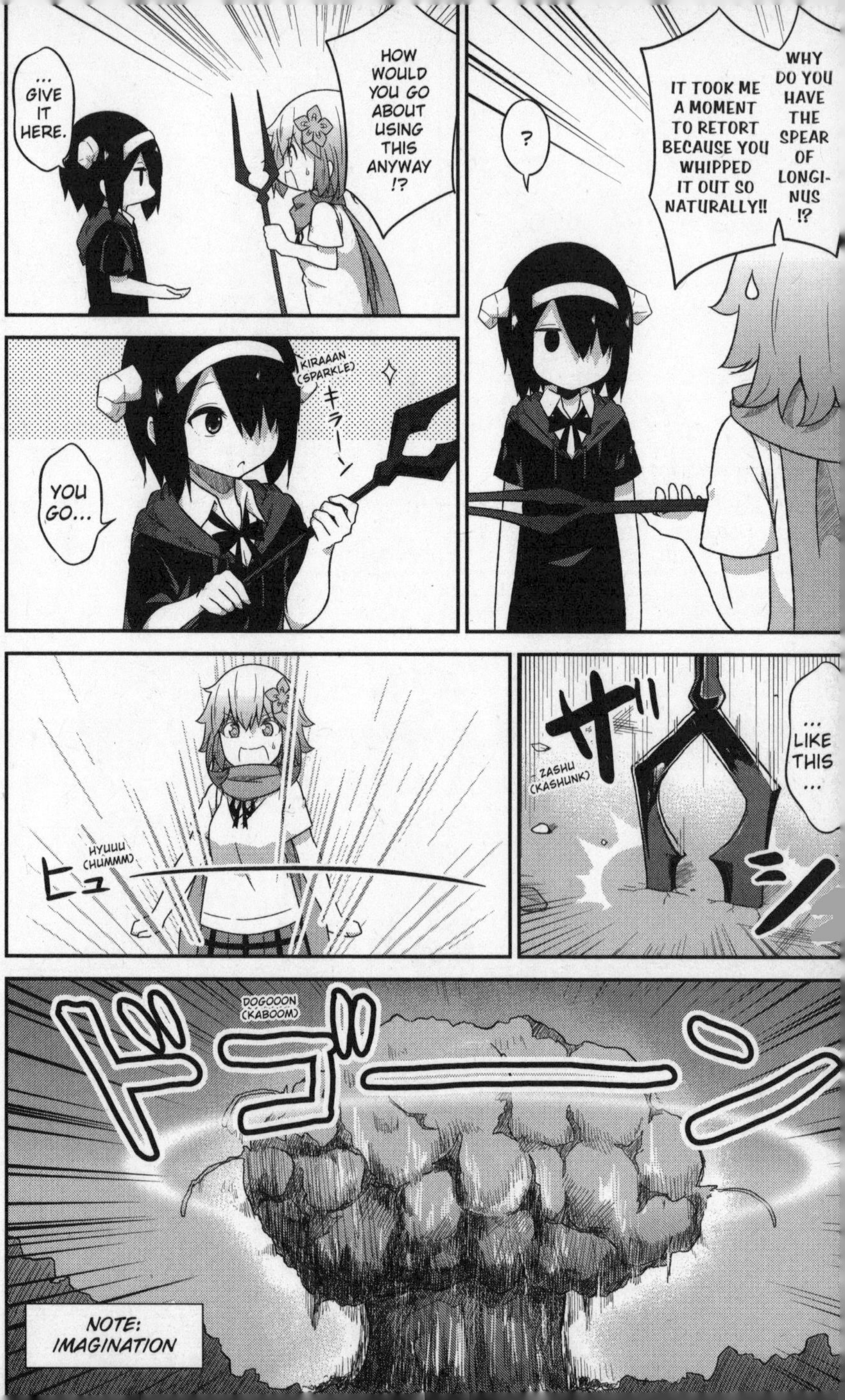
WHY DO YOU HAVE THE SPEAR OF LONGINUS !?
IT TOOK ME A MOMENT TO RETORT BECAUSE YOU WHIPPED IT OUT SO NATURALLY!!
?
HOW WOULD YOU GO ABOUT USING THIS ANYWAY !?
...GIVE IT HERE.
キラーン
KIRAAAN (SPARKLE)
YOU GO...
...LIKE THIS...
ザ
ZASHU (KASHUNK)
ヒュ
HYUUU (HUMMM)
ドゴーン
DOGOOON (KABOOM)
NOTE: IMAGINATION

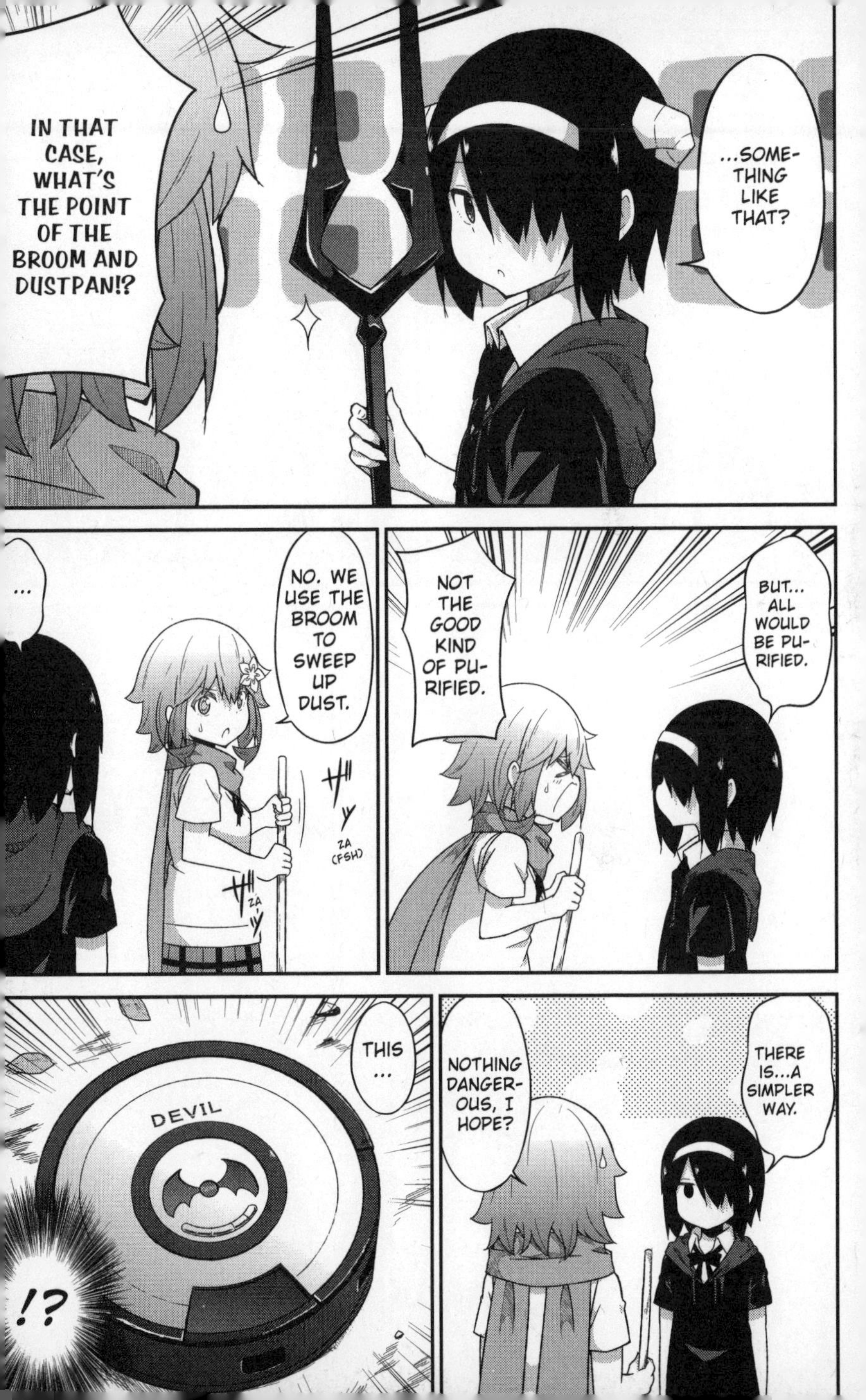
...SOMETHING LIKE THAT?
IN THAT CASE, WHAT'S THE POINT OF THE BROOM AND DUSTPAN!?
BUT... ALL WOULD BE PURIFIED.
NOT THE GOOD KIND OF PURIFIED.
NO. WE USE THE BROOM TO SWEEP UP DUST.
ZA (FSH)
ZA
...
THERE IS...A SIMPLER WAY.
NOTHING DANGEROUS, I HOPE?
THIS ...
DEVIL
!?

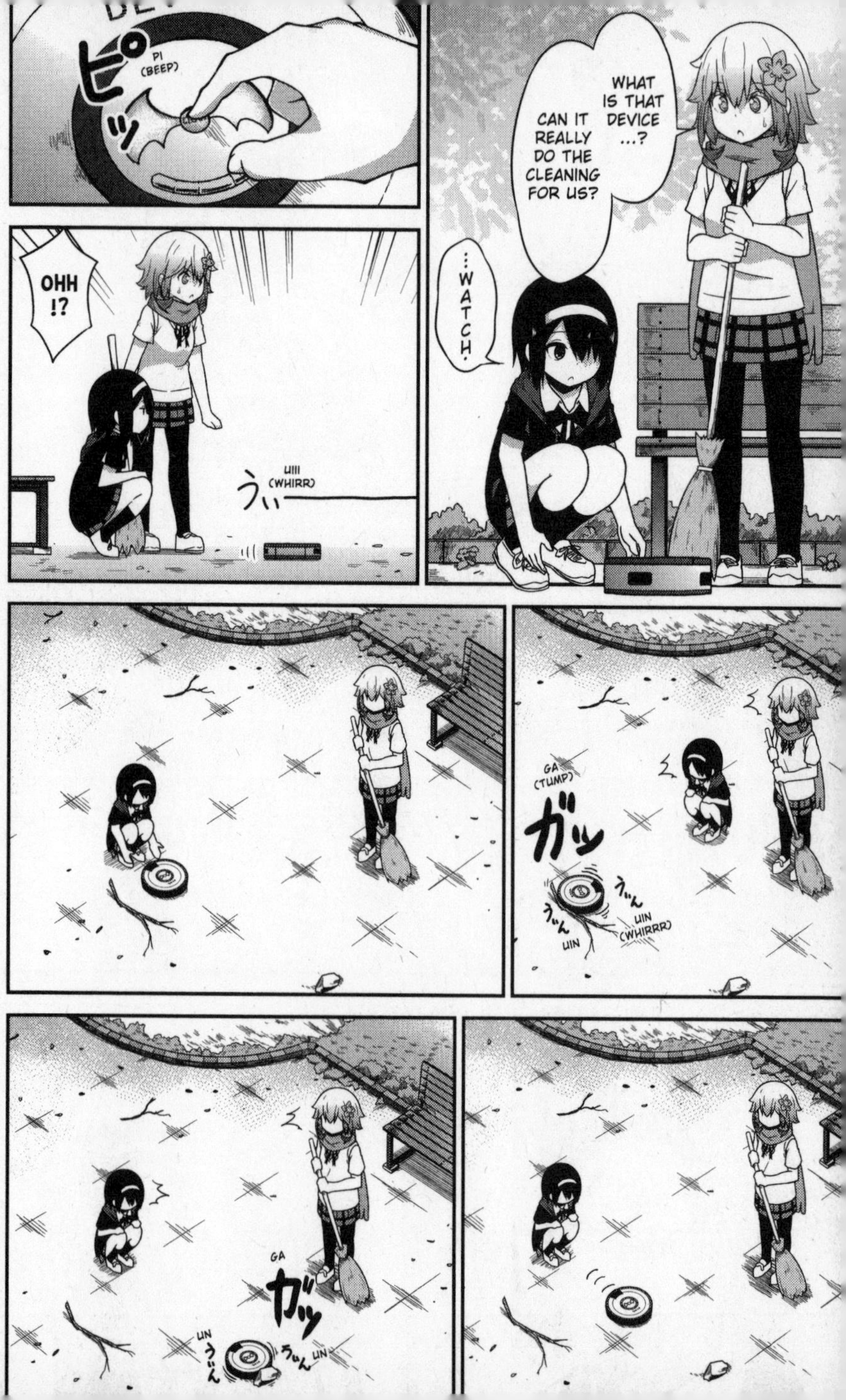
WHAT IS THAT DEVICE ...?
CAN IT REALLY DO THE CLEANING FOR US?
...WATCH.
ピッ
PI (BEEP)
OHH !?
うぃ
UIII (WHIRR)
GA (TUMP)
ガッ
うぃん
UIN (WHIRRR)
うぃん
UIN
GA
ガッ
UN
うぃん
うぃん
UIN

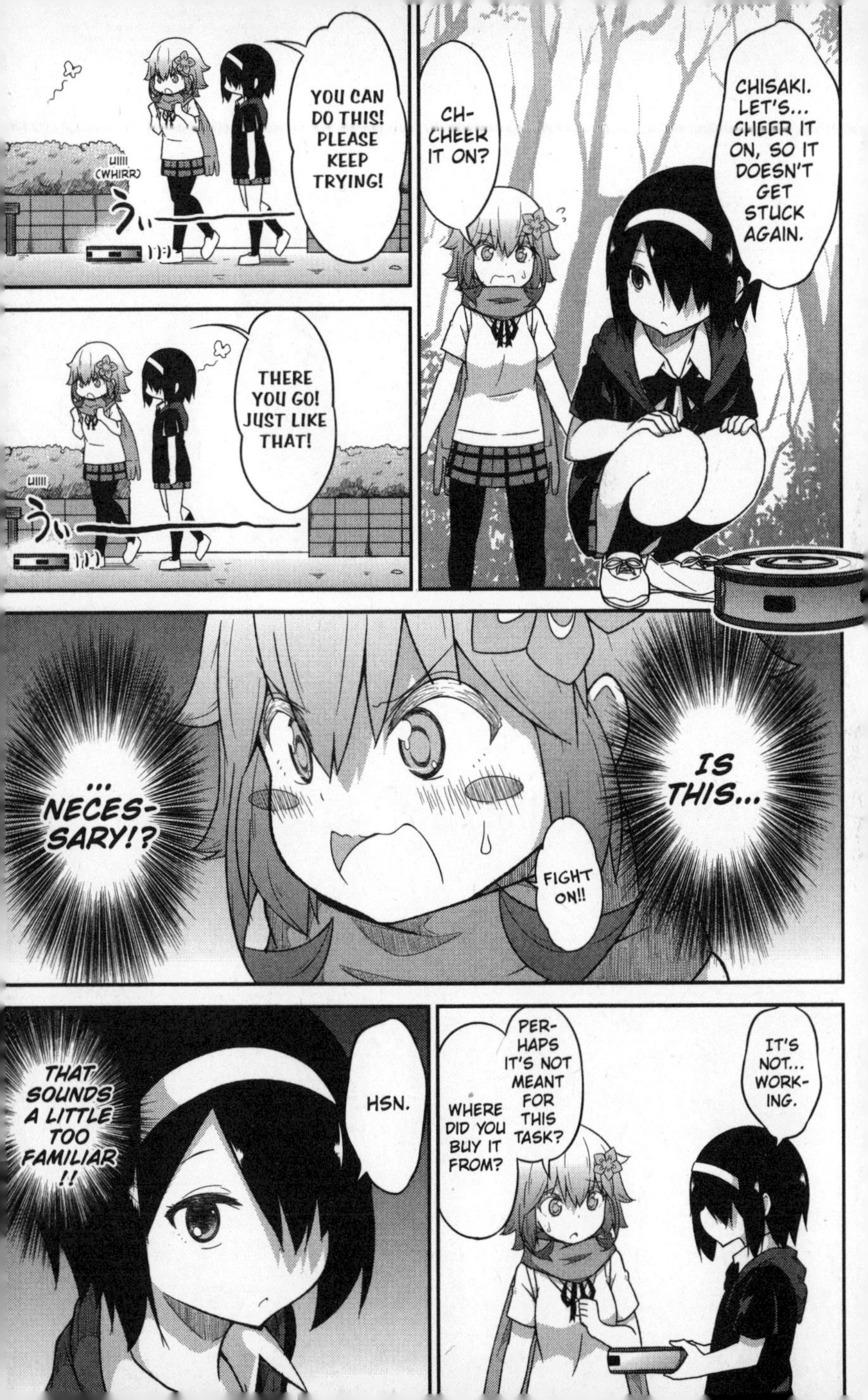
CHISAKI. LET'S... CHEER IT ON, SO IT DOESN'T GET STUCK AGAIN.
CH-CHEER IT ON?
YOU CAN DO THIS! PLEASE KEEP TRYING!
UIIII (WHIRR)
THERE YOU GO! JUST LIKE THAT!
UIIII
IS THIS...
FIGHT ON!!
...NECES-SARY!?
IT'S NOT... WORK-ING.
PER-HAPS IT'S NOT MEANT FOR THIS TASK?
WHERE DID YOU BUY IT FROM?
HSN.
THAT SOUNDS A LITTLE TOO FAMILIAR!!

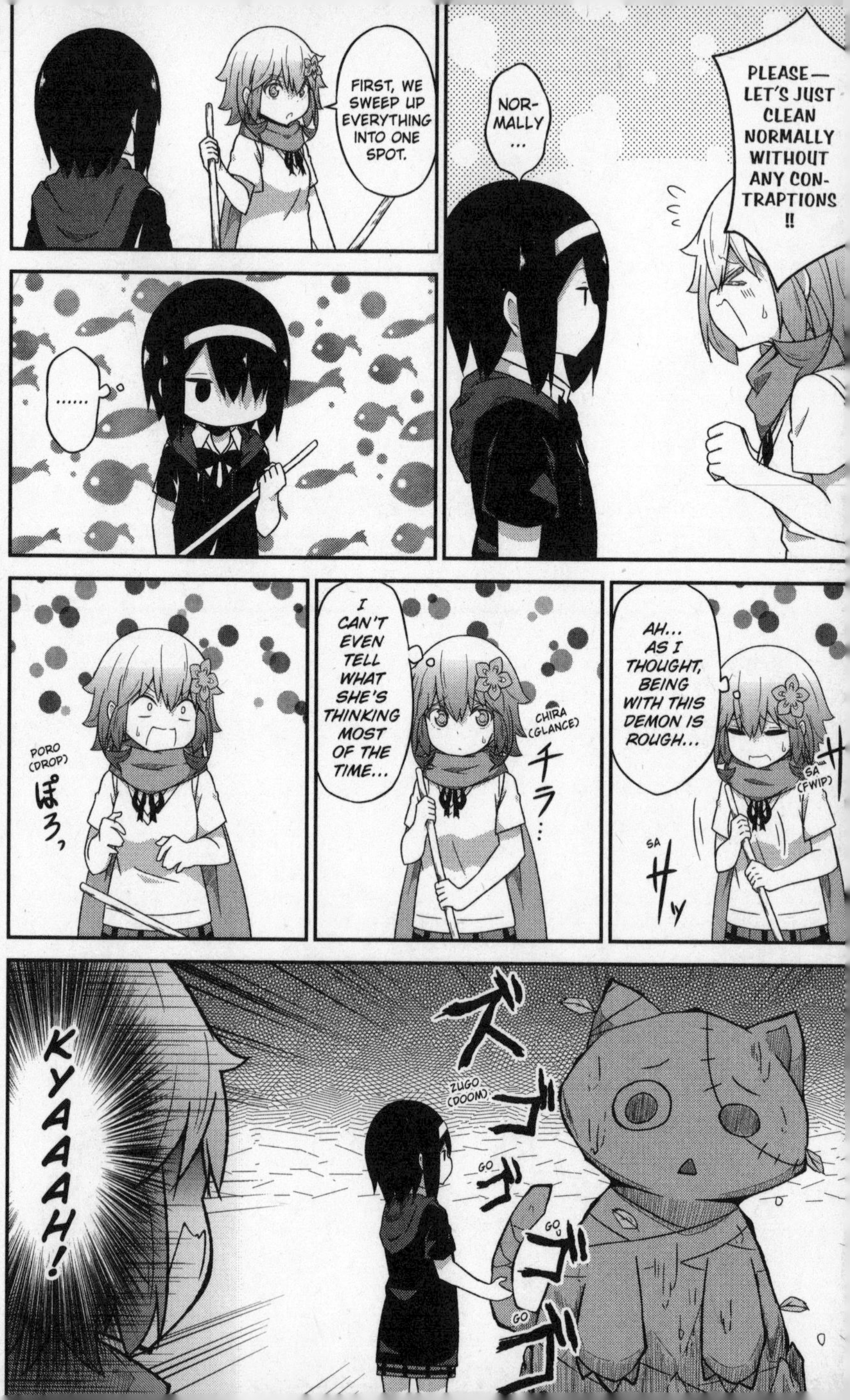
PLEASE—LET'S JUST CLEAN NORMALLY WITHOUT ANY CON-TRAPTIONS!!
NOR-MALLY...
FIRST, WE SWEEP UP EVERYTHING INTO ONE SPOT.
......
AH... AS I THOUGHT, BEING WITH THIS DEMON IS ROUGH...
SA (FWIP)
サッ
SA
サッ
I CAN'T EVEN TELL WHAT SHE'S THINKING MOST OF THE TIME...
CHIRA (GLANCE)
チラ…
PORO (DROP)
ぽろっ
ZUGO (DOOM)
ズ
ゴ
GO
ゴ
GO
ゴ
GO
ゴ
KYAAAAH!

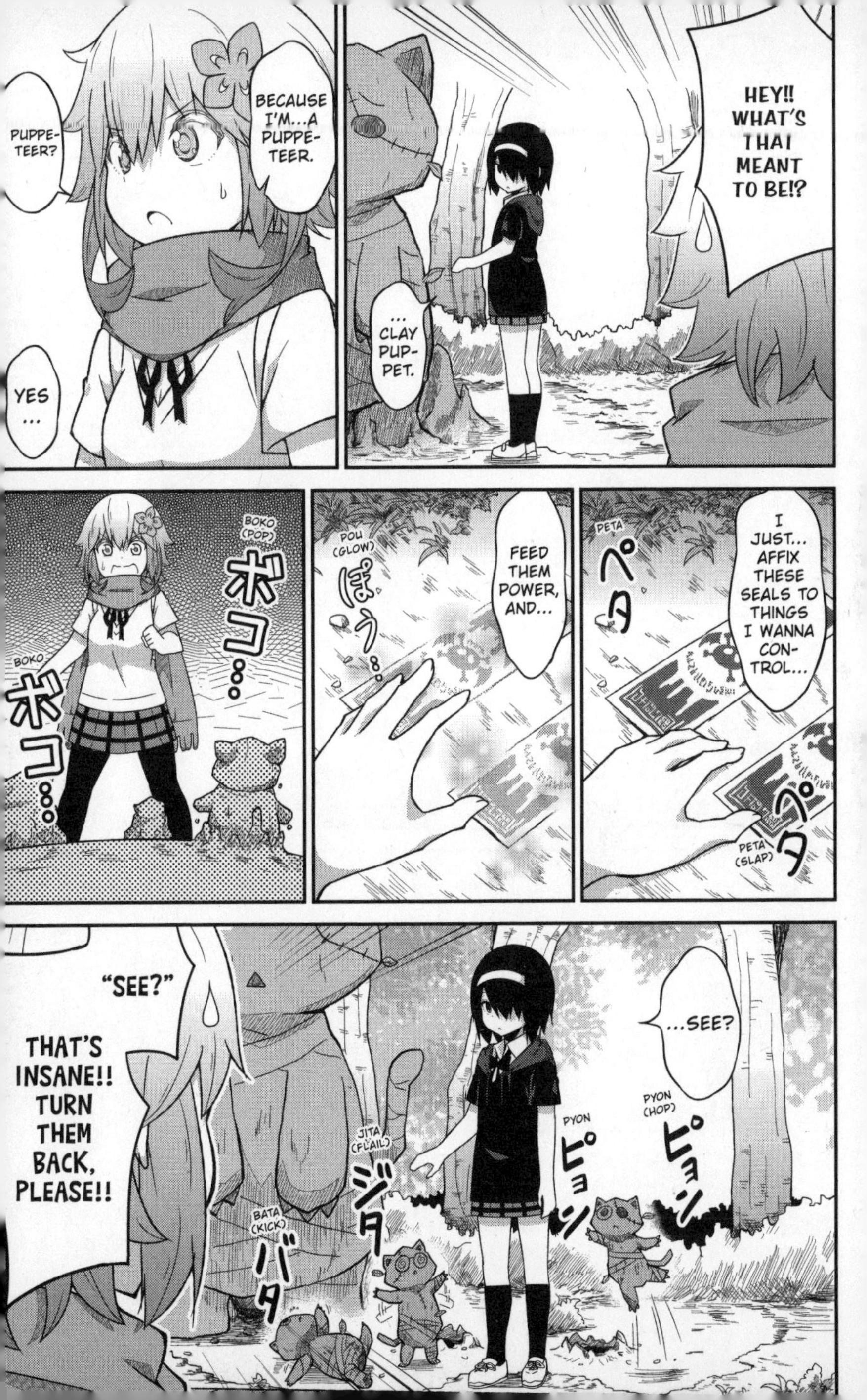
HEY!! WHAT'S THAT MEANT TO BE!?
...CLAY PUPPET.
BECAUSE I'M...A PUPPETEER.
PUPPETEER?
YES...
PETA
ペタ
I JUST... AFFIX THESE SEALS TO THINGS I WANNA CONTROL...
PETA (SLAP)
ペタ
POU (GLOW)
ぽう
FEED THEM POWER, AND...
BOKO (POP)
ボコ
BOKO
ボコ
...SEE?
PYON (HOP)
ピョン
PYON
ピョン
JITA (FLAIL)
ジタ
BATA (KICK)
バタ
"SEE?"
THAT'S INSANE!! TURN THEM BACK, PLEASE!!

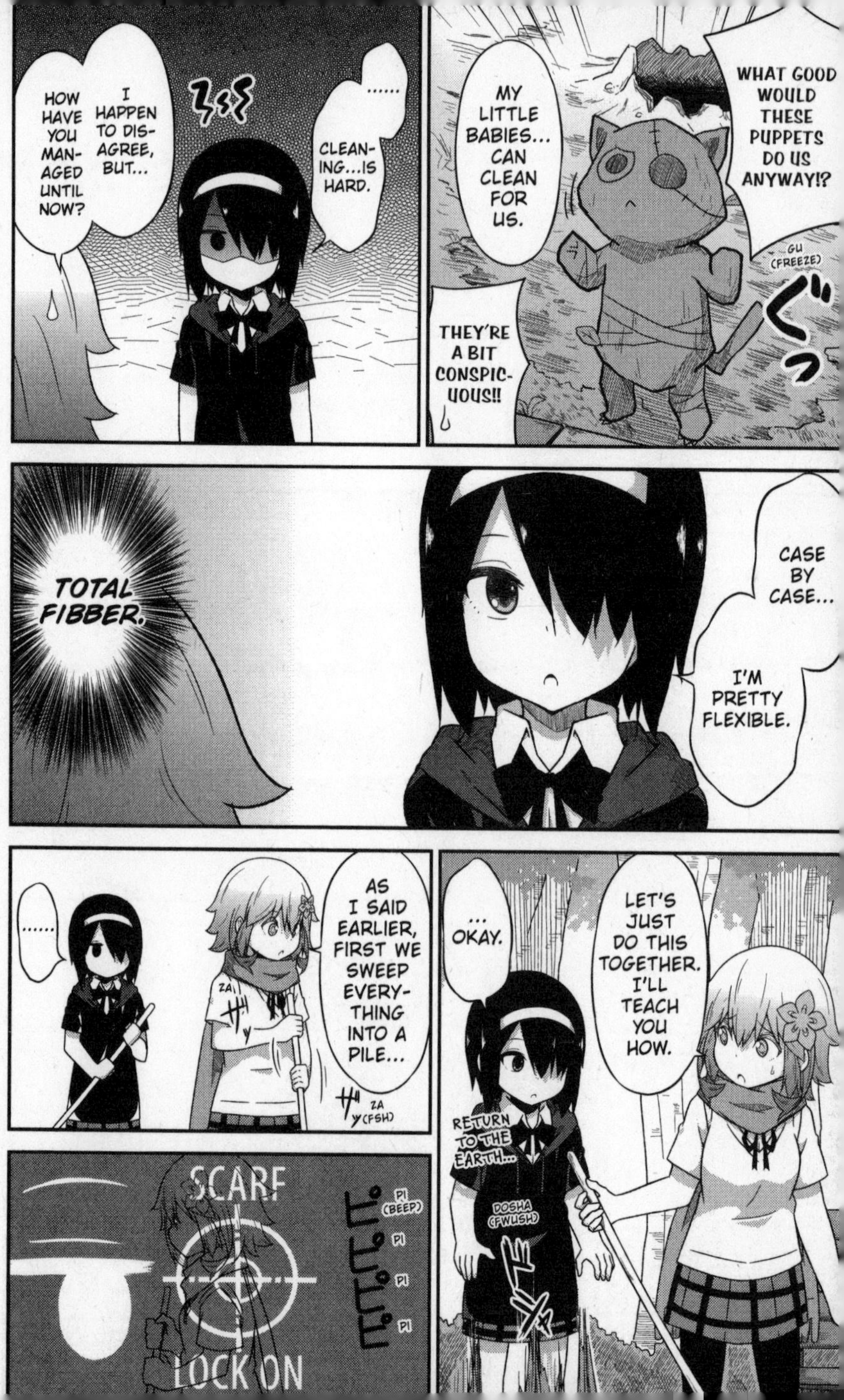
WHAT GOOD WOULD THESE PUPPETS DO US ANYWAY!?
MY LITTLE BABIES... CAN CLEAN FOR US.
GU (FREEZE)
THEY'RE A BIT CONSPIC-UOUS!!
......
CLEAN-ING...IS HARD.
I HAPPEN TO DIS-AGREE, BUT...
HOW HAVE YOU MAN-AGED UNTIL NOW?
CASE BY CASE...
I'M PRETTY FLEXIBLE.
TOTAL FIBBER.
LET'S JUST DO THIS TOGETHER. I'LL TEACH YOU HOW.
... OKAY.
RETURN TO THE EARTH...
DOSHA (FWUSH)
AS I SAID EARLIER, FIRST WE SWEEP EVERY-THING INTO A PILE...
ZA
......
ZA (FSH)
PI (BEEP)
PI
PI
PI
SCARF
LOCK ON

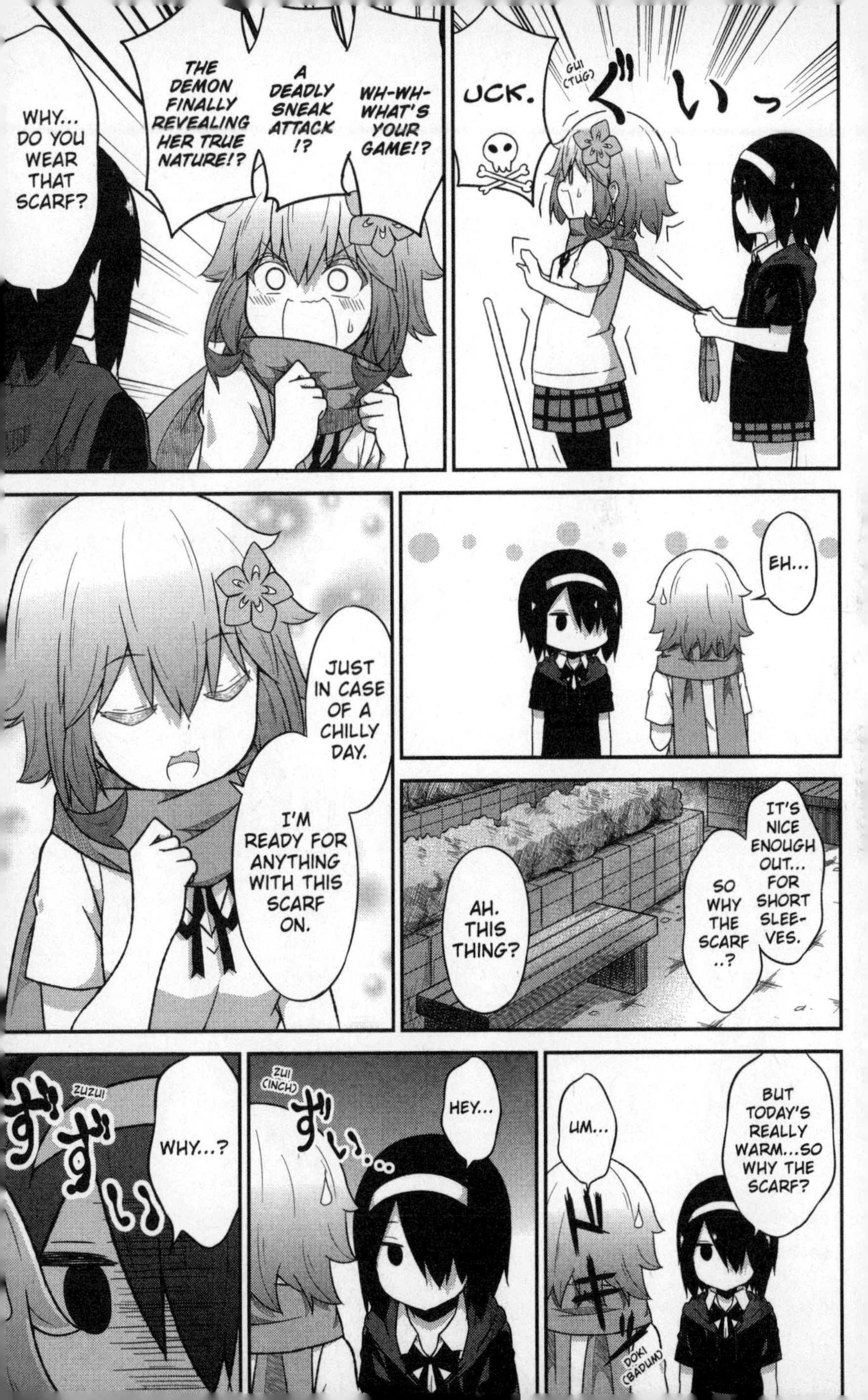
GUI (TUG)
ぐいっ
UCK.
WH-WH-WHAT'S YOUR GAME!?
A DEADLY SNEAK ATTACK!?
THE DEMON FINALLY REVEALING HER TRUE NATURE!?
WHY... DO YOU WEAR THAT SCARF?
EH...
IT'S NICE ENOUGH OUT... FOR SHORT SLEEVES.
SO WHY THE SCARF..?
AH. THIS THING?
JUST IN CASE OF A CHILLY DAY.
I'M READY FOR ANYTHING WITH THIS SCARF ON.
BUT TODAY'S REALLY WARM...SO WHY THE SCARF?
UM...
DOKI (BADUMP)
HEY...
ZUI (INCH)
ずい…
WHY...?
ZUZUI
ずずい

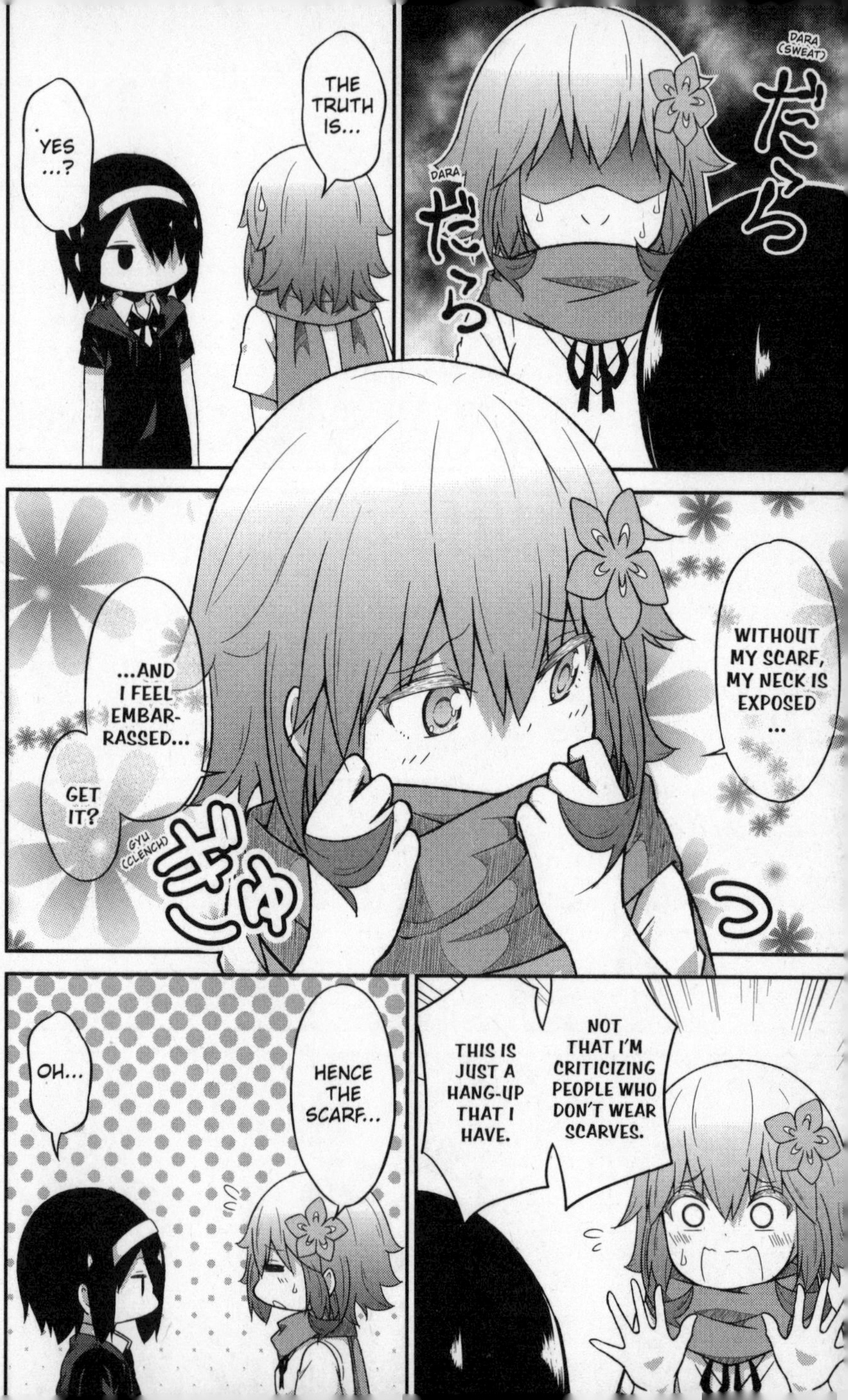
DARA (SWEAT)
だら
DARA
だら
THE TRUTH IS...
YES ...?
WITHOUT MY SCARF, MY NECK IS EXPOSED ...
...AND I FEEL EMBARRASSED...
GET IT?
GYU (CLENCH)
ぎゅっ
NOT THAT I'M CRITICIZING PEOPLE WHO DON'T WEAR SCARVES.
THIS IS JUST A HANG-UP THAT I HAVE.
HENCE THE SCARF...
OH...

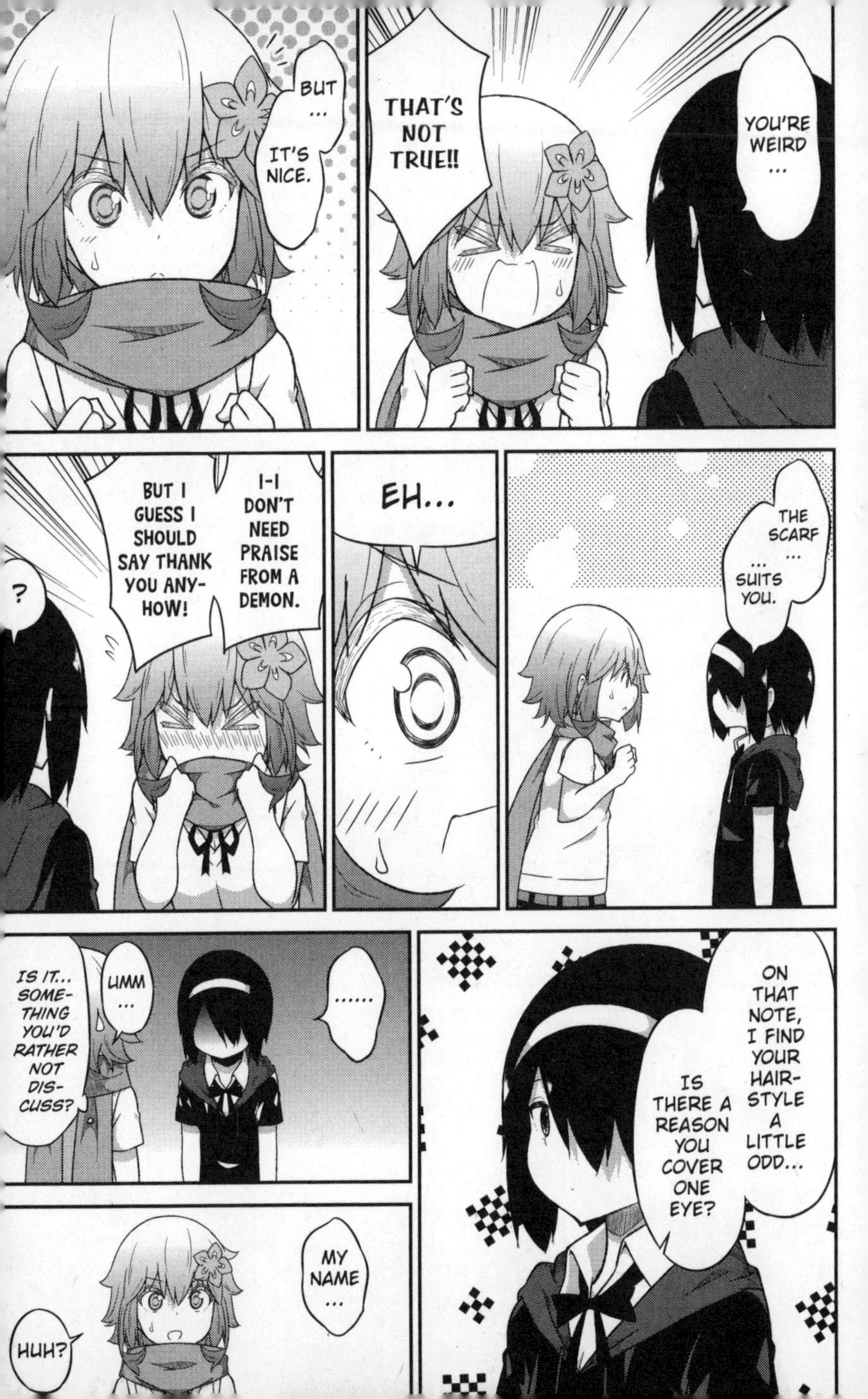

YOU'RE WEIRD ...
THAT'S NOT TRUE!!
BUT ...
IT'S NICE.
THE SCARF ... ... SUITS YOU.
EH...
I-I DON'T NEED PRAISE FROM A DEMON.
BUT I GUESS I SHOULD SAY THANK YOU ANY-HOW!
?
ON THAT NOTE, I FIND YOUR HAIR-STYLE A LITTLE ODD...
IS THERE A REASON YOU COVER ONE EYE?
......
UMM ...
IS IT... SOME-THING YOU'D RATHER NOT DIS-CUSS?
MY NAME ...
HUH?

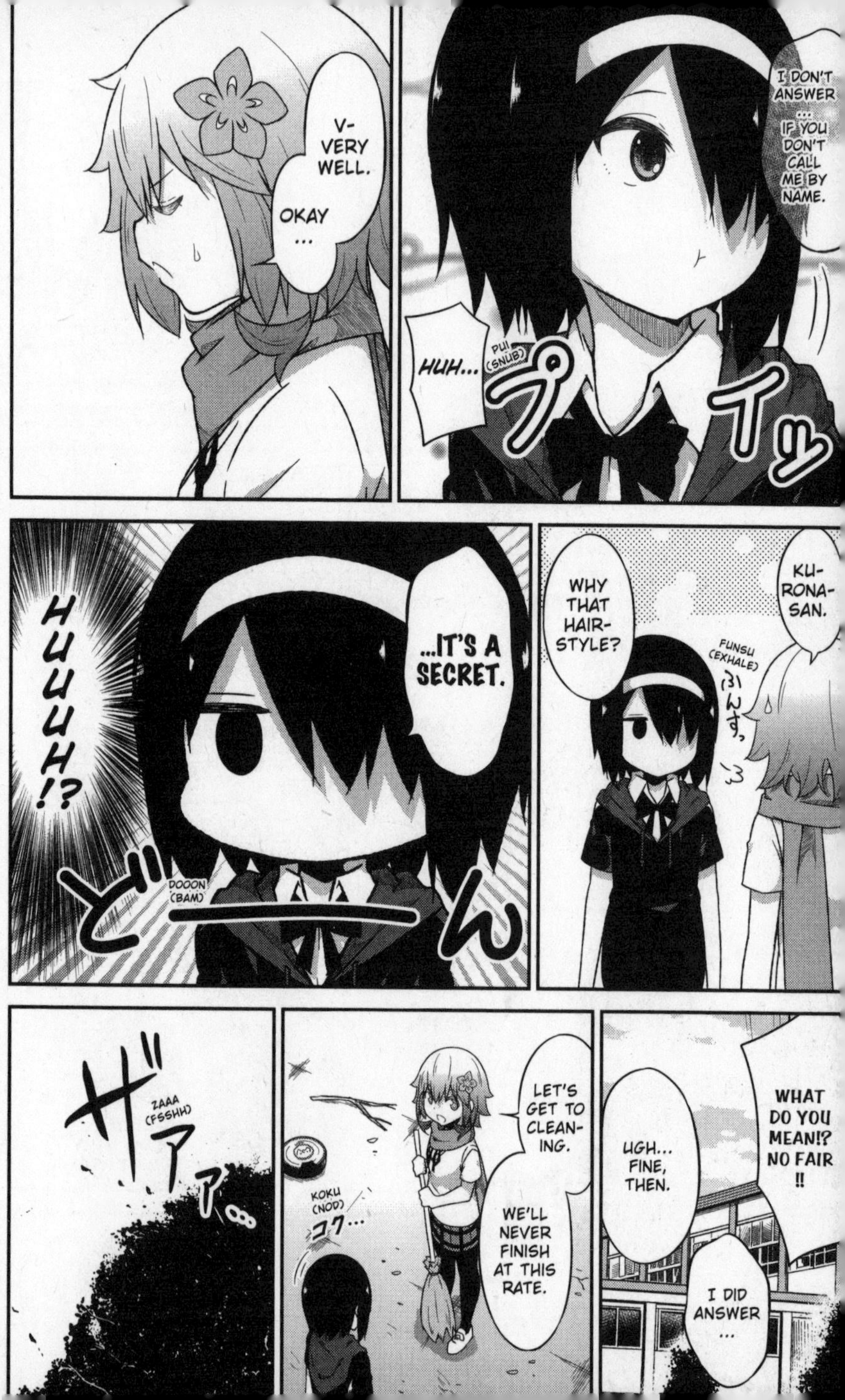
I DON'T ANSWER ... IF YOU DON'T CALL ME BY NAME.
PUI (SNUB)
HUH...
V-VERY WELL.
OKAY ...
KU-RONA-SAN.
WHY THAT HAIR-STYLE?
FUNSU (EXHALE)
...IT'S A SECRET.
HUUUUH!?
DOOON (BAM)
WHAT DO YOU MEAN!? NO FAIR !!
UGH... FINE, THEN.
I DID ANSWER ...
LET'S GET TO CLEAN-ING.
WE'LL NEVER FINISH AT THIS RATE.
KOKU (NOD)
ZAAA (FSSHH)

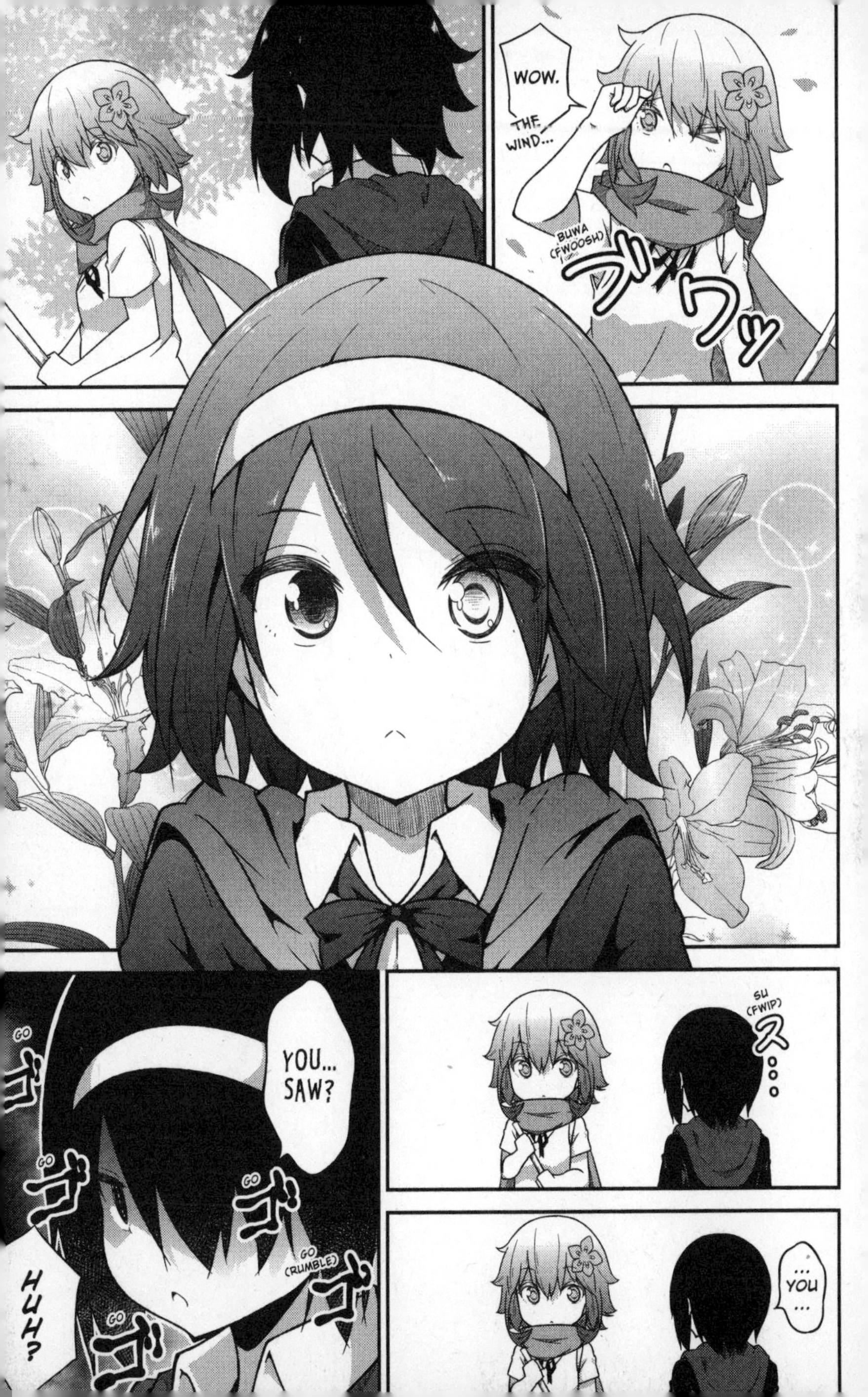

WOW.
THE WIND...
BUWA (FWOOSH)
ブワッ
SU (FWIP)
ス…
... YOU ...
YOU... SAW?
GO GO GO GO (RUMBLE) GO
HUH?

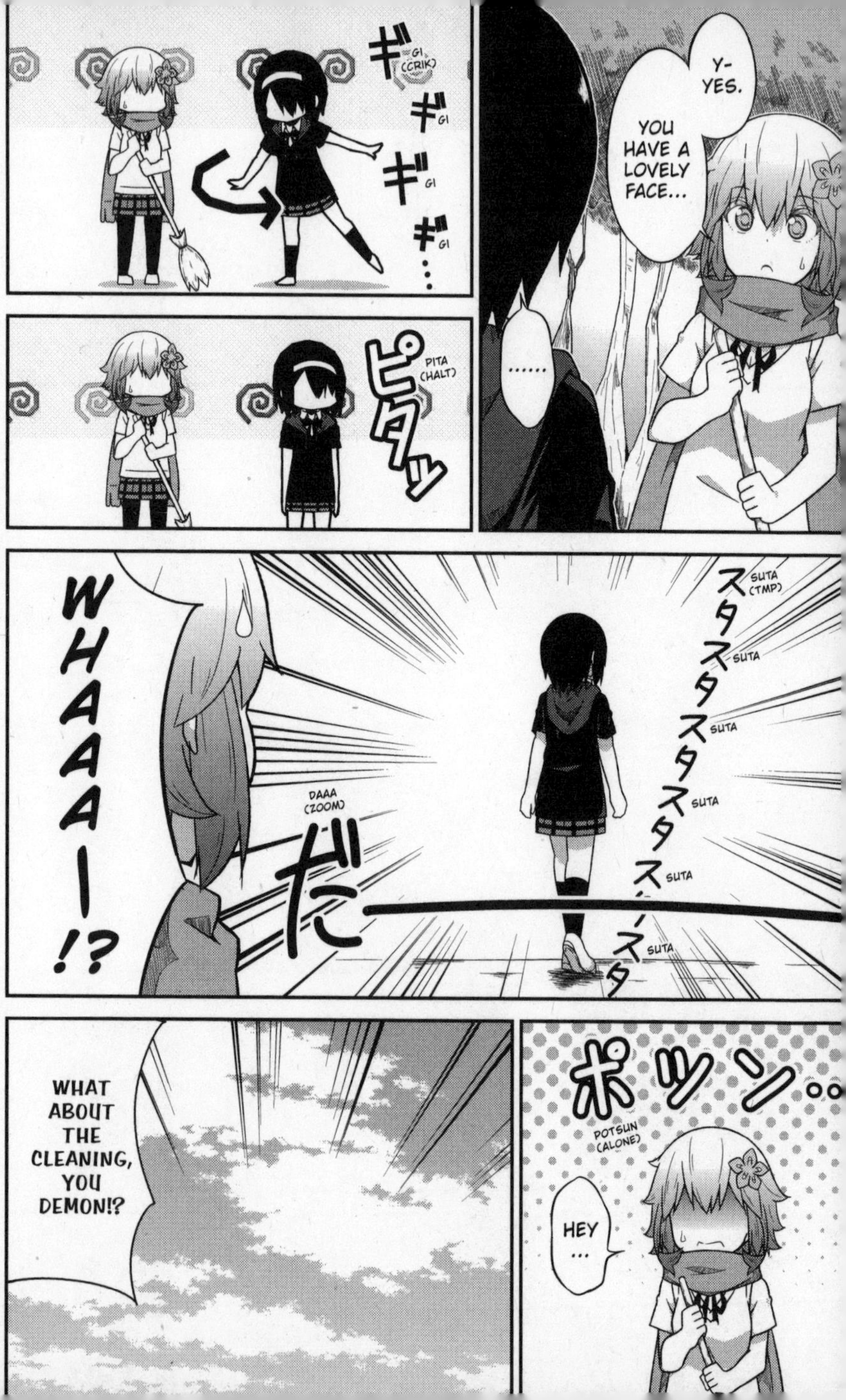
Y-YES.
YOU HAVE A LOVELY FACE...
......
ギギギギ...
GI (CRIK)
GI
GI
GI
ピタッ
PITA (HALT)
スタスタスタスタスタスタ
SUTA (TMP)
SUTA
SUTA
SUTA
SUTA
SUTA
だ
DAAA (ZOOM)
WHAAAA—!?
ポツン..
POTSUN (ALONE)
HEY ...
WHAT ABOUT THE CLEANING, YOU DEMON!?

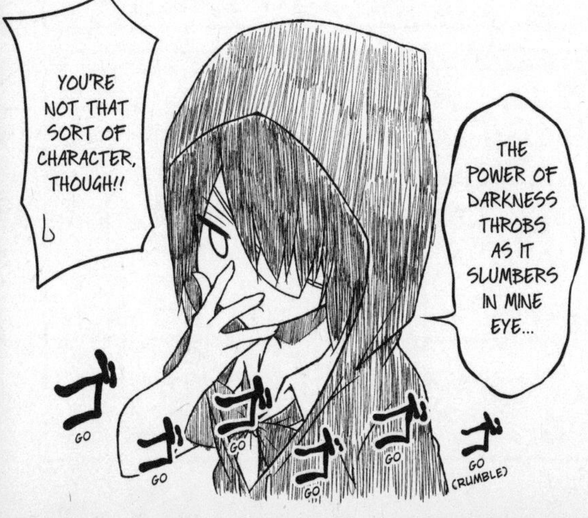
THE POWER OF DARKNESS THROBS AS IT SLUMBERS IN MINE EYE...
YOU'RE NOT THAT SORT OF CHARACTER, THOUGH!!
GO GO GO GO GO GO (RUMBLE)

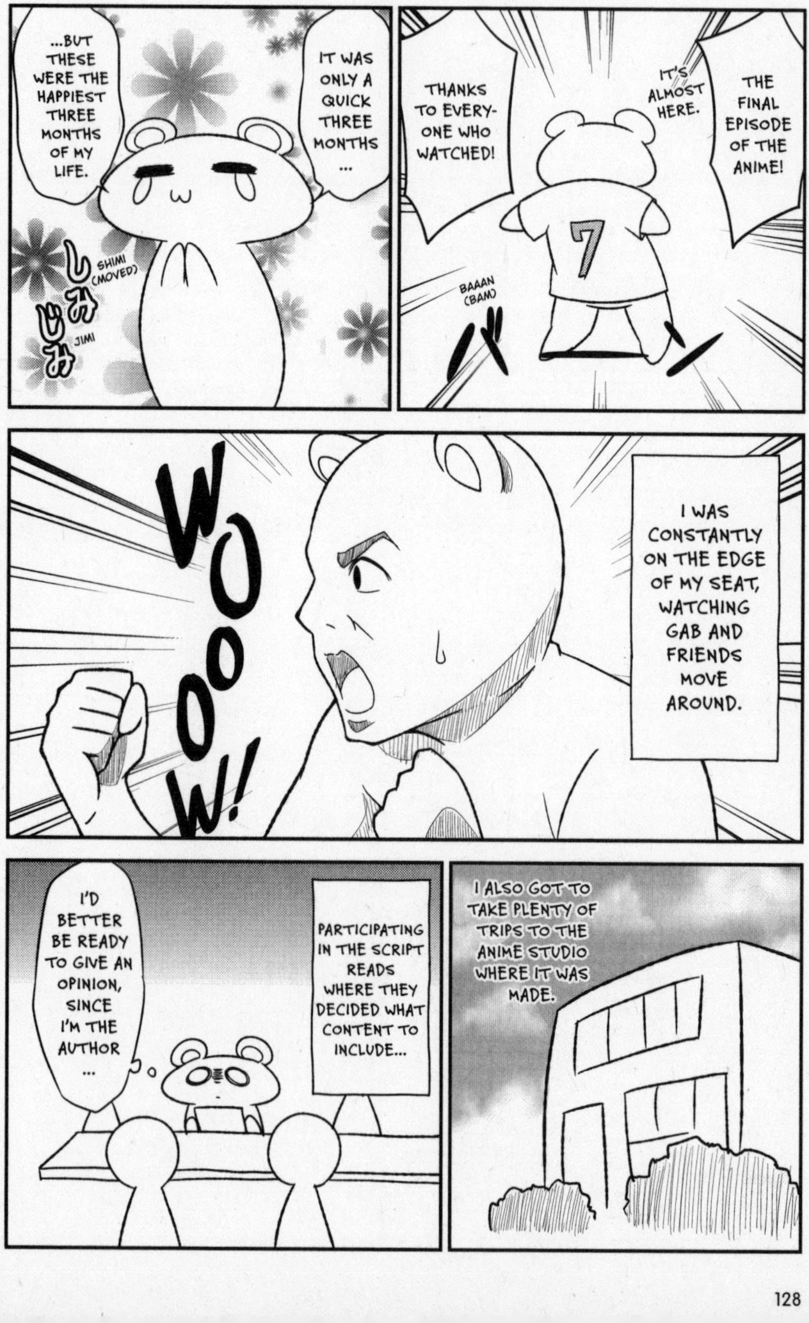
THE FINAL EPISODE OF THE ANIME!
IT'S ALMOST HERE.
THANKS TO EVERYONE WHO WATCHED!
BAAAN (BAM)
バ
IT WAS ONLY A QUICK THREE MONTHS...
...BUT THESE WERE THE HAPPIEST THREE MONTHS OF MY LIFE.
しみじみ
SHIMI (MOVED)
JIMI
I WAS CONSTANTLY ON THE EDGE OF MY SEAT, WATCHING GAB AND FRIENDS MOVE AROUND.
WOOOW!
I ALSO GOT TO TAKE PLENTY OF TRIPS TO THE ANIME STUDIO WHERE IT WAS MADE.
PARTICIPATING IN THE SCRIPT READS WHERE THEY DECIDED WHAT CONTENT TO INCLUDE...
I'D BETTER BE READY TO GIVE AN OPINION, SINCE I'M THE AUTHOR...

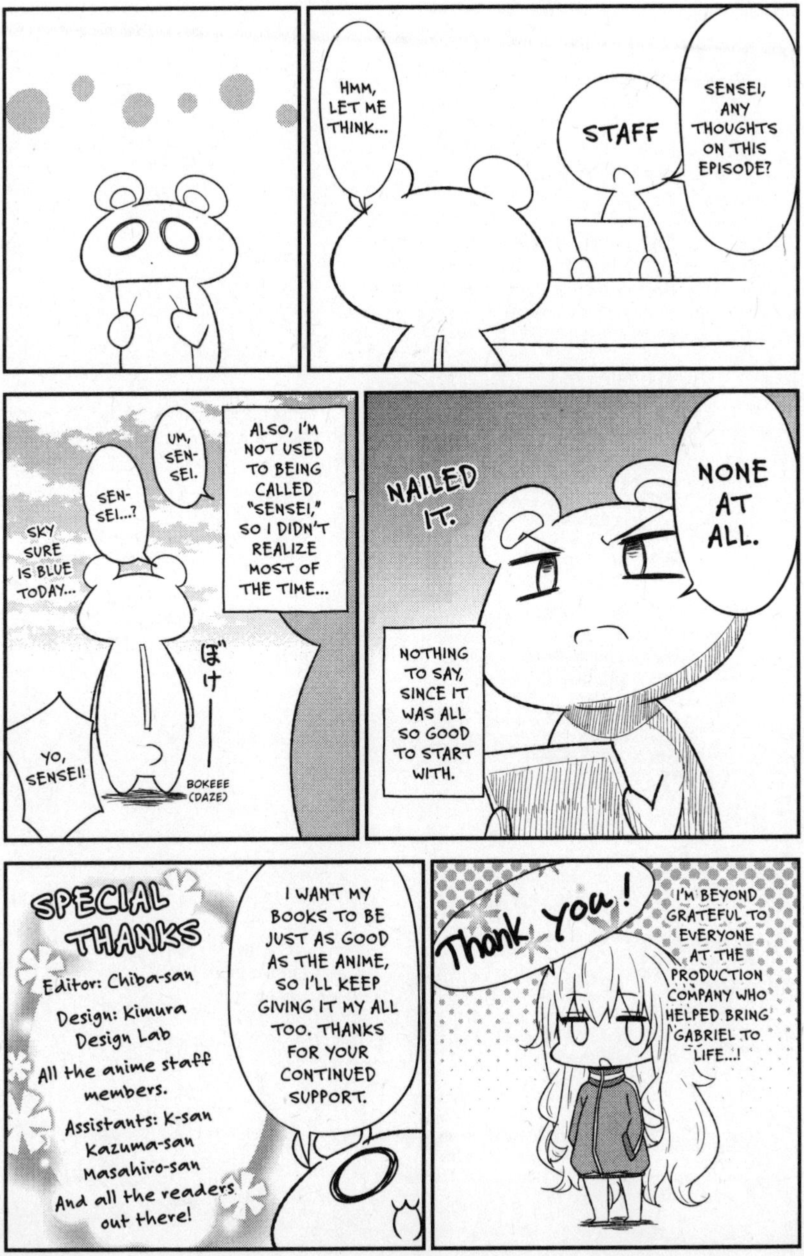
SENSEI, ANY THOUGHTS ON THIS EPISODE?
STAFF
HMM, LET ME THINK...
NONE AT ALL.
NAILED IT.
NOTHING TO SAY, SINCE IT WAS ALL SO GOOD TO START WITH.
ALSO, I'M NOT USED TO BEING CALLED "SENSEI," SO I DIDN'T REALIZE MOST OF THE TIME...
UM, SEN-SEI.
SEN-SEI...?
SKY SURE IS BLUE TODAY...
ぼけー
BOKEEE (DAZE)
YO, SENSEI!
Thank you!
I'M BEYOND GRATEFUL TO EVERYONE AT THE PRODUCTION COMPANY WHO HELPED BRING GABRIEL TO LIFE...!
I WANT MY BOOKS TO BE JUST AS GOOD AS THE ANIME, SO I'LL KEEP GIVING IT MY ALL TOO. THANKS FOR YOUR CONTINUED SUPPORT.
SPECIAL THANKS
Editor: Chiba-san
Design: Kimura Design Lab
All the anime staff members.
Assistants: K-san
Kazuma-san
Masahiro-san
And all the readers out there!

UKAMI

Translation: Caleb Cook ⁄ Lettering: Rochelle Gancio

Gabriel Dropout Vol. 5
©UKAMI 2017
First published in Japan in 2017 by KADOKAWA CORPORATION, Tokyo.
English translation rights arranged with KADOKAWA CORPORATION, Tokyo through TUTTLE-MORI AGENCY, INC., Tokyo.

English translation © 2018 by Yen Press, LLC

Yen Press
1290 Avenue of the Americas
New York, NY 10104

Visit us!
⁄ yenpress.com
⁄ facebook.com/yenpress
⁄ twitter.com/yenpress
⁄ yenpress.tumblr.com
⁄ instagram.com/yenpress

First Yen Press Edition: October 2018

Yen Press is an imprint of Yen Press, LLC.
The Yen Press name and logo are trademarks of Yen Press, LLC.

The publisher is not responsible for websites (or their content) that are not owned by the publisher.

Library of Congress Control Number: 2017945425

ISBNs: 978-1-9753-8243-8 (paperback)
978-1-9753-8244-5 (ebook)

10 9 8 7 6 5 4 3 2 1

WOR

Printed in the United States of America